Week in Week out ❋

WEEK
IN
WEEK
OUT

5²

seasonal
stories

Simon Hopkinson

Pictures by
JASON LOWE

For Jason, naturally — and with love

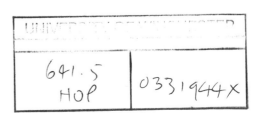

FOREWORD

The great writers, in my book, are simply those who compel you to read on. Easiest for dramatists and novelists with exciting stories at their command. Trickier for the others, the essayists, let us call them. Yet there are masters who constantly enthrall us: Max Beerbohm on anything, and nowadays Richard Dawkins on science, Miles Kingston on every manifestation of human frailty, and on cookery Simon Hopkinson.

I can read on into Simon's evocations of dream dinners for hours. Greed is only part of it. I know exactly which pans I'm going to use, and Jason's pictures only make it more compelling. One of these days I'm going to toddle up to bed with a contented smile having quite forgotten to cook anything at all. Simon will not be pleased.

Simon's signature enthusiasms (aubergines, cèpes, scallops, etc.) are not on every domestic menu. But then every menu needs to be re-invigorated. Cookery, like life itself, requires constant renewal. 'Stale and passé?' In life it's an insult. In Simon's kitchen it's already in the bin. Every larder, every fridge, every freezer needs a bit of Simon Hopkinson space. 'Only the best' I hear him saying into my ear, 'and spanking fresh please.'

There is something reassuring about following an organised plan. Both Simon and I did it with *The Cordon Bleu Cookery Course* published in weekly parts in the 1960s. Since then we have Global Warming ('and thorough this distemperature we see the seasons alter'). Don't be too inhibited, though. Follow the seasons all the same, cook what Simon says, and you'll never be disappointed. And for miles around you'll be famous, if you are generous enough to share your cooking with friends. But that's half the fun. When Simon cooks in my house the sheer bonhomie of it all spreads contagiously. With this handsome book he'll soon be cooking in yours and the joy will be just as infectious.

MICHAEL BIRKETT

INTRODUCTION

Saturday lunch, in Ball's Cross, we always think, is the very nicest one of the week and it usually begins with a couple of Michael Birkett's stupendously good (ie. almost lethal) Martinis around about 12.30pm — although it can be a little later if he is titivating one of his excellent, summer fruit tarts; a raspberry one being one of the finest. I will usually be putting together a lunch to be eaten around about 2.30pm. Friends will have arrived about an hour earlier, been given a Bloody Mary (not many imbibe in a Michael Martini if wishing to drive home safely) or a glass of fizz, and then lunch will meander long into the afternoon, beginning to wind down between, say, 5 or 6pm. Proper lunch, we call it. Grown-up lunch.

It was to be post one of these long Saturdays with Michael, and with the two of us still sitting at the kitchen table (his guests having recently bid their farewells) in his old Sussex farmhouse when the scrapbooks came out; early 2006, possibly February, but I can't be sure. So I just sat there poring over them for a couple of hours whilst Michael went upstairs and enjoyed a snooze.

There were eight of these scrapbooks to be precise, all meticulously compiled by Michael ('stuck-in' would seem a rude description), of about eight and a half years of articles I had written for *The Independent* Saturday magazine (a collection of part of these, as some of you may know, have already been used to produce a previous book called *Gammon and Spinach*, published by Macmillan in 1998). But it was not really the articles that first caused me to sit there and ponder, but the quite extraordinary, wonderful quality of two hundred or more pictures of, until then, forgotten food and dishes which the photographer, Jason Lowe, had so beautifully captured, uniquely illustrating my cooking of the recipes.

Two aspects which particularly occurred to me, however, were quite how well they had aged — not dated, in other words — and that every single one of them appeared as if from just a couple of weeks ago, even though they were simply cut-out pieces of old newsprint. 'Just imagine how they could appear in a book, displayed on high-gloss printed pages', I thought to myself over a glass of delicious Gewürztraminer and an early evening cigarette. Michael reappeared shortly, poured himself a whiskey and I related to him my excited thoughts…

The next thing to do (Michael was as excited as me, naturally), we decided, was for me to invite Jason down to lunch to look at the scrapbooks and decide as to whether he, too, would be as fond of the idea as we had so quickly become. Well, of course, he was thrilled to bits — even a little ecstatic. So, we had another Saturday lunch, Michael Martini-ed, I cooked something or other and then Jason and I took the scrapbooks back with us to London. A most happy and rewarding day.

The book you now hold in your hands is the result of that special gathering. I very much hope that you will enjoy reading it, cooking from it and, although I know it is colourful, glossy and coffee-table in size, I really won't mind if it becomes well-stained from regular use.

SIMON HOPKINSON, APRIL 2007

EELS AND OYSTERS

For the past several years it is the dinner eaten on New Year's Eve that gives the most pleasure to me over the festive season. This is the night for grown-up gastronomic fare: a slice or two from a superb terrine of fresh foie gras, perhaps; the very first taste of a few shavings from the Périgord black truffle; maybe a smear of caviar and some smoked fish; fine poultry; a fully ripened cheese and a rich pudding. It is *the* night to push the boat out and, with all thoughts of funds plundered being the very last consideration foremost in one's mind, there are also some oysters to be eaten...

Having recently returned from a five-day trip to Paris, I was introduced to a serving of nine of the finest *spéciales* it has long been my pleasure to consume. I ate

these Chez Lipp and was proudly informed by those who know – and they know, here, they really do – that these particular oysters originate from the local Atlantic waters that lap around and about the shores of the Ile d'Oléron on the west coast of France. *Spéciales 'Perles Blanches'* are what you are looking for.

Most often it is the flat Belon oyster from the Brittany coast of France to which I am initially drawn when in Paris during their season. So it was to be nine of these that I chose to eat as a beginning to my first, extremely late Lipp lunch (followed by two oil-soaked, smoked

herring fillets with potato salad and, to complete, three profitéroles filled with vanilla ice cream and flooded with lots of hot chocolate sauce) accompanied by half a bottle of sprightly Sancerre. Although they were a welcome hors d'œuvre to the city, these particular Belons were not as good as I had remembered them to be.

I shall certainly be eating oysters tomorrow night, that's for sure. However, in the meantime, here is a suitably glamorous three-course New Year's Eve dinner for you to be thinking about, just in case you are last-minute types.

Rowley Leigh's smoked eel and bacon salad

SERVES 4

The ground-breaking chef of London's Kensington Place restaurant, one Rowley Leigh, has finally given us his first cookery book. And what a joy it is, to be sure! He has named it *No Place Like Home* (Fourth Estate, 2000) and it is, as the title suggests, a generous collection of professionally inspired recipes that have been suitably adapted for the home cook. In point of fact, once one looks into the collection more closely, it soon becomes abundantly clear that the majority of dishes here are those that Rowley has always seen as simply excellent ideas in their own right. In other words, whether it be executed from restaurant range or dished up out of the Rayburn, the results will be sound.

I remain, however, perplexed that this salad, one of the earliest fixtures on his opening menu during the latter months of 1987 (Kensington Place opened just one week after Bibendum, in November of that year) does not feature in his book. I ate it many times during those early days and, with respect, this is how I remember it. And it is every bit as delicious at home, too.

2007 – Rowley has now left KP and is due to open Le Café Anglais in Bayswater, in September.

1 small salad frisée, its outside greener tendrils removed and the remaining heart well washed and dried
a squeeze of lemon juice and the merest splash of light olive oil just to dress the leaves
salt and pepper
200g smoked eel fillets, very thinly sliced horizontally into wafer-thin strips
8 very thin rashers of rindless, smoked streaky bacon, grilled until crisp
1 heaped tbsp finely chopped chives

for the beurre blanc:
2 shallots, peeled and very finely chopped
4 tbsp white wine vinegar
4 tbsp white wine
4 tbsp water
250g very cold, fine quality unsalted butter, cut into small chunks
salt and freshly ground white pepper

First make the beurre blanc. Using a small stainless steel or enamelled pan, mix together the shallots, vinegar, wine and water. Allow this to reduce over a moderate heat until almost no liquid at all remains. Turn the heat down to very low indeed and then, using a small whisk, begin to incorporate the butter chunk by chunk, allowing each chunk to melt and homogenise before adding the next. Continue in this fashion until all the butter has been used up and the sauce has the consistency of a light, slightly jellied-looking custard, and also of a similar hue. Season, and keep warm on the side of the stove.

Tear apart the frisée leaves into thin tendrils and place in a bowl. Lightly dress them with lemon juice and olive oil and then season. Divide amongst four large plates, evenly spreading the leaves to cover. Arrange the eel strips on top, snap the bacon strips into small pieces and distribute around the edge of each serving. Spoon the warm sauce in and around as a further dressing and finally, decoratively sprinkle with chives.

Poached chicken
with
truffles
and celery

—

SERVES 4

After all those crusted roastings of poultry skin or pig's crackling, potatoes and parsnips, sausages and bacon that have gone before, I can only see this poached fowl as a most welcoming relief to all of that. One might say that so soft and yielding, perfumed and savoury it is as a centrepiece to this dinner, that almost its sole kick may be that of simply soothing the tired of tooth. But when further combined with such flavours as these two, it fair lavishes the tastebuds.

Along with the thoughts of many other like-minded folk, it is clear that celery and truffles have a certain affinity with each other. As another, slightly lesser example of this, I have long known that traditional braised celery is enhanced enormously by the elementary inclusion of a few slices of mushroom added to the rest of its braising ingredients – and whether it be cultivated or couture fungi, each will gladly enhance the finished dish.

A generous amount of dried cèpes or other desiccated variety (previously soaked in luke-warm water for 20 minutes, drained and their soaking water added to the cooking juices) would be a most admirable substitution for truffles here; just so long as you don't envisage the finished dish as ever being one and the same thing.

1 x 1.5kg free-range chicken
1 litre light chicken stock
2 onions, peeled and halved
3 cloves garlic, crushed
1 bouquet garni
1 rounded tsp salt

4 celery hearts, peeled
50g cold, unsalted butter, cut into
   small chunks
1 large fresh black truffle, sliced, or a
   large handful of dried porcini

Poach the chicken in the stock, together with the onions, garlic, bouquet garni and salt. Simmer, covered for around about 1–1½ hours. Lift out and keep warm in a low oven, covered with foil, or in a steamer if you have one big enough.

Strain the chicken-cooking liquor through a fine sieve (discard all solids) and return it to the pan. Allow to settle and lift off any grease with kitchen paper. Bring up to a healthy simmer and drop in the celery hearts. Simmer for about 20–25 minutes until tender. Lift out and keep warm with the chicken.

Now reduce the chicken broth until it is well flavoured (watch out for excess salt) and just starting to become syrupy. Over the merest thread of heat, whisk in the butter bit by bit until the liquid is lightly thickened and has a gloss to it. Slip in the truffle slices and allow simply to warm through.

Carve the chicken onto a serving platter and arrange the celery hearts around the edge. Spoon over the truffle juices and serve at once.

Chocolate bavarois

————

SERVES 4

Tragically, it seems the only 'set' dairy dessert (a blancmange, in other words and therefore stiffened with gelatine) one ever encounters on a restaurant menu these days is the Italian one known as pannacotta. There is nothing wrong with this *per se*, but whatever has happened to the jolly little bavarois — that wobbling confection of set milky custard mounted with whipped cream? There are endless variations on the basic theme, but it is this chocolate one which remains a great favourite.

4 leaves gelatine
500ml milk
175g dark chocolate, broken
   into pieces

4 egg yolks
75g caster sugar
50g cocoa powder
250ml double cream

First place a roomy bowl in the fridge to chill and also lightly oil four ramekins or dariole moulds.

Immerse the gelatine leaves in cold water and leave until soft and spongy.

Warm the milk and chocolate together in a small pan, stirring occasionally, until the chocolate has melted. Whisk together until fully amalgamated and creamy. Set aside for a few moments. Beat together the egg yolks, sugar and cocoa in a small bowl until very thick and khaki-coloured. Gently whisk in a little of the milk/chocolate mixture just to loosen it and then return all of this to the pan. Set upon a gentle heat and, stirring constantly, cook until thickened to the consistency of a rich custard. Remove from the heat, lift out the softened gelatine leaves and stir into the custard to melt. Now strain the mixture through a sieve into the previously chilled bowl and vigorously whisk to assist a quick cooling of the mixture. Place in the fridge until set to *just* a wobble.

Whip the cream in another bowl to the 'soft-peak' stage. Gently re-beat the chocolate mixture to break up its stiffness and then deftly fold in a small amount of the whipped cream to loosen it. Fold in the remaining cream until fully incorporated and any streaks of cream have disappeared into the chocolate custard. Spoon into the moulds, cover each one with a small sheet of clingfilm and place in the fridge to set for at least 4 hours. Once set, un-mould by running a small knife around the inside of the moulds and turn out onto four small, chilled plates. Serve either with a bowl of whipped cream or a well-chilled custard that has been flavoured with a dash of Cointreau or Grand Marnier.

CHOICE TASTING

In this country, where it seems that the festive season continues relatively unabated from Christmas Eve right through to the early days of January (sometimes longer, depending upon how the weekends happen to fall), it seems to me that surely a modicum of relief is necessary on the food front, 'twixt Christmas and New Year celebrations. Whether this be a welcome remission from interminable plates of cold cuts, turkey curry or bubble and squeak (though the latter seems to have reinvented itself as a dish that is now cooked from scratch – I mean, *really*), but what is abundantly clear to me, is that any sort of domestic daily sustenance should surely, by now, be veering towards occasional moments of 'choice tasting' rather than fully fledged lunches and dinners. Here are four little numbers to be going on with.

Cold ham soufflé
with
Cumberland sauce

SERVES 4

I first learnt of this charming and delicate hors d'œuvre – as they then used to be called – from the menu of a small restaurant in Newport, Pembrokeshire in the early 1970s. It was called The Pantry and was, at the time, a place of note. It was expensive, with reference to the time, for the rather simple seaside town where it was and also with regard to my wages: £25 per week. Four of us, who all worked in the same hotel some miles away, saved up for such treats and went whenever we felt the urge to splurge.

I grew to like the place so much that I applied for a job. It lasted four weeks and then I was sacked. It was the only time this has ever happened to me and, to this day, I have never been entirely sure why. At least I managed to garner a good recipe whilst briefly employed.

4 leaves gelatine
175ml hot, not boiling water; or better still, ham stock, previously boiled
200g cooked lean ham
100g cooked salted ox tongue
freshly milled white pepper
2 egg whites
250ml double cream

for the Cumberland sauce:
2 oranges
2 lemons
150ml port
1 jar redcurrant jelly (around about 300g-ish)
1 large knob of fresh ginger, peeled and grated
2 tsp English mustard powder
1 tsp arrowroot

First make the sauce. Thinly pare the rind of the oranges and lemons, cut into very thin strips, blanch quickly in boiling water, then drain and rinse under cold running water. Dry on kitchen paper and reserve. Squeeze the juice from the oranges and lemons and put into a non-reactive saucepan. Add the port, jelly and ginger, bring to a simmer and allow to cook for 10 minutes. Strain through a fine sieve and then pour back into the same (cleaned) pan. Mix the mustard and arrowroot together with 2 tbsp water until smooth. Add to the port/jelly liquid and whisk together thoroughly. Bring to a simmer and cook for a few minutes until shiny and thickened. Stir in the reserved orange and lemon rind and leave to cool completely.

To make the mousse, first soften the gelatine leaves in cold water and then fish them out and put into a bowl. Pour over the hot water or ham stock and stir to dissolve. Pour through a fine sieve and leave to cool to room temperature. Purée the ham in a food processor until smooth and tip into a roomy bowl. Cut the tongue into tiny cubes and mix into the ham thoroughly, together with the gelatine liquid, until all is a homogenous mass. Generously season with white pepper.

Beat the egg whites until stiff-ish – but not over-beaten – and fold into the ham mixture. Put into the fridge for about 1 hour, the surface covered with clingfilm, until starting to set but not solid (keep an eye on this setting process). Loosely whip the cream until just floppy. Remove the mousse from the fridge and fold in the cream carefully but swiftly.

I like to serve the mousse in individual ramekins, piled in so that the mixture stands proud from the dishes in soft peaks. Loosely wrap with clingfilm and put in the fridge to set. Serve with brown toast, lightly buttered, together with the Cumberland sauce handed round separately in a bowl.

Jansson's temptation

SERVES 3—4, FOR A LIGHT LUNCH

I think it may have been my learned friend Alastair Little who first informed me of the delights of the Swedish potato dish known as 'Jansson's temptation'. Consequently, for many years since – and in the most absurdly vicarious fashion – I have forever been singing its praises as 'one of the most delicious potato dishes I know' without ever having the slightest idea of how it tastes, or the dickens of an idea as to how to make it.

That which I had always implicitly recalled, however (one just does), were the ingredients used to make the dish – as if they had somehow been stamped upon my brain all the time. To have any success with the recipe, I was strictly informed, it was absolutely essential that *only* Swedish preserved anchovies should be used, as opposed to the more readily available, dark pink Mediterranean slivers that we had long known as the only tinned anchovy fillets. And, quite simply, these will not do here. At all.

Fifteen years on. West Sussex. Lunch with fine cook and good friend, Michael Birkett – and on a clear-blue sky, just gorgeous Saturday, two-dry-Martini lunchtime, as it happened. So, I finally sat down (very carefully) to eat Jansson's temptation for the first time, all freshly baked and bubbling from the top oven of the Rayburn. Michael possibly said something like 'Will this do?'. To which I replied, 'Don't be so silly... this looks lovely.' However intoxicated, I never, ever forget that memorable moment when one has eaten something truly delicious for the very first time.

Michael buys his anchovies at Ikea, don't you know – and I think the particular canners go under the popular brand name of 'Abba'. If you decide to stock up, always keep them in the fridge.

50g softened butter

2 onions, peeled and finely chopped

2 x 125g tins Swedish anchovies, including the juice from only *one* of the tins

6 medium-sized, red-skinned potatoes (Desiree), peeled, cut into thick matchsticks, briefly rinsed, well drained and dried

a little salt and some freshly ground white pepper

400ml whipping cream

2 tbsp fresh white breadcrumbs

Preheat the oven to 190°C/375°F/gas mark 5.

Grease a shallow, ovenproof dish (handsome enough to transfer from oven to table) with half of the given softened butter. Fill the base of it with the onions. Using a pair of scissors, snip the anchovies into small pieces (three snips per fillet should do it) and distribute them over the onions. Pour over the juice from one of the tins. Cover with the prepared potatoes, press them down lightly and season. Pour over the cream and then quietly tap the dish a couple of times upon a wooden surface to settle the assembly. Sprinkle the breadcrumbs evenly over the surface and dot with the remaining softened butter.

Bake in the oven for anything between 45 minutes to 1 hour, or until the surface of the dish is nicely gilded, crusted and bubbling around the edges. Serve as it is, all on its own.

Creamed mussels
with
fenugreek and
crisp garlic bread

———

SERVES 4

The following tasty number is a variation on my dad's famous 'Twiddled prawns'; well, it was hugely famous in all parts of south Lancashire during most of the 1960s, I can tell you. As much as mum was always the provider of traditional family dishes that gave sustenance and familiar flavours, it eventually transpired that, in dentist dad, there was also this playful, mildly frustrated cook aching to pull off a decent curry, crisp sweet and sour pork or a remarkably authentic paella. I just hope that he approves of this recent adaptation; knowing him, however, he will probably have something rude to say...

NOTE: **The kneaded butter (*beurre-manié*) used in this recipe is a very useful thing to have around; stored in a sealed pot in the fridge, it will keep for a week or so. Simply mix together equal quantities of soft butter and flour to a paste. This mixture, finally, is nothing more than an un-cooked roux.**

1 medium onion, peeled and chopped
2 cloves garlic, peeled and chopped
50g butter
2 tbsp tinned, chopped tomatoes
1 tbsp white wine vinegar
100ml dry white wine
1kg mussels
2–3 tsp kneaded butter (*beurre-manié*)

1 dsp dried fenugreek leaves (available from Indian food stores)
150ml double cream
freshly ground white pepper

4 thick slices of baguette, spread with garlic butter and baked, or grilled, until crisp

Using a roomy, lidded pot, fry the onion and garlic in the butter until pale golden and then stir in the tomatoes. Add the vinegar and boil the contents of the pan until reduced to a thick paste. Pour in the wine, allow it to bubble for a couple of minutes and then tip in the mussels. Stir them around a bit and then cover the pot. Leave the mussels to steam for a few minutes and then shake the topmost layer to the bottom, so revealing those from beneath (already opened) on to the surface. Replace the lid and cook for a few minutes longer.

Once all the mussels are clearly open, tip them into a colander – suspended over another pan or bowl – and leave there for 5 minutes, so allowing their cooking liquor to fully drain. Strain the result through a fine sieve into a medium-sized saucepan. Shell the mussels – checking for any remaining stubborn beards – into a bowl (discard shells) and put to one side.

Now start to add the kneaded butter to the strained mussel juices, whisking as you go. Add the fenugreek leaves now, and leave the sauce to simmer and thicken for a good 5 minutes. Stir in the cream and continue to simmer until the consistency is of a coating consistency. Check for seasoning. Pass once more through a fine sieve; if, at this stage, you wish for a smoother, creamier consistency, give the sauce a whiz in the liquidiser. Re-heat the reserved mussels in the sauce and spoon each serving over a crisp slice of garlic bread.

Homemade taramasalata
with
boiled eggs and black olives

—

SERVES 4

I am of an age that pre-dates ready-to-dip, plastic pots of pink taramasalata; those that are now so readily available in almost every grocer, supermarket and the tiniest corner shop possible – from Land's End to John O'Groats. So ubiquitous have these become, that you will most often find such a thing stacked tight up against the milk, the butter and the processed cheese. Have no fear, I have nothing against this pink paste; so much so that I am moved to purchase the odd pot or two from time to time. But it doesn't bear any relation to the real thing.

The recipe that follows, purists might argue, is not the real thing either, and that a true 'tarama' is made from the salted roe of a type of Mediterranean grey mullet. Certainly, it would not have been fashioned from the crimson-hued lobes of smoked cod's roe that we, those keen cooks of the late 1960s and early '70s were so instructed to find with which to make our tarama. But we did. And we liked the result. Maybe it turned out a bit pink as a result. But, surely, it was never the Strawberry Angel Delight pink that we see now?

½ small onion, peeled and chopped
1 clove garlic, peeled and chopped
juice of 1 lemon
200g freshly smoked cod's roe, skinned
2 heaped tbsp fresh white breadcrumbs
freshly ground white pepper

150–200ml olive oil
a little salt, if necessary

2 boiled eggs (try to keep the yolks soft-ish), shelled and halved
black olives
toast, pitta etc…

Place the onion, garlic and lemon juice in a food processor and purée to a paste. Tip this paste into a sieve – previously suspended over a bowl – and vigorously press out the juices using the back of a small ladle. Discard the vegetable solids, rinse out the processor bowl and return to it the extracted juices. Introduce the cod's roe, breadcrumbs and pepper and pulse-purée to a rough paste. Once mixed, and with the motor running moderately, begin to introduce some of the olive oil (about half of it) in a thin stream until the mixture has visibly thickened. Have a little taste, now, and then choose to decide as to how much more oil you wish to add. The more oil you use, the thicker and more 'mayonnaise-like', smooth and bland the taramasalata will become. Only you can decide, at this critical point. Decorate with the eggs and olives and start toasting the pittas.

FAT CHANCE

Something controversial this week. Foie gras. I felt nudged into talking about it after last week's chicken terrine recipe. Although the only real similarity between the two is of layered and pressed meat, I experienced a fleeting lapse of taste, thinking that a strata of melting and rich foie gras might, momentarily, have added a further dimension to the simple notion of just chicken.

But I would have been wrong. The chicken needed nothing more than its hint of lemon, garlic and basil to lift it; the addition of foie gras would just have turned it into yet another restaurant 'pressed terrine'. Of late, there have been rather a lot of these. They are usually layers of either duck *confit* (*everything* seems to be bloody *confit* just now: *confit* lamb, *confit* salmon, *confit* garlic, *confit* tomato, *confit* egg and lettuce sandwich); some sort of salted pork – trotter, cheek or, most popular of all, hock; artichoke and potato; even aubergine. But they usually all have layers of foie gras with which to cement the other components together. FG is best all on its own.

All is lost here (aubergine should never have been found in the first place), because the thing with foie gras – the only thing really – is it's downright, all in your face, slip across the tongue, clog those arteries, RICH. It does not let up, foie gras. Its fat, perfectly pink, lumps of liver attend upon the palate like no other sybaritic food – save that of the finest Beluga.

Don't misunderstand this admission of an over-healthy greed for luxury foods as flippant. Moreover, I can only take deliciously small helpings of foie gras these days; smearings rather than slabs. The first time I was presented with some as the initial dish of a six-course lunch was at a one-star Michelin restaurant in Chartres, in 1981. Two rosy slabs had been hewn from a whole terrine, which surely could not have been much smaller than a pale pink Patrick Cox shoe box.

I ate it all, spread thickly onto golden slices of toasted brioche. As I recall, the fourth course was carved duck breast in a cream sauce. I did not eat again that day.

To make a simple – and I mean that in the purest, rather than in the constructional – terrine of foie gras taste good, it needs to be marinated and seasoned by a few aromatic ingredients. Port, a good amontillado, and either Armagnac or Cognac provide the correct alcoholic bath for the liver. A warm spice mixture called *quatre épices* has been found, by many cooks, to be the ideal seasoner. It is easily made in the home kitchen (I have never seen it for sale here, let alone France) by grinding together peppercorns, cloves and nutmeg, and then stirring in powdered ginger. Quantities will follow later.

Not wishing to beat about the bush, foie gras is not 'simplicity itself' (horrible phrase and often misleading) to make in the home. It's really quite difficult; I still find it quite tricky sometimes, even after having been making it on and off for around about 15 years or so. But it *is* worth having a go, and – once you have mastered the thing – is *so* much cheaper than buying it ready-made or paying even more for a slice or two of it in a restaurant.

I hope this humble encouragement is certainly a more tactful approach to the home cook, than was a chef recipe I read recently. It was grandly insisted upon, for the finished dish, that 'Our elaborate garnish of *fromage blanc* with fresh herbs and caviar is too complicated to prepare in your own kitchen, but you can replace it with a small salad garnish and mayonnaise'. Oh, well deary me!

When making this terrine, I had just bought some late season black truffles, so included a few slices within. These will make the foie gras taste particularly good and are a classical inclusion – if you are feeling flush, that is.

Fresh foie gras terrine

———

SERVES 8, PERFECTLY

The wizard wheeze for making your very own fatty liver parcel of joy, is to use the individual take-away carton. Naturally, this should be an un-used, pristine carton, by the way; not one that has been scraped of its fragmentary smears of sweet and sour prawn balls, chicken and cashews or anonymous curried matter.

1 x 650–750g fresh foie gras (it will arrive vacuum-packed; also try and keep within the weight parameters if possible, as this is right for the carton size)

2 tsp Maldon sea salt

1 rounded tsp caster sugar

1 rounded tsp *quatre épices*

2 tbsp port

1 tbsp medium sherry

1 scant tbsp Cognac or Armagnac

for the quatre épices:

125g white peppercorns

10g cloves

30g ground ginger (or whole dried ginger)

35g whole nutmeg (crush slightly before grinding)

Firstly, make the *quatre épices*. The best machine to use is a small coffee grinder. Once you have ground the spices as far as you think fit, tip into a sieve and sift over a sheet of greaseproof paper. Tip into a screw-top jar and label it; it is surprising how quickly one forgets what you have put into an empty spice jar.

First of all, remove the liver from its vacuum packet. Slip into a bowl of cold water and, using your fingers, gently massage the liver clean of juices that have collected in the packet. Carefully ease the two lobes apart (one is much bigger than the other), rinse in between them and then lift out of the bowl. Chuck away the water. Fill the bowl with clean water and re-immerse the liver. Sprinkle in a little salt and leave the liver to soften up for about 1–1½ hours, at kitchen temperature.

Drain the liver once more and pat dry thoroughly with kitchen paper. In between the two lobes, you will see a distinct fatty nerve that holds them together. Cut through this with a small sharp knife to separate them (you will need this knife throughout the preparation). Place the large lobe onto a chopping board and turn over, its smooth side down.

Now then, its time to remove the veins – and this, honestly, is the most tricky of all. First of all, remove a uniform lump of liver from the middle of the lobe – you can just pull this away and put on one side. Then, using the back of the small knife, start to work the soft flesh of the liver away from the centre of the lobe, where you will begin to see a network of pinky-red veins, heralded by one large one that you can hold between two fingers. Having grabbed this, continue to cut back the flesh (remember to keep using the *back* of the knife, otherwise you will sever the veins rather than lift them away) so that the veins reveal themselves rather like the Nile delta.

Once you cannot see any more veins, gently lift the network away, by lightly tugging and easing away with the knife. Once these veins have been removed, there are more… Up at the top, narrower end of the liver, you will find another prominent beginning to a network of veins (keep going…). Once again, seize the beginning of the vein and start to proceed as you did before. This network, in fact, travels underneath the ones you have just removed. Finally, check around for any stray ones that you may have missed.

You may be shocked as to how the lobe looks now, but worry not, as it all melts back together later on in the process. Carefully place onto a shallow tray and simply put any stray lumps of liver on top, including the first lump that you put on one side. Take the other smaller lobe now, and treat it in exactly the same way as the larger one; the network of veins lies in similar distribution here too. Put this one onto the tray with the larger lobe.

Whilst the two lobes are displayed, gashes prominent, upon the tray, sprinkle with about half of the given amount of salt, sugar and *quatre épices* (if you wish to insert slices of black truffle, do so now). Close up the flaps of cut-away liver, enclosing the seasoning within, and try to reform the original shape to the lobes. Place the livers, smooth side up this time, into a deep-ish porcelain oval dish, or similar, that will take them snugly. Spoon over the alcohols, and sprinkle evenly with the remaining seasoning. Cover with clingfilm and put into the fridge to marinate for at least 12 hours and as much as 24, turning once half way through.

Preheat the oven to around about 100°C – or equivalent.

Allow the liver to come up to room temperature – for about 1 hour, until they feel soft. Loosely cover with foil and put into the oven for about 45–50 minutes, checking, from time to time, using your finger, to check the internal temperature: it should only be warm, not hot, and the livers will have an almost jelly-like consistency. Do not be alarmed over the amount of deep yellow fat that has accumulated, this you cannot help. Remove from the oven and have two portion size, foil take-away cartons handy (available from supermarkets).

Allow the foie gras to cool for half an hour in its dish. I know it looks a bit odd now – all sort of flobbery – but do be brave. When cool enough to handle, lift out first the smaller lobe, using a fish slice and your hand, and slip it into the foil carton. Then take the larger one and flop it on top of the other with the nicest looking, smooth side uppermost. Tuck and jiggle it around, so that the surface looks nice and neat. Do not worry that it may be slightly proud from the rim of the carton; this is the idea. Place the lid onto the carton, silvered side against the liver, and clamp around the edges, *but not the corners*. Do not discard the fat and juices from the porcelain cooking dish.

Now put the empty carton into another dish, upside down, and then deftly place the carton containing the foie gras, upside down, onto the empty carton. The action of this, will, all under its own weight, press the livers together. Leave like this, the juices and excess fat dripping out of each corner of the carton, for at least 1 hour. Then, without budging the thing, place in the fridge for 4 hours. Scrape the liver's cooking fat and juices from the dish and place in a small pan.

Remove the liver from the fridge and revert. Chuck out the empty carton and add the fat and juices that have collected in the bottom of the dish, to the small pan. Put this on to warm through; the fat will rise to the top. Set aside. Remove the lid from the foie gras and spoon enough of the fat over the surface to seal and cover. Place in the fridge like this, for 30 minutes, for the fat to harden, then wrap in clingfilm and put back into the fridge. I like to leave it there for 2 days, at least, before eating. It will keep, well covered, for about 10 days.

To, serve, cut around the edge of the fat (it may crack a little, but you are not going to serve it – at least, I don't), tip out the terrine onto a surface, by pulling away the sides of the carton (another very good reason for using a disposable vessel). Dip a sharp knife into hot water and slice the foie gras thick. Serve with thin, hot, crust-less toast.

FRYING TONIGHT

There was a mad Welsh woman who used to live at the end of my road (when I lived in Welsh west Wales) who preferred to cook certain things in the garage rather than her kitchen. Well, of course, she wasn't *really* mad at all and was, in fact, perfectly sane and nice… But, let's face it, most sane people do, usually, prefer to use a kitchen in which to make dinner, as opposed to… well, any other room in the entire house, I would think. 'But it's the smell, bach, you see.' (Spoken with a strong Welsh accent, for best effect.) Yes, yes, that worrying smell of food being cooked! She just couldn't bear all that nasty odour permeating through her – naturally – immaculate house.

People who knew Mrs. Jones (the names have been changed to protect the soft furnishings) better than did I, gossiped of only ever seeing salads and such like being put together in the kitchen itself; a high-tea salad, that sort of thing, with beetroot, lettuce, spring onion, cucumber, sliced boiled egg (would the egg have been boiled in the kitchen, do you think?). All stews, fried food and boiled vegetables, however, once prepared for actual cooking, would swiftly be transported out through the kitchen door and down a few steps which led directly into the safety of the cold, thankfully draughty garage.

Furthermore, I seem to recall that the garage was also bereft of the car it was built to house (a pale blue Triumph Stag lived in the drive at all times, dutifully washed and polished with much vigour by Mr. Jones thrice weekly), so safe in the knowledge that the vehicle's interior upholstery would also not be tainted by the stench of cabbage, beef stew or – heaven forbid! – some such thing as a small piece of fried fish.

I was reminded of mad Mrs. Jones when Jason the Snapper (formerly Jason the Camera) had left after photographing the pictures of deep-fried fish that illustrate this week's ramble. And I suppose that, if I am honest, I wouldn't have minded having an adjacent garage in which to fire-up the deep fryer and cook my sole, mussels and whitebait – even though there is, for a domestic London apartment kitchen, a relatively powerful extractor fan fitted over the stove-top where I locate the machine when choosing to use it. But the fug pervades my entire living space all the same; and

woe betide me if I have also forgotten to remove my freshly laundered clothes, silently drying above me on the rails of the overhead Dutch airer, conveniently placed just a few feet askew from the offending fumes…

My mother also had a Dutch airer placed directly over the Aga. And we had a chip-pan too. Once my brother and I were old enough to cook for ourselves, we would make late-night chips in this chip-pan. And, as was the norm in those days, the grease we used for frying was manufactured from pure beef dripping. My, but they were the best chips! We also had a fairly new-fangled gadget that allowed one to neatly fit a peeled potato in it, pull down a handle with a good, strong grip whereupon immaculate fat sticks of raw potato would magically emerge on the other side, forced as they were through a sharp, metal grid affair. We would then cook them in hot dripping until they seemed just right. Occasionally, they would be a bit raw in the middle and too brown on the outside (fat too hot), but once salted and dipped in ketchup… well, we liked them anyway. Naturally, we never thought to notice the freshly ironed garments then either, adroitly airing as they were above our carefree, teenage bonces.

When fresh food is expertly deep-fried it can emerge, without doubt, as one of the finest gastronomic treats imaginable. It is generally understood that the finest deep-friers of food in the world are the Chinese, particularly when it comes to seafood. The Japanese are also renowned for their unique crisp 'tempura' batter that, most often (in the UK, that is), encases large prawns in a riot of minute bubbles of pustulated starch, so also sealing in the most effective fashion the juices of the fish within.

Good examples of tempura can be spectacular; poor ones, however, are filthy in the extreme – particularly those that are ignorantly attempted by a few home-grown cowboy chefs, keen to impress as to their recently acquired knowledge of all aspects of Japanese cookery ('Oh yeah, that old tempura batter is a synch!') yet haven't the slightest clue as to how carefully it should be cooked or traditionally presented. The real tragedy, however, is how surprised they are when people say 'Thank you very much, we actually don't like this at all.'

Crisp green mussels

SERVES 4

Not, as you might first think, a recipe using those gross, green-lipped mussels imported all the way from New Zealand, but a little bit of a Hoppy creation – if I may be so bold. I was very excited indeed to find quite how successful these diminutive fishy morsels turned out to be, once they had emerged from the deep fryer. It is the pure mussel juice that surprises one, as it exudes into the mouth when eaten. Granted, a fiddly and time-consuming recipe, but I think you will find the results well worth the effort.

2007 – It is surely ironic that a mussel flown all the way to the UK from New Zealand could be labelled 'green', now. This is one of the most absurd imports I know and should be banned right away. I wouldn't mind if they were nice to eat. In fact, they are as tasteless as they are unwelcome. Do we honestly not have enough of our own mussels both here and around all the coasts of France, Spain and Italy? And those from Holland, too, of course. Just when will this sort of nonsense cease?

40–50 mussels, lightly steamed and shelled (keep the mussel shells); it is important that the mussels emerge slightly underdone, remembering that they will be cooked once more, immersed in the hot oil
a little flour
very fine (sieved, in other words) dry breadcrumbs

oil, for deep-frying
lemons

for the parsley purée:
1 large bunch of parsley, picked
1 egg
1 clove garlic, peeled and chopped
1 tsp Pernod
1 tsp flour
salt and a pinch of cayenne pepper

Preheat the deep fryer to 180–185°C.

Once shelled, lay the mussel meat onto a tea-towel to dry. Process all the ingredients for the parsley purée in a food processor until very smooth. Have a little flour and some breadcrumbs, each arranged in two shallow bowls and the purée in another one. Dip each mussel first in the flour (very lightly), then in the purée and, finally, in the breadcrumbs. Deep-fry in batches (say, 10) for 2–3 minutes, or until pale golden and with the green coating still clearly visible beneath the crumbs. Arrange as depicted in the accompanying photograph.

Goujons of sole
with
dipping sauce

SERVES 2

An Asian take on the French fish finger.

175–200g Dover sole (or lemon sole)
    fillets, cut into thin strips
seasoned flour
1 egg, beaten
fresh white breadcrumbs
oil, for deep-frying
salt

for the dipping sauce:
a handful of coriander leaves
10–12 mint leaves
1 red chilli, de-seeded or not
    (depending upon your heat
    threshold), chopped
1 clove garlic, peeled and chopped
1–2 tbsp fish sauce
juice of 1 large lime
1 tbsp stem ginger syrup (or 1–2 tsp
    caster sugar)
a little water

Preheat the deep fryer to 180ºC.

To make the dipping sauce, briefly process all the ingredients together with a little water until the texture of English mint sauce.

Dredge each strip of fish in the seasoned flour, shaking off any excess, then coat in the egg, roll in the breadcrumbs and carefully lay the fish out on to a tray; this operation can be done up to 30 minutes in advance. Fry the strips for about 3 minutes, in batches, or until crisp and golden all over. Lift out, allow to drain and then tip onto folded sheets of kitchen paper. Sprinkle with salt and serve the dipping sauce in small bowls alongside.

Devilled whitebait

SERVES 2

Quite why a few crisp, freshly fried whitebait do not make more appearances as a restaurant pre-dinner nibble is a question I have frequently asked myself, of late. Rather this any day than the now ubiquitous coffee-cup of frothy, truffle oil-slicked soup that one is forced to sip with much irritable yawning.

350–400g fresh whitebait (although
    good quality frozen can be
    surprisingly good)
milk
self-raising flour, generously
    seasoned with cayenne pepper and
    a little salt

oil, for deep-frying
salt and extra cayenne pepper,
    for dusting
lemons

Preheat the deep fryer to 190ºC.

Put the whitebait into a bowl and pour enough milk over them to just cover. Leave them submerged for 10 minutes or so, then drain in a colander or sieve. Discard the milk. Put the seasoned flour in a large plastic bag and tip in the drained whitebait. Toss them around in it, shaking the bag well until each and every tiny fish is thoroughly coated. Suspend the frying basket over the sink and then lift small handfuls of flour-coated fish directly into the basket – but only fry *one* portion of fish at a time; to over-crowd the fryer when cooking whitebait will end in absolute disaster: a sorry mass of soggy fish. Slowly lower the basket into the oil and fry for no more than 1–2 minutes, or until the fish are pale golden and super-crisp: they should rustle well, when shaken. Sprinkle with salt and a little extra cayenne, depending how devilish one is feeling at the time. Drain onto folded kitchen paper and serve with lemon.

STAYING PUT

In the old days one could rely on it being very cold indeed just now (*January 2001*) and I would expect, at the very least, for there to be snow on the ground and ice on the roads from time to time. During the severe winter of 1963, I recall that a couple of large Westmoreland lakes transformed themselves into free-for-all skating rinks with several derring-doers cycling across them with glee – albeit with a touch of anxiety apparent on their brightly beaming, scarf-wrapped ruddy faces. Not any more, however. An early British February now seems to be nothing more than dreary and damp. Would that I were to be proved wrong this year. But, as it is already a relatively mild January as I write, all I can envisage are liquid lakes with their shores decorated by hosts of slightly confused daffodils being further surprised by a suffocation from the stink of a host of early wild garlic leaves.

The beginning of any British February will always be a testing time for those who are both keen to cook and who also choose to reside here. Well, whilst the timid may be more tempted by the temperate climes of the Caribbean or Cairns, we hardy natives carry on regardless. We make good with the occasional woodcock (a rarity indeed, these days); enjoy the delights of the first of the forced rhubarb, all pink and stewed in Pyrex bowls; savour the occasional blistering hot servings of braised chicory wrapped in ham, covered in rich béchamel and glazed with cheese; are dazzled just the once by a small, imported fresh black truffle from Périgord (at their absolute peak just now) finely shaved over a plate of scrambled eggs; a few worthwhile days spent potting up jars of Seville orange marmalade. Let me tell you, it beats a bowl of dull, green and tepid calalo soup eaten in blistering hot sunshine any day of the week. And, furthermore, endless glasses of rum punch will never, ever be a substitute for Claret, Burgundy, Chablis and Riesling, come rain or shine.

So, feeling soggy, irritable but stoic to the last, what is it to be that will add zing and zip to the cooking of the dark months? Here are a couple of savoury numbers to be getting on with.

Fragrant duck 'pilaf'
with
lemon and mint

—

SERVES 2

I have chosen to call the following preparation a 'pilaf' simply because the end result of this particular pulse, once cooked, seems so redolent of a pot of savoury rice that to call it 'baked duck with dal, lemon and mint' would surely fail to attract even the most informed fans of the farinaceous. Moong dal, used here, is possessed of such lightness of starch that it can even display some of the characteristics of a fine biriani. The traditional Pakistani cook, naturally, would passionately disagree with me here, but I think that my comparison remains a relatively sound observation nonetheless.

However, having now wittered on about all of that with reference to an Asian influence, to flavour a duck with mint and lemon was first introduced to me by a fine fellow called John Marfell, now long late as chef of a once grand Cotswold restaurant called Cleeveway House, in the village of Bishop's Cleeve, Gloucestershire. Christopher Driver, then editor of the 1972 edition of *The Good Food Guide* (Hodder & Stoughton, 1972), had wittily chosen to illustrate various establishments of note with wickedly accurate caricatures of their proprietors or chefs, with the bespectacled Marfell depicted as an absolute dead-ringer for a coming-of-age Harry Potter – I kid you not! Other distinguished worthies of the era are a Victor Spinetti-like Franco Taruschio and an Eddie Izzard clone of Robert Carrier, if you please.

4 duck legs
salt and freshly ground black pepper
a little oil or duck fat
1 large onion, finely chopped
4 cloves garlic, sliced
1 scant tsp ground cumin
a healthy pinch of dried chilli flakes
40g butter
350g moong dal, well rinsed and drained
500ml chicken or duck stock
the thinly pared, pithless rind of 1 small lemon
2 tbsp freshly chopped mint
1 lemon, cut in half, to squeeze over the finished dish

Preheat the oven to 180°C/350°F/gas mark 4.

Season the duck legs and, using a lidded, cast-iron (or similar) oven-proof pot, gently fry them in the oil or fat, skin side down, until golden and crisp. Then turn over and lightly colour the other sides. Remove to a plate.

Discard all but 2 tbsp of the rendered fat and then add the onion and garlic. Gently fry until pale golden and then stir in the cumin and chilli. Add the butter and stir around for a little longer before tipping in the dal. Coat the grains with fat using a stirring and folding motion, until all are glistening. Pour in the stock all at once, bring up to a simmer and stir in the lemon rind and mint. Cut the duck legs in half through their natural joints and slide into the mixture, along with any of their exuded juices. Put on the lid and bake in the oven for 30 minutes. Remove, but leave the lid on for a further 10 minutes before peeking. Now lift off the lid, fluff up the grains with a fork and serve at once, with the lemon halves alongside and, perhaps, also with a lightly dressed green salad.

Chilli crab salad
with
grapefruit and avocado

SERVES 4

There was a time when I would have instantly recoiled from such a dish as described above. Grapefruit with crab? Avocado with grapefruit? Crab with avocado, maybe, but it was this assembly of shellfish with breakfast fruit that had always struck me as a little crook, to say the least. This quandary continued unabated for years until the day I sat down to lunch at the Oriental Hotel in Bangkok, and was then moved to rapturously applaud a spirited plateful of crab meat, pomelo (related to the grapefruit), traditional Thai salad garnishings dressed up with indigenous herbs, chilli, fish sauce and all manner of further aromatics.

Moments of conversion such as this give me the greatest pleasure – and it could only have happened there, I guess. Any attempt to recreate such a thing in some dodgy West End 'Pacific Rim' joint, composed by some spunky, imported Aussie lad with loud chequerboard trousers would not, I feel, have been the same thing at all. Unconvinced I would have remained, which would have been a shame.

leaves from hearts of 2 Little Gem
   lettuces, or similar, washed and
   drained
1 pink or red grapefruit, rind and
   all pith removed with a knife,
   then neatly segmented and seeds
   picked out
1 just-ripe avocado, peeled and sliced
4–5 heaped tbsp fresh, white crab meat

for the dressing:
leaves from 1 small bunch of coriander
leaves from 6 mint sprigs
2 cloves garlic, chopped
4–5 small green chillies, seeds
   removed (or not), chopped
1 tbsp caster sugar
juice of 4 large limes
8 tbsp oriental fish sauce
8 tbsp tepid water

To make the dressing place all the ingredients in a liquidiser (preferably) or food processor and whiz to a pale green sludge. Decant into a bowl and allow the flavours to mingle. Neatly arrange the lettuce, grapefruit, avocado and crab upon four individual plates and generously spoon over the dressing.

WINTER WARMERS

Dad always, but always, liked to have a tin or two of butter beans in the kitchen cupboard. I am the same with tins of Farrow's marrow-fat peas. 'Just in case', he would say. And so do I.

I seem to remember that my brother and I were not *that* keen on the old butter bean, as children. It might have been the sort of crumbly, floury texture that we found a bit of a struggle. I still find chestnuts difficult for similar reasons and I know I will continue to deeply loathe the highly overrated *marron glacé*, almost more than anything else. But I grew to love butter beans, and I still like them out of a tin, along with flageolets, haricots, borlottis – and Heinz baked beans, naturally.

The bean, whether it be dried or processed in a can, is one of the most important storecupboard ingredients I know – and particularly so at this time of year. These early New Year months, dark and cold, wet and windy and, frankly, dank and dreary, are just the right moment to rip open a bag – or pierce a can – of pulse, be it bean, lentil or pea. These tummy warmers of the inevitable British winter months, give every good reason to spend them in the warmth of your very own kitchen, radio on and pinny tied.

Considering how cold and dismal we find ourselves and our surroundings just now, it is, these days, slightly depressing to find that we are now happier depending upon recipes from the continent, to supplement our own ways with these familiar staples. So, inevitably, the majority of us cannot get enough hummus, cassoulet and polenta these days. There is a *salade de lentilles* for us to marvel at under each and every small-fish-assembly first course. Chickpeas, chorizo and mussels are used to make soups that have their roots in the Iberian peninsula, and flageolets to accompany roast lamb. A dish of borlotti beans transports Tuscany to Twickenham on a chilly February day, along with first pressing, extra virginal oils, flat-leaf parsley and garlic. And I would

be happy to eat all those dishes, every single one of them. Yet split pea and ham soup is the only home-grown warmer I can think of just now.

But there is one stupendous dish, created by my friend Leigh Stone-Herbert several years ago now. He took a simple ham hock, which he poached precisely, some perfectly ordinary green lentils (not a pulse from Puy anywhere in sight) cooked in the ham liquor and served as a winter salad, with some winter leaves from the garden. These prime ingredients were then dressed with a piquant emulsion, based upon the pungent, very English yellow mustard powder. My word was it good!

I first tasted this particularly English salad in the dining room of Gravetye Manor, near East Grinstead in leafy Sussex, the hotel which his father, Mr. Peter Herbert, is about to celebrate 40 years of proud ownership. It is one of the very finest examples of true excellence in that curious world of endeavouring to make eating, drinking and sleeping the best they can be. Peter Herbert, in his inimitable way, refers to it as 'The Pub' – albeit with an ironic twinkle – and it is one of the loveliest places on earth. The gardens, created by William Robinson in the early part of this century, are a constant joy to behold, and include a magnificent and huge walled garden, where most of the manor's fruit and vegetables are grown.

Now then, have you ever eaten boiled lamb's tongues? Well, I wouldn't suggest that you simply eat a bowl of them, naked and undressed, of course. But how about quietly poaching some with vegetables and a little wine, then making a parsley, egg and caper sauce to add a little piquancy, and serving them up with some slippery soft butter beans? Sounds just dandy to me. I don't see any reason at all why you might not use a tin of butter beans here, but, when you think about it, why not soak some dried ones overnight, and cook them ever so gently in the resultant stock from the tongues?

Poached lamb's tongues
and butter beans,
with parsley, egg and
caper sauce

—

SERVES 4

The finest dried butter beans I have ever found are Spanish ones. It is the melting quality of these, together with thin and tender skins, that make them so good to eat. Never cook soaked, dried beans or lentils with salt, as this can toughen the skins. The stock for cooking the beans will be improved if you slip in a few lamb bones, but this is not essential.

250g dried butter beans

for cooking the tongues:
10–12 very fresh lamb's tongues
1 large carrot, peeled and chopped
3 sticks celery, peeled and chopped
2 small leeks, trimmed, thickly sliced
   and rinsed
bouquet garni, to include a healthy
   bunch of parsley stalks
3 cloves
1 small glass of white wine
a couple of chopped up lamb bones
   (optional)
salt

for the sauce:
1 large bunch flat-leaf parsley,
   leaves only
10 mint leaves
1 tbsp capers, squeezed dry to rid
   them of excess vinegar
1 dsp anchovy essence
3 spring onions, chopped
1 scant tbsp Dijon mustard
75ml sunflower or peanut oil
2 hard-boiled eggs, finely chopped
a little salt to taste, if necessary, but
   plenty of pepper

Put the beans to soak in plenty of cold water and leave overnight.

Place the eight ingredients for cooking the tongues into a roomy, lidded pan. Cover with cold water and bring up to a simmer. Just as the liquid is about to roll, whip off the scum that has formed with a large spoon, and leave to tick over, covered, for about 1 hour. Check to see whether the tongues are tender using a skewer. If not, cook for a little longer.

Lift out the tongues and put onto a plate to cool for 5 minutes. Peel off their skins (this must be done whilst they are still moderately hot, as cold tongues can be difficult to skin) and put into a smaller pan that will just take them in one layer. Strain the stock into a bowl and rinse out the pan. Discard the vegetables (and bones, if used). Pour a little of the stock over the peeled tongues and add salt. Leave on one side.

Put the beans into the rinsed out pan and cover with cold water. Bring up to the boil and then drain in a colander. Rinse under cold running water to rid them of clinging scum and put back into the pan. Cover with the remaining tongue stock (if there is not enough to cover them, simply top up with water). Simmer very gently until nearly tender – about 1 hour. Add salt now and continue to cook for another 15 minutes or so, until fully tender. Keep warm, covered.

Whilst the beans are cooking, make the sauce. Put the first six ingredients into the bowl of a food processor and pulverise to a coarse paste. Add the oil, with the motor running, until emulsified. Scrape out into a bowl and stir in the eggs and seasoning. Don't be tempted to put the eggs in the processor as they will lose their texture in a trice. Also, another warning, there is a strange reaction that takes place between cooked egg and onion: they are just fine together when freshly mixed, but if left to sit for much longer than an hour or so, this happy marriage will soon turn sour.

To serve, re-heat the tongues and slice in two lengthways. Dish up five or six pieces onto hot plates, pile on some of the beans, using a slotted spoon, and put some of the sauce on the side. Finally, moisten with some of the cooking liquor.

Leigh Stone-Herbert's Gravetye ham hock
and lentil salad

SERVES 4

I have taken the liberty of interpreting Leigh's dish, here, and we served it with pride at Bibendum on many occasions – only, that is, when I was sure we had it just about right.

for cooking the ham hock:
1 ham hock
1 carrot, peeled and chopped
2 sticks celery, chopped
1 onion, peeled and stuck with 3 cloves
2 bay leaves
2 sprigs fresh tarragon
a sprinkling of peppercorns
1 small glass of white wine

5 tbsp large green lentils
3 spring onions, trimmed and finely chopped
1 clove garlic, peeled and finely chopped
1 tbsp freshly chopped parsley

for the mustard dressing:
1 tsp English mustard powder
1 dsp Dijon mustard
½ tsp caster sugar
1 dsp tarragon vinegar
salt and pepper
150ml sunflower or peanut oil

some winter salad leaves – lamb's lettuce, chicory, say

Put the hock into a pan and cover with cold water. Slowly bring to the boil and then lift out the hock with a fork and rinse under cold running water. Discard the water and put the hock back into the pan. Add the vegetables, herbs, spice and wine, and cover with water. Bring up to a simmer, skim off any scum with a spoon and cook gently for about 1¼ hours; the meat should be very tender and soft.

Lift out the hock and put onto a plate. Strain the cooking liquor into a bowl. Once the hock is cool enough to handle, lift off the meat in lumps, allowing a little skin and fat to fall off too (lots, if I have anything to do with it), and place in a small pan. Cover with a little of the ham liquor and keep warm on the back of the stove, covered.

Put the lentils in another small pan and cover generously with some more of the ham liquor. Bring up to a simmer and cook until tender. Strain the lentils over the bowl of stock, and put the lentils into another bowl. Stir in the spring onions, garlic and parsley.

To make the dressing, combine the mustards, sugar, vinegar and seasonings in (yet another) small bowl. Whisk together and then start to add the oil in a thin stream, continuing to whisk, as if making mayonnaise. The end result should be fairly thick. *Note*: You may make this in a food processor if you prefer. Add this dressing to the lentils, loosening it if you like, with a little of the ham liquor. The final consistency should be quite sloppy.

To serve, arrange the salad leaves onto four luke-warm plates, distribute the pieces of ham on top and spoon over the dressed lentils. It is really a matter for you, as to whether you make the dish very wet, or just moist and meaty.

TWO'S COMPANY

I was extremely gratified to hear from a sprinkling of last year's readers who were, once again, very pleased to be furnished with festive recipes that might suit a smaller gathering rather than that which is more usually offered around this time of year: that of the contented child-less couple who, against all odds, had happily chosen to remain indoors, quietly prepared a delicious Christmas lunch just for themselves, drunk a couple of bottles of really fine wine before finally retiring to bed with either The Queen or Bond.

Unashamedly, all three recipes I am offering are pretty damn rich. But, after all, this is just fine when it's only the two of you: you may indulge and please yourselves. There are no aunts or grannies, no permanently dieting teenage daughters and no 'little darlings' who will, respectively, worry, shrink away or have tantrums and be horribly sick. Just think, this freedom further allows you to pull six crackers each, giggle stupidly over the jokes without embarrassment and, with genuine affection, may lovingly offer up a tiny folding set of miniature screwdrivers in exchange for lipstick and eye-shadow tightly folded up within a floral handkerchief without, for once, the inevitable 'I wanted that!' followed by sulks. And you don't need to put a paper hat on your head if you really don't want to.

A very Happy Christmas to one and all! – and especially to two and no one else at all.

Braised pheasant

with cabbage, garlic and fat bacon

—

SERVES 2

25g butter

4 thick slices of very fat, streaky bacon, cut into squares

1 dressed pheasant

salt and pepper

10 large cloves garlic, peeled

a generous splash of Madeira or medium sherry

75ml white wine

100ml chicken stock

3–4 sprigs thyme

1 small, hard green cabbage, divested of tough outer leaves then cored and quartered

Preheat the oven to 140°C/275°F/gas mark 1.

Heat the butter in a large cast-iron pot (a lidded Le Creuset pot is perfect, here) and add the bacon. Allow the pieces to gently sizzle away until a generous amount of fat has exuded from them. Lift out and set aside. Season the pheasant with salt and pepper, place it in the pot and carefully allow to colour on all sides, until golden and crusted. Lift out and also set aside.

Now tip in the garlic and stir these against the crusty bits in the bottom of the pot, hoping to vaguely pick up scraps of residue in the process and until they have also taken on a little colour themselves. Tip off most of the collected, residual fats and pour in the Madeira (or sherry) and white wine. Using a stiff whisk, scrape up all the remaining bits and then add the stock and thyme sprigs. Bring to the boil and put in the cabbage. Simmer until the cabbage begins to wilt and lose its stiffness, then push it to the sides of the pot to make room for the pheasant. Bury the bird into this simmering brew and tuck the bacon pieces around it, pushing them well down into the pot.

Cut a piece of greaseproof paper to fit inside the pot (a *cartouche*) with a little room to spare, so that it comes up the sides a little; a few snips around the edge with a pair of scissors helps the thing to fall into place. (I used to think this contraption a waste of time but now, do not, as it really does add a secondary muffle to the proceedings in addition to the lid.) Put the lid on and place in the oven to braise for about 1–1½ hours. Remove from the oven but leave the lid in place for 20 minutes, or so, allowing the bird to settle and rest prior to carving. Serve with plainly boiled potatoes, nothing more.

Roast duck
with cider, cream and apples

—

SERVES 2

An unseasonably gruff note by way of introduction, but it is one that has been heavy on my mind for some time and fits, here. Although fully aware that each of the metric measurements for the quantities of cider and cream given for the duck sauce may look absurd, it is only because this happens to be the way in which they are sold in the supermarket: a quaffing can of Woodpecker cider is a curious 440ml and a pot of double cream comes in at an even more absurd 284ml.

Truly, I now see these lingering translations from imperial as nothing less than a joke, never mind how much they continue to irritate the modern day, go-ahead recipe writer. It may seem mildly pathetic to point this out, but it only needs just another three or four tablespoons of cider to take the present contents of this can up to the frighteningly neat figure of 500ml. And, as if you didn't know, 284ml of cream is exactly equal to half a pint, yet it requires even less to get this one up to a mere 300ml: a single tablespoon!

In retrospect, and with this in mind, I now guess that there may have been occasional moments prior to these revelations when you have cursed me over what I consider to be my sensibly ordered amounts. Perhaps the supermarkets, in all their supreme wisdom have long been busy analysing this interesting situation. Considering that most sane recipe writers these days now choose to metrically 'round up' their millilitres (it is rarely down), I can only guess that this dilemma can only gently force the more timid shopper to further purchase more, therefore making up the shortfall. Don't get taken in! As near as dammit, a tablespoon or so either way in all recipes will make little or no difference to the finished result. But, truly, I think something should be done very soon with reference to these increasingly outdated, unhelpful measures, don't you?

1 fresh duck, dressed weight about 1.5kg,
   or so
salt and pepper

for the apples:
3 Granny Smith apples, peeled, cored
   and cut into large dice
25g butter
1 level tbsp golden caster sugar
squeeze of lemon juice
a splash of Calvados

for the sauce:
1 x 440ml can of sweet cider;
   Woodpecker, for preference, as that is
   the brand I have used since 1972
1 x 284ml pot of whipping cream

Regular readers will know that the Chinese method of pouring boiling water over the surface of a goose and then hanging it up to dry prior to roasting is one of the best ways to achieve a crisp, dry skin. The same method equally applies to duck where, by tradition, its skin is first deftly punctured many times with the point of a thin skewer or sharp knife (and that is *just* under the skin, not gaily onward into the flesh too), placed upon an inverted bowl, or similar, within the confines of the sink and fully drenched all over with boiling water poured directly upon it from the kettle.

You will then observe that those little holes you so carefully made will have opened up upon contact with the boiling water, thus allowing the subcutaneous layer of fat beneath to later flow out as it cooks. The bird should then be allowed to dry (a pleasing amount will also drain away during this process too). I find that the best way to do this is to either rest it on a wire rack or hang it up on a meat hook; whichever method you choose, the close proximity of a breezy open window will enormously assist and speed up the process: 3–4 hours will just about do, but overnight will give the finest results.

Preheat the oven to 230°C/450°F/gas mark 8.

First give the duck the treatment as described above. Then rub salt all over the skin and sprinkle some inside the cavity as well, together with a little pepper. Now put the duck on a wire rack placed inside a roomy roasting tin and slide into the oven. Roast for 20 minutes and then turn the temperature down to 180°C/350°F/gas mark 4. Roast for a further 40–50 minutes, or so. No basting is required, but as the fat runs from the duck into the roasting tin periodically pour it off into a metal bowl (use this fat to roast potatoes). Once the roasting time is complete, remove the duck from the oven and allow to cool. Leave the oven switched on.

Whilst the duck is cooking, prepare the apples and sauce.

For the apples, melt the butter in a small pan, stir in the apples and sprinkle over the sugar and lemon juice. Allow to stew gently, stirring occasionally (trying not to crush them) until both soft and also touched with occasional golden burnishes here and there. Splash with the Calvados and stir in.

To make the sauce, pour the cider into a stainless steel pan and bring to the boil. Simmer, allowing the cider to reduce until very dark and syrupy. *Note*: You *must* watch the final stages of reduction like a hawk as, before you know it, all that will be left is a stinking, blackened mess – and a ruined pan to boot. Pour in the cream and whisk together. Bring back to a simmer and further cook until slightly thickened: the consistency of cold, pouring cream. Set aside.

Completely remove each half of the duck from its carcass using a small, sharp knife. Place each half of duck into a roomy, preferably oval and shallow, oven-proof serving dish and pour over the sauce. Cluster the cooked apples as two small piles into any obvious gaps between the duck and contours of its dish. Return to the top of the oven and re-heat for around about 20–25 minutes, or until all a-bubble and the duck skin is nicely glazed. Serve at once, perhaps with a sharp watercress salad and some small roast potatoes.

Sirloin steak

with

green peppercorn sauce

———

SERVES 2

2 x 200–225g thick (this is essential), well marbled sirloin steaks their edge of fat remaining fully intact
salt
25g butter
1 dsp green peppercorns (in brine)

1 tbsp Cognac
a small clove of garlic, crushed to a paste with salt
2 tsp fine Dijon mustard
100ml whipping cream

Take a thick heavy-based frying pan (cast-iron, for preference) and allow it to become hot over a naked flame. Generously season only the fatty edges of the steaks with salt and then, pressed together as one double thickness steak, place them fatty-edge down directly into the dry pan. Over a moderate heat allow the fat to quietly crisp up, so exuding its grease into the pan (the steaks should not, assuming you took note of thickness being a priority, topple over) of which there will, exactly, be sufficient to finally fry the meat itself. Once the fat is sufficiently crisp, turn up the heat and fry the steaks as you normally would and to your liking. Lift out and keep warm on a plate whilst the sauce is made.

Tip up the pan and remove the pool of fat with kitchen paper (don't wipe out the crusty bits, please!). Add the butter to the pan, allow it to froth and add the green peppercorns. Partially squash some of them into the butter using the back of a wooden spoon and then stir in the Cognac and garlic (there is no real need to flame the alcohol). Allow to combine for a few moments and then whisk in the mustard and cream until all is smooth. Simmer gently – whilst also continuing to occasionally whisk – until the copious amount of bubbles formed during this final process begin to reveal an increasingly brown tinge to their edges and the sauce seems of just the correct, creamy consistency to nicely coat the steaks.

UP AGAINST IT

'And would madam enjoy her grouse on, or off, the bone?' is the question all head waiters will have regularly asked during the soon-to-expire feathered game season at Bibendum. They will also, no doubt, have similarly requested the same of strapping butch sirs too, so timid have husbands, boyfriends, fathers, uncles and brothers become as the years have slipped by. I suppose it is a rather sad combination of ignorance and laziness that now defeats the modern gentleman when faced with a small, roast bird on his plate; and let me tell you, if any vague attempt is actually made, the result looks like dinner had been road kill rather than legally shot game. The sole remaining benefit (for the cook, that is) forthcoming from this now all too common reverted-to-kitchen task, is that the carcase stays stove-side and can easily be slipped into a quietly simmering game stock pot, later to be lightly thickened for gravy or soup.

To combat this burgeoning ineptness, nanny chefs now see fit to remove the breast meat from such birds even before cooking, choosing, therefore, to deftly sauté or grill them as neat little lozenges, so removing in a trice any trace whatsoever of passing fugitive flavours and aromas that might have been transferred to them from a gut-smeared carcase. The very worst example of this is when rare woodcock is treated so, ruined in an instant and with such ignorance it beggars belief. The common wood-pigeon is given similar treatment on an almost daily basis, I would imagine, its breasts neatly sliced and draped over dinky, designer salads. It is the equivalent of intercourse with a blow-up doll: tasteless, bouncy, spineless.

Roast quails
with butter and lemon

SERVES 2

Let it be understood here and now that the taste and savour of the little farmed quail, quietly roasted, should not be underestimated. Mind you, given the choice, be sure to search out those that have been reared in France.

4 fine quails
a little melted butter, plus a large knob
salt and pepper
lemon

Preheat the oven to 220°C/425°F/gas mark 7.

Brush the quails with melted butter and then season with salt and pepper (the reason for melting the butter is primarily to allow the seasoning to stick). Place in a tin and roast for around about 20 minutes. Add the knob of butter and squeeze over a generous amount of lemon juice. Baste thoroughly and roast for a further 5–7 minutes or so, until the birds are well browned and crisp of skin. Very good eaten with creamed potatoes and a bowl of lightly dressed watercress.

Braised oxtail
with onions, anchovy, vinegar and parsley

SERVES 4

One large oxtail is going to yield about three large joints, two medium ones and one, or possibly two, tiny tail-end pieces. All may be used within the same dish and it would also be rare indeed for a butcher to either sell you just the large bits or to allow you to leave his premises without first having expertly jointed your tails.

2 large oxtails, jointed
salt and pepper
flour
a little dripping or oil and butter mixed
2kg onions, peeled and thinly sliced

3 bay leaves
2 tbsp anchovy essence
2 tbsp red wine vinegar
4 tbsp freshly chopped parsley

Preheat the oven to 140°C/275°F/gas mark 1.

Season the oxtail and then dust with flour all over. Heat the chosen fat in a deep, cast-iron casserole dish that also has a lid. Gently fry the oxtail on all surfaces until crusted and golden. Remove to a plate. Tip off all but a couple of tablespoons of the fat. Turn the heat down to almost nothing, lay half of the onions in the bottom of the pot, reintroduce the oxtail in one layer together with the bay leaves and then cover with the rest of the onions. Lay a buttered sheet of greaseproof paper (butter side down) upon the surface and put on the lid. Place in the oven and leave there for 2–3 hours – or until about to fall off the bone.

Remove from the oven and pick out the oxtail. Place the pot back on to a moderate heat and stir together the onions, which will now have collapsed to a golden goo. Stir in the anchovy essence, vinegar and parsley and return the oxtail, burying it in the onions. Put the lid back on, return to the oven and cook for another 20 minutes. Serve directly from the pot.

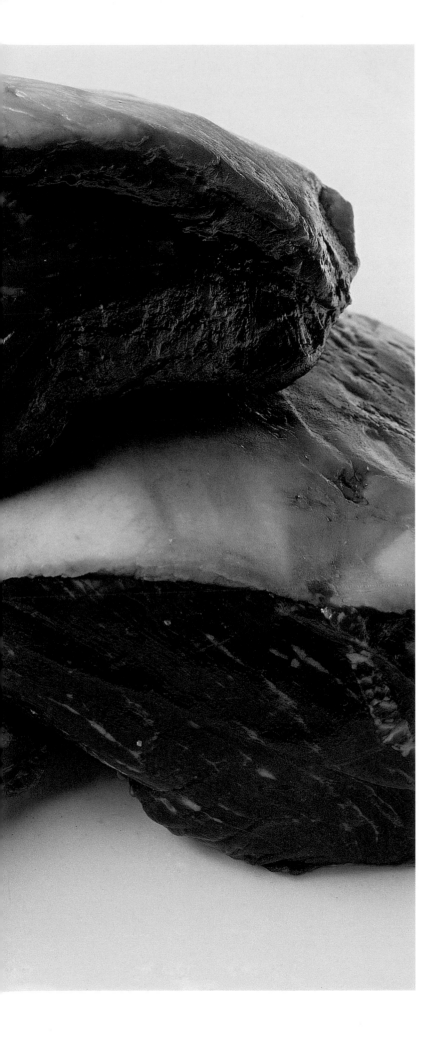

TAFELSPITZ

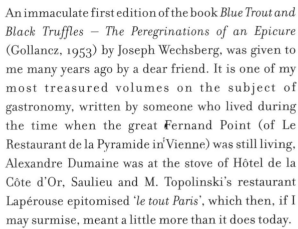

An immaculate first edition of the book *Blue Trout and Black Truffles – The Peregrinations of an Epicure* (Gollancz, 1953) by Joseph Wechsberg, was given to me many years ago by a dear friend. It is one of my most treasured volumes on the subject of gastronomy, written by someone who lived during the time when the great Fernand Point (of Le Restaurant de la Pyramide in Vienne) was still living, Alexandre Dumaine was at the stove of Hôtel de la Côte d'Or, Saulieu and M. Topolinski's restaurant Lapérouse epitomised '*le tout Paris*', which then, if I may surmise, meant a little more than it does today.

One of my favourite chapters in the book is entitled '*Tafelspitz* for the Hofrat'. Here, Wechsberg delights the reader with the glories of the boiled beef of Vienna, particularly that served at the restaurant Meissl & Schadn (sadly, now an office building), and which Wechsberg goes on to tell us, '… was held in high esteem by local epicures for its boiled beef – twenty-four different varieties of it, to be exact.' He then goes on to list these, starting with *Tafelspitz* and finishing with *Ortschwanzl*; the 22 other cuts named in between as meaningless to me – though I am sure absolutely gorgeous and delicious – as they will be to most of you. But I *do* know about the first one, *tafelspitz* – and have done for some time now. You will, I'm afraid, have to find a copy of the book to learn more about the Hofrat.

During my apprenticeship at the Normandie restaurant, in Lancashire, I was very lucky to have been given an extremely good grounding in all aspects of butchery – and French butchery exactly. Now this bears almost no relation whatsoever to the Dewhurst way (R.I.P. Red, dead and badly bred; neat meat, but no treat) or some of the supermarket hacksmith's untidy knives and ugly band saws. In contrast, the methods employed by any self-respecting *boucher* and (most) *hypermarché* are, at the very best, almost surgical or, at least, respectful to the meat. I hasten to add that there *are* some excellent butchers in Britain, it is just that they are becoming more and more difficult to find. This, of course, is partly due to the stomping supermarket leviathan, some local butchers who couldn't care less and, embarrassingly, the British shopper: the majority simply don't know what they are shopping for any more.

Only the other week, whilst in a (supposedly) classy butcher just off Chelsea Green in London, I remembered I needed to buy a pound and a half of best mince, with which to clarify beef broth for a *bœuf en gelée*. Well, honestly, it was just a mess in there – and, what's more, the mince cost me £3.40! Much of it was spilling over into other trays of meat: a motley pile of lamb's kidneys, some undistinguished and indistinguishable cuts of veal which, in turn, were languishing over a tray of sad looking lamb's hearts. A couple of dry and dismal, darkly crusted lamb chops lay lonesome in their metal tray and some of the sausages looked as anaemic as might a dead finger. I didn't say anything, didn't buy anything, I just fled, feeling very depressed.

But to return to the Normandie. Boning out a well-hung rump of beef was one of my very first tasks. Actually, my initiation duty was to make 3 kilos of garlic butter for *escargots*, by hand, which, apart from the butter and other aromatics, included a mulch of five heads of finely chopped garlic, enough Pernod to last an afternoon's boules match and a small meadow of finely chopped parsley. But the prize from that boned rump – the 'butchers perk', the 'rump cap', *le triangle*, *l'aiguillette*, the *tafelspitz*, to list the nomenclature that are now familiar to me – was left to me to lop off in quantity, from several rumps, for the family suppers about once every couple of weeks.

It is a most delicious cut of beef and truly is triangular (*le triangle*) in shape. When you next buy your ready-cut rump steak from the supermarket shelf, look at the meat carefully when you come to cook it. The piece that is aching to be un-tethered, held only by the merest thread of sinew, is part of this corner piece. The French butcher will already have removed his, selling it in its own right (or keeping it for his dinner) and then will sculpt the remainder of the rump to make neat and tidy, tight and trim muscular sections, for presenting his immaculate *romsteak 'extra'*.

Wechsberg goes on to say that, '…the technical expressions denoting various cuts of beef differ from land to land. Vienna's *tafelspitz* (which, curiously, he translates as 'brisket'), for instance, is called *tafelstück* by the Germans and *huft* by the German-speaking Swiss'. Perhaps my suppliers of their *tafelspitz* are confused too, but they label it so and it is very, very good.

At any rate, my *tafelspitz* travels down to London direct from Donald Russell in Inverurie, Aberdeenshire. This highly efficient company of butchers packs together prime-quality cuts of beef, vacuum-sealed and delivered to your door in insulated polystyrene boxes. It's a super service, with the added advantage that this airtight meat will keep in your fridge for up to 15 days. For more information, telephone 01467 629666.

2007 – I have left the above information for Donald Russell intact, here, because this company remains as one of the very best purveyors of Scotch beef and, of course, a reliable source of *tafelspitz*.

I went about cooking my *tafelspitz*, so:

SERVES 4

1–1¼kg *tafelspitz*, in one piece

1 pig's trotter, split lengthways

150g celery, washed and cut up into
    short sticks

200g carrots, peeled and cut into
    quarters

150g flat mushrooms, thickly sliced

2 medium onions, peeled and each
    stuck with 2 cloves

2 bay leaves

1½ dsp Maldon sea salt

Put the meat and trotter into a solid, lidded pot that you know will accommodate it (and later on the vegetables too) snugly; it should also be able to sit directly on a flame. Cover with cold water and, very slowly indeed, bring it up to the merest simmer. *Note*: Some also suggest that you might put the meat directly into boiling water and then simmer, the immediate heat sealing in the juices. However, I am not sure as to whether this will achieve a good clear broth once the meat has finished cooking. I have yet to try this method, but you may, by all means.

Preheat the oven to 140°C/275°F/gas mark 1.

As the water comes up to simmering point, a large amount of scum will form. When it resembles a thick blanket, start to carefully remove it with a large spoon. Allow the meat to carry on simmering – or, rather, effecting the odd shudder – and continue to remove any further despumation. Once you are happy with the clarity of the broth, only then introduce the vegetables, bay leaves and salt.

The vegetables will throw off further scum, so remove this too and then, once the broth is clear again, put on the lid and place in the oven for 1¼ hours, checking from time to time that the broth is only making polite blips rather than uncalled for eruptions; turn the temperature down further if this is the case.

Whilst the beef cooks, prepare the following:

8 medium-sized, really nice carrots, peeled
4 celery hearts, trimmed and with the outside ribs peeled
4 small onions, peeled
12 small, waxy potatoes, peeled
1 tbsp chopped chives

Once the beef has had its 1¼ hours, remove it from the oven. Very carefully lift out the meat and put onto a plate. Scrape off any clinging vegetable matter and then strain the meat broth through a colander into another vessel, allowing it to drip for a good 10 minutes (discard the vegetables and trotter). Wipe out the original pot and then strain the broth back into it using a fine sieve. Return the beef to the pot and add the carrots, celery and onions. Slowly bring up to a simmer once more, removing more scum when it arises, put the lid back on and return to the oven once more. Cook for a further 40 minutes and then add the potatoes. Continue for 20–30 minutes longer, or until the potatoes are tender when pierced with a small sharp knife.

By now, the meat should be almost jelly-like in its fondancy. And be warned, it needs very careful carriage from broth to plate or carving surface. Use a long, very sharp knife when slicing the meat, arranging it on a heated serving dish neatly surrounded by the vegetables. Spoon over some of the broth and sprinkle with chopped chives.

Note: Carve the meat across the grain, starting at the widest and most meat-prominent part of the triangle. Once you have reached about half way, change to slicing the meat in a downwards direction; this is traditional, according to Wechsberg. In some circles, it is also considered proper to have a bowl of the delicious broth as a first course. Capital idea.

Now then, I love to eat this with a large dish of freshly made creamed horseradish and gherkins or fat dill pickles. Wechsberg mentions a further tradition of serving apple sauce too. In fact, an American friend – who knows a good deal more than I do about Viennese boiled beef – makes a horseradish and apple sauce for his table, which although may sound curious to some, is a perky and most pleasing relish.

Apple and horseradish sauce

——

MAKES ENOUGH FOR THE BEEF

2 large Bramley apples, peeled, cored and chopped
3 tbsp caster sugar
4 tbsp water
3 cloves
juice of ½ large lemon
120g, or thereabouts, piece of fresh horseradish root, peeled and finely grated

Put the first four ingredients into a solid bottomed pan and allow to come to the boil. Once the apples start to collapse begin stirring from time to time, then cover and put onto a very low light indeed. The sauce will start to erupt somewhat as it thickens. Cook for about 45 minutes, until thick and semi-smooth – you do not want it to end up as baby food. Once cooled, stir in the lemon juice and horseradish and mix well.

VINUM IN REDUCTUM

Making sauces from, and braising in, red wine, was one of the first serious cooking processes I learnt to do, both in the home and, soon after, as a young apprentice in a French kitchen. I have a feeling it was a very creditable *coq au vin*, in fact, that was one of Dad's early forays into 'Continental' cookery. I wonder whether it may have been a touch purple looking (wine not 'cooked out' enough?), the sauce was a little watery (chicken not coated in flour?) and, as this was the early 1960s, the cooking wine itself was not particularly special (Hirondelle?). But, hey, at least he had a bash at it! How many dads are cooking *coq au vin* today? Well, of course, there is no need. You may buy it ready-made in the supermarket.

Guinea fowl in red wine

———

SERVES 4

In essence, *coq au vin* made with guinea fowl. However – and it is an important however – the method of preparation is similar to that of the French *salmi*, whereby the bird is first briefly roasted, left to rest, the joints removed from the carcass and the latter roughly chopped and stewed in the wine, vegetables, aromatics and so on.

This, I believe, is an excellent way to prepare such a dish, as it benefits hugely from the slow stewing of bones. And, furthermore, the texture and shape of the flesh also seems improved by employing such procedures.

2007 – These days I like to introduce a roughly cleavered small pig's trotter to the 'stewing of bones'. It adds both body and richness to the final assembly. You may either discard it with the spent bones or, of course, save it and lift off the delicious morsels of meat to nibble on later. Well, that's what I do.

1 guinea fowl	8 thin rashers of streaky bacon
salt and pepper	1 liqueur glass of Cognac
25g butter	½ bottle of full-bodied red wine
1 tbsp olive oil	200ml chicken stock
4 flat, dark-gilled mushrooms	1 carrot, peeled and chopped
1 large onion, peeled and cut into	1 large stick celery, chopped
4 thick slices – across the rings,	1 bay leaf
rather than from top to bottom	1 tsp redcurrant jelly
a little flour	a little chopped parsley (optional)

Preheat the oven to 200°C/400°F/gas mark 6.

Season the guinea fowl and fry in the butter and olive oil on all sides in a deep 'pot-roasting' type of dish, until golden brown. Transfer to the oven, un-covered and roast for 40 minutes, turning once. Remove the guinea fowl from the pot and leave to rest on a plate until cool enough to handle – about 20–25 minutes. Dust the mushrooms and onion slices with flour and gently fry in the residual fats until they are well coloured on each side. Now joint the guinea fowl into two breasts and two leg/thigh portions, neatly cutting them away from the carcase. Arrange them upon the mushrooms and onions, packing them well into the pot, and then cover the joints with rashers of streaky bacon. Place the pot upon the heat once more and, once the sound of sizzling has reached a moderate pitch, add the Cognac and ignite the fumes with a match. Switch off the heat, allow the flames to die down and place to one side. Reduce the oven temperature to 170°C/325°F/gas mark 3.

Roughly chop up the guinea fowl carcase, place in a medium saucepan and add the wine, stock, carrot, celery, bay leaf and redcurrant jelly. Bring up to a simmer, skim off any resultant scum and cook, gently for 1 hour. Strain through a fine sieve over the pot of guinea fowl. Bring the entire assembly up to a simmer, put on the lid and braise in the oven for about 1 hour, removing the lid for the final 20 minutes, or so, to allow the bacon to colour somewhat. Allow a quarter of the bird per person, together with the onions, a mushroom each and some bacon. If serving up in the cooking pot or arranged on a serving dish, finally sprinkle with chopped parsley. Eat with plain boiled or mashed potatoes.

Filet de boeuf à la Bordelaise

———

SERVES 2

As classic as top flight French cookery can be. The simple combination of a fine, grilled and crusted fillet steak, *just* melting bone-marrow and a rich red wine sauce is truly quite marvellous. Some might say that the correct cut of meat here is a sirloin steak – as in *entrecôte à la Bordelaise*. Absolutely and indisputably proper, no question. I just adore the soft and luxurious texture of a fillet, here, however much talk is banded about concerning its lack of flavour. If a piece of fillet is well hung, its flavour will come through time and time again.

4 large slices bone marrow
2 x 200g thick, fillet steaks
salt and pepper
a little olive oil

for the sauce:
½ bottle of decent claret (or use a whole bottle and drink the other half with the steak)
100ml good, strong beef or veal stock – or, at a pinch, good quality canned beef consommé (it has worked tolerably well for me in the past)

1 small shallot, peeled and very finely chopped
2 sprigs thyme
1 dsp crème de cassis (low-alcohol blackcurrant syrup, most often used for making *kir*)
½ tsp *fécule de pommes de terre* (potato flour), slaked with a little extra red wine
salt and pepper
25g cold butter, cut into tiny pieces

Note: You will need two index finger length marrow bones for this dish. Soak them in a bowl of lightly salted, room temperature water for 30 minutes, or so and then, using your thumb, simply push the marrow out of the bone in one neat, ruddy pink and cylindrical extrusion. Chuck out the bone and cut the freed marrow – using a sharp knife that you have dipped into hot water – into thick slices.

Preheat a stove-top, ribbed grill (or solid-bottomed, cast-iron frying pan) until very hot.

First make the red wine sauce. Pour the wine and stock into a small, stainless-steel saucepan and add to it the shallot, thyme and crème de cassis. Bring up to a simmer and reduce by three quarters. Whisk in the potato flour and season. Allow to simmer for a further 5 minutes, or so, until lightly thickened and syrupy. Fish out the exhausted thyme sprigs and put the sauce to one side.

Lightly season the steaks and rub well with olive oil. Place upon the hot grill and leave there for 2–3 minutes, or so. Turn through 45 degrees and repeat. Turn over and give the other side the same treatment. This will result in two rare steaks. To cook further, turn the heat down a little and cook the steaks for longer. Place on two hot plates and keep warm. Re-heat the sauce and whisk in the butter bit by bit until glossy and syrupy-looking. Slip the slices of bone marrow into the sauce, but only just to warm through and soften them. Spoon over the steaks, taking care that the bone marrow sits on top. Thin, crisp and salty chips are a must here, I reckon.

Skate and potatoes
with red wine vinaigrette

———

SERVES 2

Skate, for me, has always partnered red wine very well indeed. In this particular case – where there are also hot potatoes and a flavour of raw onion involved – the dish becomes something really quite special: all at once, a piquant hot fish salad masquerading as a substantial main course.

1 portion size skate wing
salt and pepper
vinegar
2–3 medium-sized scrubbed potatoes (red-skinned, if possible), steamed or boiled and then peeled
a little olive oil
sliced spring onions or snipped chives

for the vinaigrette:
200ml red wine
1 tbsp red wine vinegar
1 small shallot, peeled and finely chopped
1 small bay leaf
pinch of sugar
salt and pepper
50–75ml olive oil
squeeze of lemon juice

Bring a large pan of water to the boil. Add salt and a good splash of any old vinegar. Slip the wing into the water, bring back to a bare simmer, cover and then switch off the heat. Leave to finish cooking in the hot water. Thickly slice the cooked potatoes, season them and put to fry ever so gently in a frying pan using a little olive oil, turning them occasionally until lightly gilded on each side.

Meanwhile, make the vinaigrette. Put the red wine and vinegar into a small, stainless-steel saucepan together with the shallot, bay leaf and sugar. Bring up to a simmer and allow to reduce by about three-quarters. Allow to cool in the pan, season and then whisk in the olive oil as if making a normal vinaigrette. Add lemon juice to taste and then strain the result into a small bowl.

To serve, arrange the potatoes onto two hot plates. Lift the skate from its cooking water, ease off the flesh from the cartilage in thick strips and lay onto the potatoes. Spoon the vinaigrette over each serving and scatter with the spring onions or chives. Delicious eaten with a large dollop of garlic mayonnaise (*aïoli*). Perfect as a simple supper or light lunch.

PARTICULAR TREATS

I enjoyed an early upbringing that was easy with offal. This may have been due to both place and period (Lancashire in the late 1950s and early '60s) but, largely, it was really down to Dad and his liking for very particular delicacies. Mostly, however, these were cooked as a breakfast treat rather than for lunch or dinner and mostly at weekends. Nothing seemed to appear as being unusual to me at the time about any of this; I just ate everything that was put before me. One Saturday it might be slowly braised bits of ox kidney spooned over fried bread with a big, black, grilled mushroom alongside. The following Sunday there would be a few slices of 'lamb's fry' tucked alongside crisp rashers of streaky bacon and 'a egg' (it was always 'a egg', aged 7, wasn't it?). Just in case you didn't know this, the polite North of England term 'fry' exactly refers to lamb's testicles. Now then, these were especially good.

Once Dad had decided it was going to be kidney day, he would prepare them the night before and always using a beef kidney. Possibly no more than half of one, at the most and cut up into very small pieces. Then simply dusted with flour, fried in a little dripping, salt added and moistened with nothing more than plain water. A special, small oval Pyrex dish was then brought out (only, but *only*, used for Dad's

kidneys), the kidneys poured in and all popped in the bottom oven of the Aga and left to quietly stew overnight until well done and very moreish by morning. Just delicious.

Luckily, Mum and my brother were not over-keen on the kidney front so I always managed quite a large serving. And all for just a few pence, I guess, 40 years ago. Come to think of it, a more accurate figure might now be almost impossible to back date; how about minus ninepence? In fact, the mushroom probably cost more than the kidney.

But it was a memory of those delicious breakfast kidneys which so prompted me to recall another relic of that era: kidney soup. Now, this particular muddy broth may not have been quite as well known as a similarly turbid tureen of the time, the 'Brown Windsor' (British cookery nomenclature, perhaps, at its most banal, never mind the end result), but this was of little consequence then, when the prime consideration merely required all soups to be served 'nice and hot' – whatever colour they happened to be. Kidney soup may well have been brown too, but that is where the comparison ends. For a good kidney soup, as an example of one of many traditional British meat soups now rarely encountered – if ever – can be a very fine bowlful indeed.

Kidney soup
with
bone marrow and
parsley dumplings

– and with a small bowl of beef brawn on the side, if you so desire…

———

SERVES 6

I came up with the idea to embellish the soup with dumplings, simply wishing to add interest to this intensely meaty flavoured, though slightly one-dimensional soup. Then, further inspired, I also secreted a tiny nugget of beef bone marrow inside each one. A happy result, if I may humbly say.

for the soup:

2 thick slices of beef shin
  (approximately 400–500g)
1 tbsp dripping or oil
salt and pepper
500–600g beef kidney, sliced
flour
2 onions, chopped
3 large flat, black mushrooms,
  chopped
100ml amontillado sherry or tawny
  port
1 x 400g tin of chopped tomatoes
1.5 litres any good stock

2 or 3 small pieces of veal or beef
  knuckle bone or a split pig's trotter
1 tbsp anchovy essence
1 tbsp redcurrant jelly
1 tbsp red wine vinegar
1 tbsp Worcestershire sauce
a few blades of mace
2–3 bay leaves and a few sprigs thyme

for the dumplings:

200g suet
350g self-raising flour
½ tsp baking powder
salt, pepper and grated nutmeg
2 heaped tbsp freshly chopped parsley
the reserved bone marrow

Preheat the oven to 140°C/275°F/gas mark 1.

Remove the marrow from within the beef shin bone with a small knife, wrap it in foil and reserve in the fridge. Heat the dripping in a roomy, solid pot, that also possesses a lid. Season the beef shin slices and fry until well browned. Remove to a plate. Season and generously dredge the kidney in flour and similarly fry in the dripping until golden and crusted. Also remove to a plate. Now add the onions and mushrooms to the pot (you may need to add a little more fat here) and cook until well browned. Pour in the sherry or port and add the tomatoes and stock. Reintroduce the beef and kidney and slip in the knuckle or trotter. Slowly bring up to a simmer and remove any scum that forms on the surface, using a large spoon. Stir in the anchovy essence, redcurrant jelly, vinegar, Worcestershire sauce, mace, bay and thyme. Put the lid on and cook in the oven for at least 2–3 hours.

At some stage, make the dumplings. Simply mix together all the ingredients – save the bone marrow – in a mixing bowl. Bind with 2–3 tbsps of cold water until it will just form a dough. Put in the fridge to rest. Cut the reserved bone marrow into 12 small pieces and season. Whilst forming the dough into 12 walnut-sized balls, insert a piece of bone marrow into the centre of each. Set aside.

Remove the pot from the oven. Using a slotted spoon, carefully lift out the beef and kidneys (flicking off any clinging bits) and put them onto a plate. Strain the broth through a sieve into a clean pan and leave to settle. Discard the solids. Lift off any excess fat with kitchen paper. Using your fingers, now break up the beef into shreds, put into a small bowl and spoon over just enough of the broth to cover. Place in the fridge. This will then set solid and provide you with a lovely, small pot of beef brawn to spoon out and eat with mustard and gherkins at your leisure – a more delicious sideline I cannot think of!

To continue… Bring the broth to a simmer and poach the dumplings in it for 15–20 minutes, or until visibly swollen. Remove and keep warm. Tip the kidneys into a liquidiser or food processor (the former will give you a smoother soup) and add enough broth to achieve a pouring, definitely 'soupy' consistency. Check the seasoning and ladle into hot soup plates. Add two dumplings to each serving.

Grilled veal kidneys
with creamed onions and sage

———

SERVES 4

Ah... veal kidneys. The finest of all! I first tasted these as a kitchen apprentice. And it was only when the restaurant purchased a whole side of veal – and therefore only sporting one set of kidneys – that I so experienced such a rare treat. These were always expressly reserved for chef Champeau's English parents-in-law, as part of their early evening supper. On each and every occasion that Mr. and Mrs. Jenkinson's kidney treat coincided with my occasional role as a waiter, they would, intentionally, insist on leaving me a few remaining morsels for me to eat once I had cleared their table. Bless their hearts.

75g butter

3 large Spanish onions, peeled and chopped

salt and freshly ground white pepper

50ml white wine vinegar

100ml medium dry white wine

400ml whipping cream

2 whole sprigs sage

a few extra sage leaves, chopped

a little olive oil

2 veal kidneys, trimmed and cut into 1cm-thick slices

Melt the butter in a roomy pan and add the onions. Season, and allow them to stew quietly, uncovered, for at least 30 minutes, or until very soft and melting. Stir occasionally and be careful not to allow the onions to catch or colour. Add the vinegar and continue to simmer until there is no trace left of any liquid whatsoever. Now add the wine and similarly simmer away, but this time arrest the cooking a few minutes before the wine has fully evaporated. Pour in the cream and stir in the sage sprigs. Finally, bring the mixture to its final simmer and leave to stew for about 20 minutes, stirring from time to time. Do not let the onions catch; use one of those heat-diffuser pads if you have one. Pick out the sage sprigs and discard, then stir in the extra chopped leaves. Cover the onions and keep warm.

Heat a little olive oil in a heavy frying pan until almost smoking-hot. Season the slices of kidney and briefly sear on each side until golden; the entire operation – possibly in two batches – should not take much more than several minutes, to achieve a nice pink interior to the kidneys. Spoon the onions onto hot plates and lay the slices of kidney on top. Serve without delay.

Brochette of lamb's kidneys
with bacon, thyme and potato 'worms'

———

SERVES 4

Just enough here for a light lunch or supper. You may, of course, double up the quantities if you wish for a more substantial meal. The beauty of this little dish lies in the gorgeous juices that exude into the buttery, garlic imbued potatoes, from the kidneys and bacon. A sprinkling of dried herbes de Provence may, if desired, also be sprinkled over the brochettes at the last minute, just before being placed in the oven.

4 large potatoes, peeled and cut into large chunks

125g butter

3–4 cloves garlic, bruised

8 large fresh lamb's kidneys, skinned, cored and cut into 3 equal-sized chunks

7–8 thick-ish slices of flat, rind-less, Italian pancetta, each slice cut into 24 squares

Maldon sea salt

freshly ground black pepper

4 wooden skewers, soaked in warm water for 20 minutes

Preheat the oven to 190°C/375°F/gas mark 5.

Steam the potatoes until very well cooked through. Lightly butter four individual 'eared' dishes (or similar). Gently heat together the butter and garlic and leave to infuse. Lift the potatoes out of the steamer and work the potatoes through a vegetable mill (*mouli-légumes*) or potato-ricer, directly and equally, into each dish. Do *not* press down or fiddle about with it!... and leave to cool.

Thread the kidney pieces onto the skewers alternating each one with a piece of bacon, allowing six pieces of kidney and the same amount of bacon. Lay each brochette across the middle of each dish. Sprinkle salt and grind pepper over both brochette and potato. Spoon the infused butter over brochette and potato, but reserving the majority for the potato 'worms', whilst also discarding the exhausted garlic cloves. Now place in the oven and bake for 25–35 minutes, or until the kidneys feel firm, yet bouncy, to a tweak of the fingers and also when the potato is speckled brown all over.

NATIVE TONGUE

Slices of hot, salted ox tongue remain one of my favourite meats to eat. Thoughtfully done, the results here can be magnificently good. As with traditional boiled mutton, a generous platter of fondant salted tongue may also welcome a welter of mildly piquant, judiciously creamed, English caper sauce flooded across its rosy countenance; piquant is always good with boiled tongue.

Conversely, in France it might be *sauce ravigôte* or *gribiche*, each being a thickened vinaigrette based upon strong Dijon mustard, chopped pickled gherkins or capers and emulsified with a simple oil. And, incidentally, the use here of that latter ingredient is critical; to use a fragrant oil such as olive – although it may be seen as the *sine qua non* of all oils for dressings in these days of lemming cookery – would be quite wrong here. The neutral oil is intended to carry the sauce rather than to flavour it. Please don't be tempted by the fruity olive.

Anyway, to return to the vehicle for these emulsions and ointments, the tongue. Unless it is Christmas time, when the more choosy branches of supermarkets might wish to interest their choosier clientele and provide a freshly salted ox tongue for them to cook, press and traditionally present cold in deep red slices, I hazard that your local butcher is going to be the regular place to go when you fancy tongue – even post tinsel time. Now you may need to order it beforehand, but this should cause little problem to an enterprising family butcher. But here is how to dish up some hot tongue, with our very own English caper sauce.

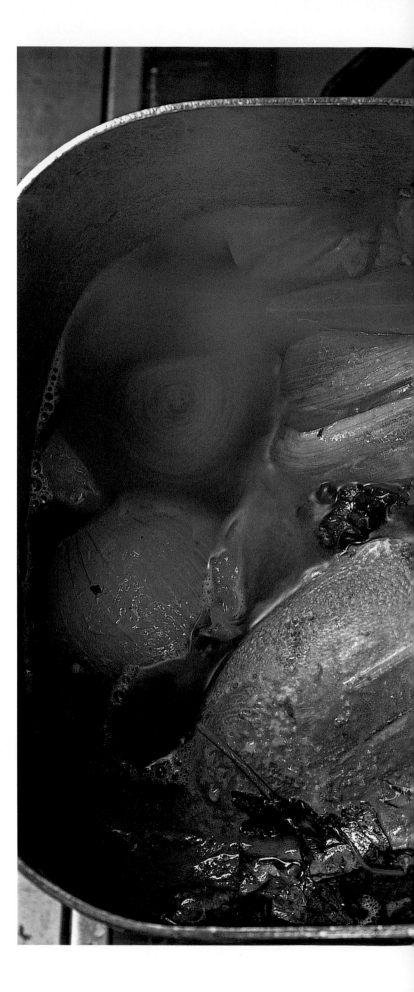

Boiled salted ox tongue
with caper sauce

SERVES 4—5

These days, salted tongues usually arrive in a plastic pouch, swimming in pink and briny juices. Firstly, cut the bag open and rinse the tongue well in warm water. Pat dry and place in a roomy pot. Cover with cold water and slowly bring to a gentle simmer. Once the surface of the water is covered with a light layer of scum, and small bubbles are breaking through, lift out the tongue with a slotted spoon and rinse under a cold running tap. Chuck out the water, clean out the pot and put the rinsed tongue back in.

Now add 2 peeled onions (one of them studded with 5 cloves); 3 small carrots, peeled and sliced in half lengthways; 2 small leeks, trimmed and washed; 3 sticks of celery, cut in half; 2 bay leaves; 2—3 sprigs thyme; several peppercorns. Cover everything with cold water and, once more, bring up to a gentle simmer. More scum will settle on the surface, so this time remove it with a spoon. Once this is done, allow the tongue to murmur gently for about 1½—2 hours, depending on its size. After 90 minutes, check from time to time by running a thin skewer right through the meat; as soon as there is little to no resistance, the tongue is then cooked.

Remove it to a dish, scrape off any bits of clinging vegetable or herb, then strain the stock through a sieve into a clean pan and keep hot over a meagre flame. Once the tongue is cool enough to handle, carefully peel off its skin and discard. Return the tongue to the steaming stock to keep hot, whilst you make the sauce.

for the caper sauce:

40g butter
1 small onion, peeled and chopped
40g flour
350ml hot tongue stock
1—2 tbsp of vinegar (decanted from the jar of capers), to taste
salt and freshly ground white pepper
1 dsp smooth Dijon mustard
1 tsp redcurrant jelly
75ml double cream
1 tbsp capers, squeezed of excess vinegar
1 tbsp freshly chopped parsley

Melt the butter in a saucepan and fry the onion until pale golden. Add the flour and cook over a low heat, stirring, for a couple of minutes until lightly coloured. Stir in the hot stock slowly, until thickened and smooth. Add the vinegar, seasoning, mustard and redcurrant jelly. Allow to simmer gently for 10 minutes. Strain through a fine sieve into a clean pan and whisk in the cream until smooth and of a custard-like consistency. Introduce the capers and stir in the parsley. Simmer once more for a couple of minutes and then spoon over the tongue, which should be served cut into fairly thick, juicy slices. Plain boiled potatoes here, naturally.

Sauces ravigôte and gribiche

SERVES 6

So, to my two best beloved alternative lotions of the school of thick, French vinaigrettes. Both, once more, include the most useful, piquant caper. And, incidentally, do not be tempted to waste your money on those expensive, teeny-weeny fellows, which should really only be used in their own right: sprinkled into a salad or maybe to garnish smoked salmon. So no, here it is the fat and juicy ones that are correct (as is also the case for the previous recipe), as they have a great deal more flavour.

Each of the following sauces can be successfully spooned over hot tongue (in France, it is more likely that the tongue will be unsalted and also that of veal rather than beef). The former is more loose than the latter, having only onion and herbs to carry in suspension, whereas the latter is bulked out and further thickened with the inclusion of chopped boiled eggs. Neither – as I have often annoyingly seen of late included in recipes from the misinformed – should include chopped gherkins. Those are for tartare.

the base sauce for both dressings:

Note: For best results, use a small liquidiser, hand-held blender or food processor here.

1 heaped tbsp smooth Dijon mustard
1 tbsp red wine vinegar
salt and pepper
4–5 tbsp warm water
150–175ml sunflower or groundnut oil

Put the first four ingredients into the goblet of your chosen machine. Switch on and blend until smooth. With the motor still running, add the oil in a thin stream until a homogenous, creamy dressing is achieved. The result should have an almost jellied consistency to it, limpid and pale yellow in colour. Tip into a bowl and stir in the appropriate garnish:

for the ravigôte:
1 tbsp coarsely chopped capers
1 scant tbsp freshly chopped tarragon leaves
1 scant tbsp freshly chopped parsley
½ small onion, peeled and finely chopped

for the gribiche:
1 tbsp coarsely chopped capers
1 scant tbsp freshly chopped chervil
1 tbsp freshly chopped parsley
2 hard-boiled eggs, peeled and finely chopped or grated

Leave both sauces to mature, at room temperature for 30 minutes, before using.

CITRUS CHRISTMAS

Three little sweet and tart citrus numbers here. For when the puddings, pies, port and all manner of piggy over-indulgences have finally caught up with you, it is recipes such as these that will hit the right note.

Mandarin granita

———

SERVES 4

For those of you who have had enough of peeling and eating tangerines, satsumas and clementines at Christmas, this wonderfully refreshing granita uses up all those left hanging around. For those of you who have not made or eaten granita before, it is, in essence, a coarse sorbet or water ice. Italian in origin (meaning 'granular'), the most famous of all granitas is the one made from strong espresso coffee. And the most delicious of these, that I have ever eaten, is one served at Tre Scalini, on the Piazza Navona in Rome.

500ml tangerine, satsuma or clementine juice, strained

125–150ml caster sugar, depending upon the sweetness of the fruit
juice of 1 small lemon

Before you start to make the granita, make sure you chill a shallow metal tray in the freezer.

Put the three ingredients together in a bowl and whisk together to dissolve the sugar. Carefully pour into the tray in the freezer, and leave there for about 20 minutes and then have a look. What you are looking for is ice crystals forming around the edge of the tray (completely opposite to ice cream or sorbets, as here the ice crystals are the essential charm of the thing). Once the crystals have formed about 2 or 3 inches from the edge, towards the middle of the tray, gently lift them with a fork into the not-so-frozen middle part. Return to the freezer. Have another look in a further 20 minutes and repeat the forking. Continue this procedure until all the mixture has formed crystals; this process may take up to 2 hours. Once fully crystallised, tip into a suitable lidded plastic container and store in the freezer until ready to use. The granita should keep its granular texture for a few days, but soon after that, it will start to firm up into a block. However, it is simple to start again by just melting the fruit juice and going through the motions once more. To serve the granita, pile into tall chilled glasses and top with a spoonful of crème fraîche or whipped cream, flavoured with a little mandarin liqueur or Cointreau, if you like.

Pink grapefruit and blood orange jelly
with Champagne

SERVES 6

A refreshing and elegant way to finish a late supper in and around the festive season. Jellies are one of the very nicest things to eat at any time of the year, particularly when using home-grown fruits in season. I rather like eating this with a thin, ice-cold, homemade custard flavoured with either Cointreau or Grand Marnier. At a pinch, you could buy a good quality, ready-made custard, thin it with a little whipping cream/milk and then add the alcohol; it is a pouring consistency that is needed, I feel.

4 pink grapefruits
5 blood oranges
5 leaves gelatine
225ml plain orange juice (strained through a fine sieve)
250ml Champagne

Cut the skin from both grapefruits and oranges right down through past the pith, using a sharp serrated knife. The best way to do this – after cutting off a slice from the top and bottom – is to stand the fruits on their ends, cutting downwards in a curved motion, following the line of the cut fruit once it has been exposed by the knife. Continue in this fashion, rotating the fruit, until all the skin has been removed. Put the leaves of gelatine into a bowl of cold water to soak until spongy.

Now, taking the fruit in one hand, slice between and against the membranes so allowing a segment to fall out, discarding pips as you go along. Collect both grapefruit and orange segments in a bowl, juice and all. Once finished, strain off excess juice into a small pan and put in the gelatine leaves. Warm over a low heat to melt the gelatine and strain once more into a measuring jug. Top up with the plain orange juice to reach 250ml, and then slowly add the Champagne to reach the 500ml mark. Stir well, but carefully, as the Champagne will froth.

Line a terrine mould with clingfilm and pile in the fruit segments. Pour over the Champagne and orange juice and gently move the fruit around with a fork to aid even distribution of solids and liquid. Put in the fridge to set for 1 hour and then cover the surface with a sheet of clingfilm, allowing it to make contact with the surface of the jelly. Leave in the fridge for at least another 4 hours, or, preferably, overnight. To serve, dip the mould into a bath of hot water for a few seconds and then carefully invert onto a chilled serving dish. Slice carefully, using a serrated knife that has been dipped into hot water.

Lemon and lime syllabub

SERVES 4

Syllabub is one of the very nicest of traditional English desserts. It should be light and almost frothy, insubstantial and tart, with the merest hint of spirit and wine in the background. To add some further interest to the previous jelly recipe, you might like to serve it with some of this syllabub, having previously halved the recipe.

zest and juice of 2 limes
zest and juice of 1 large lemon
150ml sweet white wine (sweet Alsatian would be particularly good)
2 rounded tbsp caster sugar
1½ tbsp Cognac
275ml very cold double cream

Note: Make sure there is no pith attached to the zest of the lemon and limes.

Put the zest and juices into a small stainless-steel or enamelled pan, together with the wine, sugar and Cognac. Bring up to a simmer and cook for 3–4 minutes, very gently. Cover and leave to infuse for an hour, or so. Strain into another similar pan (or rinse out the old one) and heat once more, simmering, to reduce the syrup by one-third. Leave to cool completely, in the fridge.

Pour the cream into a chilled bowl and stir in the citrus syrup. Using an electric hand beater, whisk the mixture on a slow speed until loosely thick and just holding its own shape. Pile into chilled glasses and chill once more in the fridge for 30 minutes. Serve with dainty sweet biscuits.

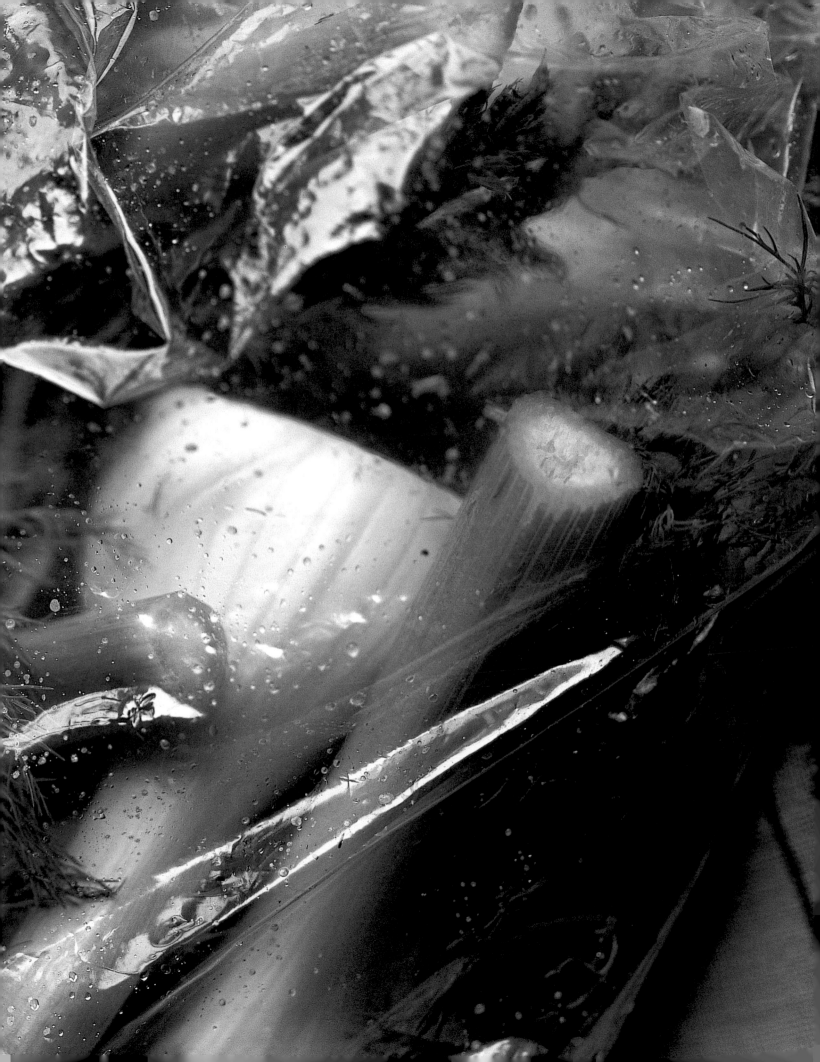

TAME AND TASTY

One of divers absurdities that I have begun to notice inexorably creeping (and, truly, it is a shade creepy) into the menu planning of almost every restaurant in the land, is that if a dish includes mushrooms as part of its composition, you can be absolutely sure that they will not be tame ones. For it seems that button mushrooms are boring, open-cups are out and those flat, wide and black-gilled saucer-sized monsters are simply seen as only being fit for adding depth of flavour and colour to endless pots of simmering *jus*. Folly, I say. But then what's new?

The forests and fields of France are positively riddled with all manner of wild mushrooms. Yet — unless I am very much mistaken — it would cause a minor rebellion if stalwarts such as *champignons à la Grecque*, *potage crème de champignons*, *sole à la Normande* or the very useful little mushroom stuffing known as *duxelles* (finely chopped shallots and mushrooms, seasoned and stewed in butter, before being reduced to a rough paste with the addition of white wine) to name but a few, no longer played a part in a long established repertoire much loved by all, simply because their essential ingredient had somehow become, how shall we say, *un peu passé*? Well, it doesn't bear thinking about. But, then, does not a populace all at peace with its domestic skills more easily embrace each and every ingredient simply because it makes for good eating, rather than as a slave to fashion?

Brit mushroom-menu speak is now only seen as serious if it involves at least two or more of some of the following fiercer fungi: cèpes, morilles, chanterelles, girolles, trompettes de la mort, mousserons and pieds de mouton. And, following that culinary cornucopia, there are then the semi-house-trained, too: pleurottes (both original blue/grey and the ever so cool new yellow), shiitake (though I am often moved to refer to these only by their first syllable, so much do I loathe them) and, for the terminally twiddled, a miniature bouquet of Japanese enoki. Finally, the occasional rare appearance of a few slices of the astonishing giant puff-ball, a clutch of chicken-in-the-woods' or a basketful of field (or horse) mushrooms.

I enjoy wild mushrooms as much as anyone. I have gathered girolles and cèpes in woods a few miles outside of the Scottish Highlands town of Nairn, and filled wicker baskets brim-full with damp field mushrooms, picked from the slightly more convenient meadows of Berkshire. And I so wish that I had also witnessed the early morning harvesting of an extraordinary display of Welsh morels that, truly as if by magic, had appeared overnight, just the once, to decorate the lawn of Franco and Ann Taruschio's Walnut Tree Inn, several years ago now.

Similarly, on another rueful occasion, I found myself no more than politely moved to bid a weak 'good morning' to a sweet Polish family at the break of dawn, as they admired each other's bounty of immaculate *boletus edulis* (that cèpe or British 'penny bun'). The fact that this exactly coincided with the very moment I chose to emerge scratched, weary and entirely *boletus*-free, from the forest, remains as a memory of failure at its most intense — and all just a crisp packet's throw from a spookily dormant Surrey stretch of the M25. 'Ah, well', I said to myself as I flung my empty basket into the boot of the car, 'I bet they've never tasted the heated contents of a nice can of creamed Chesswoods on toast...' And, you know, at the time, I *really* meant it.

Creamed mushrooms
on fried bread

———

SERVES 4

This is a little way onwards from a can of creamed Chesswoods. Sunday supper stuff at its very best. The smiling Surrey Poles are known to fancy making a nice warming soup from their bounty – well, that is, from those left over after having sold on the majority…

40g butter

4 shallots, peeled and finely chopped

500g button mushrooms, thickly sliced or quartered

150ml Madeira

275ml whipping cream

salt and pepper

juice of ½ lemon

4 thick slices of white bread, fried in olive oil

Melt the butter and fry the shallots until pale golden. Add the mushrooms and stew until limp and lightly coloured, and any excess liquid derived from the mushrooms has evaporated. Pour in the Madeira and cook until syrupy and sticky. Add the cream, bring up to a simmer and stew very gently for about 10 minutes, or until the cream has thickened considerably. Season with salt and pepper, and stir in the lemon juice. Put the slices of hot, fried bread onto four warmed plates and spoon over the mushrooms.

Cream of mushroom soup
with Parmesan

—

SERVES 4

This is a simply gorgeous recipe: the palest grey, velvety in the extreme (a *velouté*, for once, in its most accurate description) and intensely fungal. Perhaps the finest example of these three recipes in which the cultivated mushroom shines over the wayward wild ones in the woods. And, if you employ the Marigold bouillon option, a more perfect vegetarian soup I cannot think of. But, just wait until you spoon in the Parmesan... Exceedingly good soup.

175g open-cup mushrooms, wiped
    and sliced
125ml milk
125ml whipping cream
salt and freshly ground white pepper
grated nutmeg
25g butter

1 small onion, chopped
285ml Marigold vegetable bouillon
    (or light chicken stock)
squeeze of lemon juice, to taste
4 tbsp double cream
2 tbsp freshly grated Parmesan

Place the mushrooms, milk, whipping cream and seasonings in a pan and bring to a simmer. Cook very gently for 20 minutes. Meanwhile, soften the onion in the butter until pale golden and pour in the stock. Simmer for 5 minutes. Combine the two pan-fuls and liquidise until very, very smooth. Sharpen with lemon juice and check seasoning. Re-heat without boiling and ladle into individual soup bowls. Stir a tablespoon of double cream into each serving and scatter with Parmesan.

Mushrooms Arméniennes

SERVES 4

I first learnt to cook these in a small restaurant in the town of Newport, Wales. Its name was The Pantry, where I briefly cooked as a young chef for four weeks before being mysteriously sacked. To this day, I still don't know why this was so, but remain solaced by the acquisition of a number of techniques and useful recipes that I learnt there, and which were of such sensibility that I have never since forgotten them. The following dish is based upon one of those.

2007 – I since discovered that the original recipe was from the pages of Elizabeth David.

2 tbsp olive oil

4 rashers of streaky bacon, rind removed (but reserved), chopped

700g button mushrooms

4 cloves garlic, peeled and chopped

salt and pepper

300ml red wine

3 tbsp freshly chopped parsley

a little extra olive oil

Using a roomy pan, fry the bacon in the olive oil until crisp. Add the mushrooms, garlic, seasoning and the reserved bacon rind (for flavour, mainly). Stir until coated with oil and bacon fat, then leave to stew for a good 10 minutes. Pour in the wine, bring to a boil and cook rapidly for a further 10 minutes, uncovered. Tip all the contents into a colander suspended over a clean pan and leave to drip for a few minutes. Return the new pan to a high heat and reduce the winey liquid until syrupy and dark. Put the mushrooms into a serving dish, pour the reduced essence back over them, stir in the parsley and further lubricate with a little of the extra olive oil. As with the previous recipe on page 71, serve at room temperature and eat with similar crusts.

SMOKING POT

Smoking and potting are two of the very best things we do in Great Britain – and possibly do them better than anyone else. Well, the Dutch smoke good eels too, but this is mainly because they seem to grow eels bigger than we do, therefore producing a fatter, juicier morsel. And I suppose you could call foie gras potted, but then the delicacy lies within the ingredient, rather than in the individual potting or preservation of it. And badly prepared foie gras is one of the nastiest things it is possible to eat.

The two native stars of smoke and pot are shrimps and salmon. Reputedly, the best smoked salmon comes from Scotland, whilst the finest potted shrimps are from Morecambe Bay, Lancashire. Here, a certain Mr. Baxter buries them in the finest spiced butter and dispatches them mail-order all over the land. They are famously good, one of the best commercially made brands I know. The salmon story has become a little more ubiquitous.

With the onset of vast sea-vats of farmed salmon that now churn out identikit fish around our coastal waters, the taste and texture of the fish, once smoked, has now changed for ever. Its formality and consistency has been welcomed by the masses, but its character is now lost to the supermarket pre-packaging facility and the fast-food outlet; it is also a boon to the unskilled carver. With a few exceptions, it is, tragically, no longer the treat it once was.

Severn and Wye Smokery, in the Forest of Dean, smokes some of the most delicious wild salmon I have ever tasted. Now this is something else. Its texture is the first thing that really grabs you: smooth, very, very smooth, but with a density that only the powerfully muscled wild fish can ever achieve. Then you notice the flavour: deeply, naturally savoury (a piece of raw wild salmon already has this note), and with a sweetness that bears out its diet of foraged crustacea. It costs some, this wild and wonderful stuff, but I firmly believe it is worth every penny.

Severn and Wye smoke a good eel, too. Some of the wrigglers, naturally, come from the Severn and Wye rivers; others from Irish waterways. Of course, the majestic Severn river becomes world famous in the spring for its elver (infant eels) harvest, when millions upon millions upon millions of inch-long eels plough their way upstream from their source, far, far away in their spawning grounds of the Sargasso Sea. A pricey delicacy if you can ever get your hands on some, as most of the catch – often tonnage in size – is exported to eel farms as far away as Japan.

Potting shrimps is one of the best – if not *the* best – things to do to a brown shrimp. Mind you, I have always been partial to an old-fashioned English pink shrimp sauce (flour-thickened white sauce with lemon juice, parsley and the merest dash of anchovy essence), and also the very, very delicious 'shrimp croustade' that Baba Hine cooks at Corse Lawn Hotel, near Tewkesbury.

2007 – Baba recently informed me that she no longer cooks this lovely dish. I'm going to have to bully her a bit next time I see her, over this serious omission.

And finally, a lunch that consisted of a large pile of impeccable peeled shrimps, a few slices of smoked eel, some hot, peeled and buttered new potatoes and mayonnaise eaten at the Oesterbar in Amsterdam some years ago was, perhaps, one of the most perfect plates of food I can remember. The bottle of Louis Michel Chablis also at hand, made it even more memorable.

Potted shrimps

—

SERVES 6

A source of peeled shrimps is not the easiest to find. Perhaps the best way is to bully your fishmonger or, at least, ask him to make enquiries. In London, such places as Selfridges or Harrods food halls may stock them. The crustacea van at the Michelin Building on Fulham Road should also be able to help you. Failing all those options, you may just have to buy them in shell, sit down at the kitchen table with worthwhile friends and set to with nimble fingers. Open a bottle of wine and chatter amongst yourselves over the meaning of life, the Millennium Dome – why? – or how the remarkable men and women of Morecambe manage to whiz through this exacting task every day of the working week.

2007 – It is a little easier to find peeled shrimps, now. Even some farmer's market fish stalls offer them. The ones that are sold in small, plastic pouches are, I think, imported from Holland but of very good quality indeed.

Potted shrimps make brilliant picnic food, too. Make them in small, lidded plastic pots for ease of transport (ensuring that the butter is not too hot if you use these containers) and simply fork directly onto slices of good brown bread. Don't forget the essential lemons and a pepper grinder.

175g best quality unsalted butter
350g brown shrimps
salt
1 tsp cayenne pepper

1 tsp ground mace
generous scraping of nutmeg
juice of 1 lemon

In a large frying pan, melt 100g of the butter. When hot but not frothing, tip in the shrimps and stir around until heated through. Sprinkle with a little salt and stir in the spices. Squeeze in the lemon juice and remove from the heat.

Take six ramekins and divide the buttery shrimps between them, making sure you collect an equal amount of liquid and butter to the shrimps in each pot. Gently press down with the back of a spoon so that the shrimps are as submerged as possible. Place in the fridge to cool. Melt the remaining 75g of the butter and spoon over the tops to seal. Return to the fridge where they will be fine stored for up to four days.

Smoked eel
with fresh horseradish cream and warm potatoes

———

SERVES 4

This combination is heaven. Horseradish is famously good with all smoked fish, but with eel it truly comes into its own. The slice of warm and waxy steamed potato that carries the assembly seems so splendidly correct: you know, the right stuff. I should insist that the horseradish cream is freshly made, but if you are an interminable weeper, then a jar of good old Colman's is a nice and hot, easier option.

8–10 small to medium-sized waxy
   potatoes (charlotte are good)
salt
250–300g of smoked eel fillet –
   depending upon how greedy you
   feel, but not forgetting how rich
   smoked eel is too

for the horseradish cream:
175g piece of fresh horseradish root,
   peeled and freshly grated
2 tsp sugar
1 level tsp salt
juice of 1 lemon
275ml double cream

First make the horseradish cream. Place the grated horseradish in the bowl of a food processor, together with the sugar, salt and lemon juice. Work to a smooth paste and tip into a fairly roomy bowl. Add the cream and beat together with a whisk. Watch how you go, as the mixture will thicken quite quickly. Check for more salt, sugar or lemon juice and spoon into a bowl ready for use. Leave to mature in the fridge for 30 minutes.

Wash the potatoes and place in a steamer. Sprinkle salt over them and steam until tender when pierced with the point of a small sharp knife. Remove and leave to cool for 5 minutes, then peel off their papery skins using the same knife. Do not allow the potatoes to cool completely, as they can be a sod to peel. Once dealt with, put the peeled potatoes back into the still-warm steamer. Cut the eel fillets into small lozenges and put onto a plate.

To assemble: Cut the potatoes into thick-ish slices, smear with a goodly wave of the horseradish and place a piece of eel on top. You may wish to sprinkle a few snipped chives atop the assembly to pretty the thing, especially if you wish to serve this as a 'cocktail snack'. Naturally, if you decide upon this route, dimensions all round should be reduced.

Potted smoked salmon
with spring onions and soured cream

SERVES 4

This one is for those of you who were brought up on those dear little jars of Shipphams paste – and hated them so much they made you sick. I actually quite liked some of them, particularly the chicken one. But I really loathed 'sandwich spread', didn't you? I mean, sandwich spread was sick.

You may use smoked salmon off-cuts to make this dish, but they must be of reasonable quality. Fatty, discoloured, bony and skin-bits are not really good enough. It is a delicious little dish, after all, so buy the most sensibly priced real thing and do it properly.

250g smoked salmon, cut into 2cm dice
75g unsalted butter
150ml soured cream
4 spring onions, trimmed and finely chopped
1 flat tbsp chopped fresh tarragon
juice of 1 small lemon
plenty of freshly ground white pepper
good pinch of ground mace
6–7 tbsp melted unsalted butter
a few extra leaves of fresh tarragon

Melt the butter in a shallow pan and heat until hot but not frothing. Turn the smoked salmon dice through this, over a very low light, with a wooden spoon. Add the soured cream, spring onions, tarragon, lemon juice, pepper and mace. Stir together and heat through until you just see the odd bubble forming on the surface (not much longer or the mixture may separate). Also, try not to break up the fish too much, although some falling apart will be inevitable. The centre of each chunk should remain a little opaque. Remember, the fish will carry on cooking a little in its own heat, once removed from the source.

Remove the pan from the heat and pack the mixture into four ramekins. Cover with clingfilm and chill in the fridge. Once cold, spoon over the melted butter to seal the pots, dropping a few sprigs of fresh tarragon to set into the melted butter as you go. Serve from the ramekins with hot buttered toast. A glass or two of iced chilli vodka is particularly good with this one.

A BRUSH WITH BASIL

At some reckless moment during the early 1970s I chose to cook a dish entitled 'Pork Basil Brush'. I had come across this absurd recipe in my trusty old copy – well, of course, it was actually not such an old copy, then – of *The Good Food Guide Dinner Party Book* (Consumer's Association, 1971, now long out of print). And, my word, what an error of judgement that turned out to be! Pork Basil Brush was, possibly, the silliest, most pointless and dreary thing I had ever cooked – before or since (now I come to think about it, there was that dish of hot, creamed scallops with diced salami in it that was pretty dire… but then that was the work of a precocious, teenage novice. Me.) The remainder of that most favourite book, however, remains as trusty as ever.

The creators of this particular recipe were a sweetly eccentric couple, Mr. and Mrs. St. John-Brooks (I eventually ended up inspecting their restaurant, The Manor House at Gaunt's Earthcott, Gloucestershire, for *Egon Ronay's Guide* and so consequently met them). Though they did manage to make one of the finest caramel ice creams it has ever been my pleasure to consume (eventually requesting thirds) and were further possessed of a keen eye in collecting an eclectic array of antiques and bric-a-brac (everything was for sale in their restaurant, from the chair one sat on to the front door), their editors maybe shouldn't have accompanied the recipe with the following cutesy by-line: 'The St. John-Brooks's have Basil Brush's permission to name this dish after him – and a paw-marked certificate to prove it.'

I won't go into the recipe in full, but – and I suppose this was a sign of the times – it seems, even then, that to use dried basil, dried sage and powdered dill all within the one recipe was, how shall we say, mistaken?

Nowadays, of course, there are more packets of fresh basil available – throughout the year – for purchase in the supermarket than there are indigenous varieties such as parsley, sage, rosemary and thyme. And, absurdly, coriander now seems to come in second to basil as a matter of course. Yes, of course it is lovely to have such choice, but basil is so very redolent of warm weather cooking don't you think?

Tomatoes stuffed with crab
and basil

—

A nicer summer first course, I cannot imagine. The freshest crab meat, a spoonful or two of mayonnaise, seasoning and some finely chopped basil. In passing, I must say that I am getting a little tired of this insistence that fresh basil leaves may only be 'torn' or 'ripped' rather than chopped like other herbs. Yes, I understand that they are a touch more flimsy and tender than some other sprightly herbage, but I find that, finely chopped at the very last moment – as in this recipe – the basil flavours this particular composition most admirably. So there.

10 ripe tomatoes
the brown and white meat extracted
    from 2 small, preferably female
    crabs, freshly boiled (you should
    enjoy doing this yourself, but if you
    have a hard-working fishmonger or
    willing children, palm off the task
    to him or them)

a little salt
a few drops of Tabasco, as seasoning
3–4 tbsp mayonnaise
a squeeze of lemon juice
at least 1 tbsp finely chopped basil,
    plus 20 small sprigs or leaves of
    basil for decoration

Core the tomatoes and then cut each one in half horizontally. Scoop out the flesh and seeds (tip these into a small freezer bag, freeze and use for something else at another time) and then lay each tomato half cut side down on a plate – previously laid with a double sheet of kitchen roll – for 30 minutes, or so.

Fork together the brown meat with a little seasoning and a smidgen of mayonnaise, until smooth. Place a small teaspoon of this into the base of each tomato half. Do the same to the white meat, but this time add more mayonnaise, the chopped basil and lemon juice. Pile this on top of the brown meat until each tomato half is filled to almost overflowing. Decorate each filled tomato half with a leaf or sprig of basil and then place all of them on a suitable serving platter; there will be 20 pieces in all: 5 per person. Lightly toasted short lengths of baguette here, don't you think? And spread with plenty of fine butter, too.

Fagioli e fagiolini
con basilico

SERVES 4

A celebration of new beans, here: both the super-farinaceous fresh borlotti or white cannellini bean extracted from their pods, mingled together with tiny, pipe-cleaner thin, fine French green beans. The only dressing needed here is the finest olive oil you can lay your hands on, sea salt, freshly ground white pepper (for preference) and the tiniest squeeze of lemon juice. Only then may you feel free to scatter them with as much torn or chopped basil leaves as you like.

500g borlotti or white beans in pod, podded
250g finest, thinnest and freshest fine French green beans, topped and tailed
salt and freshly ground white pepper
lemon juice
olive oil
basil

Simmer the borlotti beans in unsalted water until very tender. Vigorously boil the green beans in salted water until they are also tender – and not crunchy to the bite. Leave the borlotti beans in the water until the water is warm. Thoroughly drain the green beans and tip into a roomy bowl. Lift the borlotti beans from their water using a slotted spoon and add to the green beans. Season both judiciously with salt and pepper, add a squeeze of lemon juice and douse with olive oil until all is well lubricated. Scatter with as much basil as you see fit and take to table in the bowl, complete with spoon and fork. Allow each person to serve themselves – and not without the greatest of pleasure, I reckon.

2007 – In retrospect, I think the merest hint of garlic might be welcome, here. If you agree, then I would suggest crushing a small clove and infusing it in the oil for an hour or so before beginning the recipe.

Potato gnocchi
with garlic
and basil cream

If you can find yourselves some new-season garlic for this dish then all the better. Whatever garlic you do happen to use, just make sure you remove any green shoots that may have formed inside each clove before cooking. I must say that this teeny-weeny creation of mine (well, the sauce, that is) has recently given much pleasure to the most discerning palates.

for the gnocchi:
500g potatoes – not too floury; I find
    that red Desiree work very well here
1 egg
150–200g plain flour, approximate
    weight
½ tsp salt

for the sauce:
about 15 large cloves garlic, peeled
200ml double cream
100ml whipping cream
salt and freshly ground white pepper
2 handfuls of fresh basil leaves
a little freshly grated Parmesan
    (optional)

To make the gnocchi, steam or boil the potatoes in their skins, peel, and then put through a vegetable mill (*mouli-légumes*) directly onto a floured surface or board. Do not flatten them as they should retain some fluffiness and air. Allow to cool. Once cooled, make a well in the potato with your fingers. Drop in the egg and sift in the flour (minimum amount) with the salt. Now gently bring everything together with your hands and knead deftly to a dry-ish consistency. At this stage, you may need a little more flour, both on the surface and in the mixture. The ideal consistency should be similar to very soft pastry. Now roll the dough into long sausage shapes about 2cm in diameter and then cut the sausage into 2cm pieces.

To make the garlic cream, cover the garlic cloves with water and bring to the boil. Drain and repeat the process. Return the cloves to the pan, cover with both of the creams, season and bring to a simmer. Cook ever so quietly until the garlic cloves are completely soft. Liquidise until very smooth but leave in the goblet.

Pick up one of the pieces of dough and, using your thumb, roll it down the inside tines of a fork, then flicking it off the end, to form both a ridged impression and, at the same moment, forming a depression on the other side from the thumb. This is the desired shape for gnocchi so that it holds any sauce that you decide to coat it with. Once all the gnocchi are formed, return to the floured tray.

Set a large pot of salted water on to boil and drop about a third of the gnocchi in to cook. Simmer until they float to the surface then give them a further 20–30 seconds. Lift out with a slotted spoon, drain well and put into a heated, lightly buttered dish. Keep warm and continue cooking the rest. Once all the gnocchi are cooked, fling the basil leaves into the garlic cream in the liquidiser and process until attractively green-flecked. Pour the cream over the gnocchi and gently combine, mingling all together with spoon and fork. Serve up at once, sprinkled with a little grated Parmesan, if liked.

LUNCH IN THE GARDEN

One hot and sunny Saturday morning in early August this year, Uzès market near Avignon was over-laden with prime produce. We bustled towards the fish stalls first, as these are usually the first things to pack up and go. But here, still, soon after 9am, there were some slimy and stiff daurade Royale (so named as the finest of the bream family and, furthermore, due to their flash of gold by their noses as if like a tiny coronet), trays of sloppy octopus, pearly-white ready cleaned squid, piles of *chipirons* – tiny cuttlefish the size of your thumb just waiting to be seized in hot oil and garlic – and wriggling *ecrevisses* in wicker panniers, their claws angrily reaching up, poised to pinch probing fingers.

I wrote about Uzès two years ago, and, once again, I was staying with (and, therefore, cooking for) *le docteur* Woodcock. He has inhabited Uzès for many years during the warmer months, returning to London in the winter for theatre, opera and the finer dining rooms of London. He has a tall, thin house in a narrow street just off the centre of the town, but a stroll from the main street and market place. There is a Casino supermarket on the corner, which Elizabeth David so fondly talked of in her book *An Omelette and a Glass of Wine* (Penguin, 2000), and a fine baker only four doors down, which make the finest *fougasse* filled with melted Roquefort and black olives. We quickly wolfed one of these, only because it appeared from the back of the shop, oozing and crisp from the oven. It was 10am and we were returning from the market, so this was breakfast.

Lunch was to be served in the back garden, under the shade of a voluminous almond tree, its furry green fruit ripe and dropping. Vegetable salads were to be the order of the day, to accompany the fine *colin* (hake)

that I had clocked on the best-looking fish-stall. Incidentally, why is it that you can meander around a northern market such as the one in Bury, Lancashire, and see hake stacked up to the ceiling, yet you hardly ever see it for sale in the choicest of London fishmongers? Perhaps it is always snapped up by greedy Spaniards who rate this fish above all others, and consequently export all the finest specimens that we trawl. Hey-ho.

The most important point to consider, when making a vegetable salad, is that the ingredients should be of the very finest and freshest you can find. This may be an obvious stipulation, yet it is surprising how often it is not adhered to. The courgettes in Uzès market were of such brilliant green they simply begged to be bought; so, too, were the green beans, thin as string and snapped with juice when broken. And I have always liked the way one collects produce at French vegetable market stalls; there are these brightly coloured, small plastic washing-up bowls (for want of a better description) dotted about, into which you drop your chosen vegetables. All mixed up, it matters not – so much nicer than those little plastic bags which you pull off a roll in the supermarket.

A fine bunch of mint wafted its fresh scent from another corner of the stall, and there were sprightly chives, too, destined for a warm potato salad. The mint made me think of a favourite vegetable salad from Italy, where courgettes – or zucchini – are cut into thin strips, quickly fried in olive oil until daintily gilded, and then dressed with wine vinegar, garlic, a touch more oil, and some coarsely chopped mint, all while still warm.

2007 – The lovely Doctor Patrick Woodcock sadly died in 2002.

Courgette salad
with mint and vinegar

—

SERVES 4

8 medium-sized courgettes, thinly
  sliced lengthways, preferably on a
  mandolin
a little salt
2 tbsp olive oil
a little more olive oil

2 cloves garlic, peeled and chopped
2–3 tbsp wine or sherry vinegar
a flurry of freshly chopped mint –
  as much as you like really
freshly ground black pepper

Sprinkle the sliced courgettes with salt, and mix together with your hands in a colander. Leave for 20 minutes. Rinse briefly under cold running water and dry thoroughly with a tea-towel, being careful not to crush the vegetables too much.

Heat a very roomy frying pan or wok and fry the courgette slices in olive oil, in batches, until tinged golden, but do not over-cook. After each session, drain the courgettes in a colander, and when all is done, place in a roomy bowl. Add a little more oil to the frying pan and throw in the garlic. Cook till sizzling well and pour in the vinegar. Add back the courgettes for a moment or two and toss around with the mint. Season with black pepper and tip back into the bowl. Serve at room temperature.

Fennel à la Grecque

—

SERVES 4

This is particularly good as an accompaniment to grilled fish, but is equally nice eaten all on its own as a vegetable dish or first course. It is important that the fennel is extremely fresh, with the central parts good and white.

8 small, very fresh bulbs of fennel,
  trimmed and neatly quartered
20 button onions, peeled
salt and pepper
juice of 1 small lemon
1 scant tbsp Pernod or Ricard
200ml dry white wine

1 tsp fennel seeds, dry-roasted in a
  small frying pan until fragrant
2 cloves garlic, peeled and sliced
2–3 sprigs fresh thyme
2 bay leaves
6 tbsp extra virgin olive oil
1 tbsp freshly chopped parsley

Put the fennel and onions in a large pot so that they are almost in a single layer. Season and sprinkle over the lemon juice and Pernod. Add the white wine, fennel seeds, garlic, herbs and oil and put onto a low light to cook. Stir together briefly, once it has come to a simmer and cook very gently, covered, for about 45 minutes.

By this time the vegetables will be very soft and deeply flavoured. Allow to cool to room temperature, before tasting the juices to ascertain a correct seasoning. Spoon into a serving dish and sprinkle over the parsley.

Salad of green beans
with anchovies

—

SERVES 4

1 tbsp smooth Dijon mustard
1 tbsp red wine vinegar
½ clove garlic, peeled and well crushed
4 tbsp warm water
pepper
12 anchovy fillets
150ml peanut oil
150ml virgin olive oil
400–500g extra fine French green
  beans, topped and tailed
1 large shallot, peeled and very
  finely chopped
a little extra virgin olive oil

First make the dressing. Blend the
mustard, vinegar, garlic, water, pepper
and four of the anchovy fillets until
smooth in a food processor or
liquidiser. With the motor still
running, add the oils in a thin stream
until the dressing is homogenous and
creamy. If it has become too thick,
thin with a little more warm water.

Fill a large pan with salted water
and bring to a rolling boil. Drop in
the beans and cook briskly for
3–4 minutes, or until tender – they
should not, however, squeak when you
eat them. Drain and then immediately
refresh under very cold running water.
Drain again and pat dry with a tea-
towel. Divide the beans onto four
individual plates and loosely arrange
into piles. Spoon over the dressing,
sprinkle over the shallot and decorate
with the remaining anchovies.
Trickle over a little of the extra olive
oil and serve.

STOP MESSING ABOUT

Were I really to pause and think, I would guess that it has taken me the devil of a long time to master the art of making pâtés and terrines. Part of the reason for this backward failing has been entirely of my own making: that of fiddling and messing about with that which has been made abundantly clear to me by other people; well, to be more precise, the exact instructions of other people's recipes. With hindsight, I can only view this absurd habit as having been something of a naive obsession, fuelled by a cocky desire to alter and improve that which, in fact, I actually knew nothing about.

As with mastering the complexities of pastry making and achieving a good rise, flawless crust and finely textured crumb in a simple loaf of bread, a similar set of rules applies to perfecting the construction of a good pâté or terrine. Makeshift may be okay for those moments when there are leftover scraps of cooked meat here, a little fatty bacon there, a few chicken livers at the back of the freezer, basic seasoning, a beaten egg or two… and, yes, this is all just fine, but it will never be anything more than a snack. To achieve the required texture – be it rough, smooth or somewhere in between – and deeply savoury qualities of a well turned-out terrine or pâté, ingredients must be carefully sourced and absolutely prepared from scratch.

One of my earliest meddling mistakes was to miscalculate (blatantly ignore, of course) the correct ratio of fat to meat asked for in a recipe for a rather good, but very simple, *terrine de campagne* (a 'country-style' terrine, that I think originated from an Elizabeth David book). I had been asked to make this for the regular cold buffet lunch, offered up daily within the Pembrokeshire hotel I was working in at the time. Sally Newton, the chef in residence in 1972 – or thereabouts – sternly reproached me as she returned to the kitchen from a pre-luncheon scrutiny of my platter of sliced terrine: 'You have been fiddling about with Mrs. David's recipe again, haven't you Simon?', she boomed. 'It's *far* to dry. All crumbly. I'm surprised you even managed to slice it!' She was right, of course. It had been the very devil to achieve neat slices. So much so, in fact, that I had had to do a fair bit of cementing to make them behave as slices at all.

Possibly, I might have been a little bit better at making smooth pâtés. In those days, pâté was always, but always made with chicken livers; it may have also been called *pâté maison* by those who felt happier with this homely description, but you can bet your bottom dollar it was made from chicken livers just the same. The reason I had less trouble with this one, perhaps, was that its basic ingredients were really nothing more than livers and butter. Less to fiddle about with…

I will never forget the strange case of the two Pembrokeshire farmers and their respective wives who turned up at my little restaurant one Saturday night, over 30 years ago now. And it was only ever on a Saturday night that these hard-working folk managed such outings of wild extravagance – possibly even as much as twice a year. Of several first courses available on that particular evening, one of them was pâté and another was snails, six of them. Pembrokeshire farmer requested to see me in the bar. 'Hello there', he said, as he tidily put down his glass of pale ale. 'I have two questions for you. Nawrte,' – Cymru slang for 'Now then,' – 'Are the snails brown? And is the pâté sour?' Initially struck dumb for a few seconds, I then replied: 'They are both very nice indeed, thanks very much!' And with that, I fled back to the safety of my tiny kitchen . (I was only 21!) When the order finally came through to me, it read as follows: 'Four soups; four steaks, well done'.

Chicken liver pâté

SERVES 8—10

I usually make this in two small foil take-away containers (rough capacity about 400ml each). The beauty of these useful vessels lies in how each can be neatly placed upon the other as a means of compressing the pâtés, once cooked. And, incidentally, this is not now just a blend of butter and liver. Much that I admire this perfect pink amalgam, many interpretations now resemble a slab of Spam.

Note: The aromatic French spice mixture known as *quatre-épices* (see page 25) can be made up as follows: 125g white peppercorns; 10g cloves; 30g ground ginger; 35g whole nutmegs. Mill together in an electric coffee grinder, sieve and store in an air-tight jar. A super spice mix for seasoning many pâtés and terrines – particularly that of foie gras.

500g chicken livers, coarsely minced
200g fresh pork back fat, chopped
    into tiny cubes
2 tbsp Cognac
½ tsp *quatre-épices*
25g butter
6 shallots, finely chopped
1 small egg, beaten
1 large teacupful fresh white
    breadcrumbs
2 cloves garlic, peeled and finely
    chopped
1 heaped tsp fresh thyme leaves
2 tbsp freshly chopped parsley
1 rounded tsp salt
1 tsp pepper

Pre-heat the oven to 150°C/300°F/gas mark 2.

Thoroughly mix together the minced livers and back fat in a bowl and add the Cognac and *quatre-épices*. Leave to macerate for at least 1 hour. Melt the butter in a pan and fry the shallots until softened and lightly coloured. Allow to cool. Scrape into the liver mixture and stir in. Then mix all this with the remaining ingredients.

Lightly grease the insides of the foil containers and evenly fill with the mixture. Tap down to settle the filling, lay a buttered sheet of foil over each surface and then crimp around the edges to seal. Place in a deep roasting dish and fill with hot water so that it comes two-thirds of the way up the sides of the terrine dish. Cook in the oven for about 1 hour.

Take out and carefully lift off the foil. Check to see if they are ready by inserting a thin metal skewer into the centre of each. Leave it there for several seconds, pull it out and place it on your bottom lip. If it registers a definite 'hot', the pâtés are cooked (there should also be a tiny bead of deep pink juice that exudes from the skewer's puncture). Remove from the water bath and allow to cool and rest for 10 minutes. Now place one container on top of the other and leave to press for 30 minutes. Reverse the process and repeat the duration. Cover each one with its accompanying lid (silver side down), clamp the edges over and refrigerate for 24 hours before eating. They should keep perfectly well for about 1 week.

Rabbit terrine

—

SERVES 10, AT LEAST

**I cannot see any reason whatsoever to
mess around with this recipe: I have
already seen to that.**

for the forcemeat:
1 farmed rabbit, stripped of every scrap of
    meat (including liver, heart and kidneys),
    coarsely minced, bones saved
200g veal shoulder, coarsely minced
125g piece of belly pork, skin removed
    (but saved), coarsely minced
100g pork back fat, finely diced
125g cooked ham, finely diced
50ml port
50ml Cognac
2 tsp herbes de Provence
1 level tsp ground allspice
2 level tsp salt
1 level tsp pepper

for the savoury jelly:
the rabbit bones, chopped up
1 pig's trotter, split lengthways, then
    chopped
1 large carrot, chopped
1 large onion, chopped
3 sticks celery, chopped
1 scant tsp fennel seeds
6–7 juniper berries, bruised
3 bay leaves
250ml white wine

12–15 thin slices of rindless streaky bacon
    (or Italian pancetta)

Put all the ingredients for the forcemeat into a large bowl. Using your hands,
employ clutching movements throughout the mince, turning it over as you
proceed, until it is all one homogenous mass. Leave to macerate in a cool place,
tightly covered, and for as long as it takes to make the savoury jelly.

Pre-heat the oven to 150°C/300°F/gas mark 2.

Place all the ingredients for the savoury jelly into a roomy pot. Top up with cold
water until just covered. Stir around with a wooden spoon and then slowly bring
up to a simmer. Much scum will form on the surface as the pot heats up, so make
sure you keep a beady eye over this frothing despumation, spooning it off at
regular intervals, as failure to do so will result in muddy, dirty jelly. Once you are
happy with a constant murmuring simmer, slide the pot, uncovered, into the
oven. *Note:* Do not add any salt. Cook for about 2 hours, turning the heat down if it
looks as if a bit of a boil is settling in.

Remove from the oven, place a clean pan in the sink, suspend a colander over it
and drain the broth through. Leave to settle for 10 minutes, or so, discard all
solids and then carefully remove all traces of fat from the strained liquid with
sheets of kitchen paper. Pass this through folded muslin into yet another clean
pan. Reduce over a moderate heat – once again assiduously attending to instances
of rising scum – until a volume of around about 400ml has been achieved. Leave
to cool to room temperature but do not allow to gel. Increase the temperature of
the oven to 170°C/325°F/gas mark 3.

Line a 1–1.5 litre loaf tin or deep porcelain dish (mine measured exactly
1.25 litres, as it happens) with the slices of streaky bacon, neatly overlapping and
also allowing some of them to overhang the rim of the dish; the result of which
will enable the surface of the forcemeat to be fully enclosed by bacon once it has
been packed into the vessel. So, that having been said, proceed forthwith: press
the forcemeat in with firmness, smooth its surface with wetted hands and, at the
same time, make it slightly domed. Collect the bacon ends one by one and fold
over the top, once more overlapping as much as possible.

Now carefully pour over the rich jelly, allowing it to seep down the sides of the
bacon-wrapped forcemeat, the action of which may cause it to float slightly. No
matter. Cover and seal with a sheet of foil, then bake in a deep tray filled with
water (see previous recipe) for about 1¼ hours. Remove the foil and continue
cooking for a further 30 minutes, or until the bacon has coloured nicely and the
terrine is literally floating within a moat of slightly fatty, golden liquid. As
explained in the previous recipe, check that it is completely cooked by deeply
puncturing with a metal skewer. Leave to cool completely, without pressing,
before putting it in the fridge, covered, to chill. Allow 24–36 hours before eating.
This terrine will keep well for at least one week.

Kipper pâté

SERVES 4

Fish paste to finish up with. Don't be put off by my preference for these plastic pouches of kipper fillets, complete with their flower-shaped disks of butter, as they are just dandy for this recipe. Apart from anything else, all the kipper juices are neatly sealed inside, which helps to moisten the finished pâté. Furthermore, by the time one has fully pulverised everything, who can tell whether the kipper was Manx or Craster in the first place?

2 x 200g packets of kipper fillets
150g melted butter
125g cream cheese
juice of 1 lemon
Tabasco
salt, if necessary
extra melted butter

Poach the 2 packets of kipper fillets in a pan of simmering water, cooking them for about half the time suggested. Lift out and leave to cool for 5 minutes. Snip the packets open with a pair of scissors and slide onto a deep plate or tray. Scrape away all skin and remove the minimal central cartilage. Flake all the flesh into the bowl of a food processor.

Now suspend a small sieve over the same bowl and pour all the buttery juices, skin and bits into it. Compress this debris with the back of a ladle so that every scrap of kipper essence is forced through it. Pulse the mixture for a few seconds only to break it up. Add the butter, cream cheese, lemon juice and Tabasco. Process to a smooth purée. Taste for seasoning. Spoon into small pots, smooth over the surface and seal with a little more melted butter. Put to chill in the fridge for at least a couple of hours. Eat with hot toast. Once sealed, these will keep, chilled, for 4–5 days.

FIELDS OF GREEN

I guess that the following concern of mine may come across to you as an unusually anxious one, but I truly feel that there is something deeply disturbing about the way in which asparagus grow. I mean, one day there is nothing much there at all. Then, one warm Spring morning, suddenly there they are, tentatively poking up through the soil, as if without a by your leave: 'Hey there! Here we are! Just watch us grow before your very eyes!' There is no display of foliage whatsoever, not even one tiny little sign that there will, very soon, be a whole field full of tight green sticks. Randomly. Spookily. Just there.

I see this is a kind of vegetable Greek myth. A planting of three-year old 'crowns' (the nomenclature used for an asparagus plant that has been previously nurtured for strength of growth and hopeful harvest) taking the place of a sprinkling of poisoned teeth; pretty little purple-tinged heads that poke through the earth as opposed to those of an army of shiny-helmeted invincible warriors. Was it the teeth of the terrifying Hydra, perhaps, once slain, which produced those menacing figures? Oh yes, I think it was. Native asparagus in full growth certainly smacks of the mythical to me.

Threatening, of course, they are not, these sprightly English stems. Come late April and into the months of May and June, the flat Fenland fields once more come alive with one of the most magical vegetables on earth. Time to celebrate and rejoice in them with an obscenely large serving, eaten with much melted butter and a glass or two of chilled Sauvignon (a suitable wine for this difficult conjunction – and only just, for some) for a lunch eaten out of doors.

Here is a trio of slightly more convoluted recipes, once you have become both weary of melted butter, vinaigrette and a spoonful or two of hollandaise and also relieved of paying over the odds as the season finally draws to a close. So, time to afford to play about a bit.

2007 – I would not have admitted to suggesting that anyone would become weary of melted butter with freshly cooked English asparagus, today. One of the reasons for me finding it more and more difficult to turn out new, seasonal recipes week after week was simply because I do honestly think that all an asparagus spear needs is much melted butter poured all over it.

Cold herb omelette 'pancake'
with asparagus and soured cream

SERVES 4, AS A SUBSTANTIAL FIRST COURSE

Eggs and asparagus have always been seen as excellent bed-fellows. In the following combination – all wrapped up as a sort of cosy sleeping bag affair – the result is, all at once, piquant, luscious and fresh tasting. Try to buy the best eggs you can find, for this.

16–24 spears of English asparagus,
  trimmed and peeled
salt

for the omelette 'pancakes':
4 large eggs
salt and freshly ground white pepper
1 tbsp finely chopped fines herbes
  (tarragon, chervil, parsley and chives)
2 tbsp double cream
butter

for the soured cream dressing:
½ tsp English mustard powder
pinch of caster sugar
squeeze of lemon juice
4 tbsp soured cream
pinch of cayenne pepper
1 tbsp snipped chives

Fill a large pot with water, add plenty of salt and bring to a rolling boil. Drop in the asparagus, return to the boil and cook them until just tender. Drain and refresh under cold running water. Lay out on a tea-towel to dry.

To make the omelette 'pancakes', beat together the eggs with seasoning and herbs and then stir in the cream. Melt a tiny amount of butter in a small frying pan (non-stick, for ease) over a moderate heat, add 2 tbsp of egg mixture and gently swirl it around the pan in one thin layer. Allow it to set for several seconds, deftly flip it over, count to 5 and then slide it onto sheets of kitchen paper. Continue in this fashion until you have 8 omelettes. Set aside until needed.

To make the dressing, simply fold the given ingredients together in a small bowl (too much agitation will thin the cream). Spread the dressing evenly over the 8 omelettes and place the asparagus spears in the middle of each. Roll up the omelettes quite tightly and press gently together with the tips of your fingers. Serve 2 per person, together with offerings of thinly sliced brown bread and butter handed at table.

Baked pasta
with asparagus, prosciutto and truffle

—

SERVES 2, FOR A GOOD LUNCH

I expressly chose the type of pasta for the dish in question simply because it matched the shape of the attendant asparagus spears. However, this combination of tubular white pasta, occasionally insertable stalks of green asparagus and tricksy slivers of bosky black truffle is a sublime one in terms of flavour – and maybe just a little bit rude, which is always nice.

Note: **A large handful of sliced mushrooms, whether cultivated or wild may, of course, be substituted for the expensive truffle. Simply stew them first in a little butter and lemon juice, season them and add to the pasta, juices and all.**

200–250g trimmed and peeled
    asparagus spears
salt

for the béchamel sauce:
30g butter
20g flour
150ml milk
100ml asparagus cooking water
salt, white pepper and nutmeg
2–3 tbsp whipping cream

50g butter
50g sliced prosciutto, cut into
    thin strips
100g dried tortiglioni (the Barilla
    brand seems to be about the
    right size)
1 small black truffle, sliced
    (or mushrooms)
75g freshly grated Parmesan, plus
    extra to hand at table
1 scant tbsp dried breadcrumbs

Moderately preheat an over-head grill.

Bring a large pot of salted water to the boil. Cook the asparagus until just tender and then lift out with a slotted spoon and cool quickly in a bowl of iced water. Drain off the water and dry the asparagus on a tea-towel. Cut them in half and put to one side. Don't ditch the asparagus cooking water.

To make the sauce, melt the butter in a small pan and stir in the flour. Cook gently together for a couple of minutes and then whisk in the milk and 100ml of the asparagus water. Season with salt, pepper and nutmeg and slowly bring up to a boil, continuing to whisk until thickened. Allow to simmer very gently for 5 minutes before stirring in the cream. Keep hot.

Melt half of the butter in a large (preferably non-stick) frying pan over a moderately high heat. Add the prosciutto and cook it for a minute or two, stirring constantly. Add the cooked asparagus and warm it through. Boil the pasta in the asparagus water until tender. Drain well in a colander, and tip it into the frying pan with the prosciutto and asparagus. Add the truffle (or mushrooms), briskly toss all together, sprinkle with half of the given amount of Parmesan and thoroughly mix it in.

Now spread all of this evenly into a shallow, preferably oval, white baking dish. Spoon the béchamel sauce over the surface and sprinkle with the remaining Parmesan and the breadcrumbs. Cut the remaining butter into slivers and scatter over the top. Place under the grill until the entire dish is molten, bubbling and evenly blistered by golden pustules. Serve without delay onto hot plates and pass around the extra Parmesan at table.

Lamb's sweetbreads
with wilted cos lettuce, asparagus and tarragon

———

SERVES 2, AS A LIGHT MAIN COURSE

My eyes lit up recently when I popped in to see Sid, my excellent local butcher, as there, tucked into a corner of the chilled display cabinet in a flimsy plastic bag, lurked the first lamb sweetbreads of the Spring season. Being the beady-eyed fellow that I am, however, I could see quite clearly what they were but, in retrospect, am now deeply concerned that the reason they were not on full display in the first place was simply because Sid, sister Rosie and father Michael were planning to snaffle the whole lot for their own supper that very evening. Today's final, whimsical assembly.

75g butter
2 slices of streaky bacon
½ clove garlic
2 Cos lettuce, severely trimmed of all green leaves to leave yellow hearts
salt and white pepper
1 tbsp tarragon vinegar
2 tbsp jellied chicken stock

400g fresh lamb's sweetbreads, trimmed of all skin and gristle
a little flour
150g well-trimmed asparagus spears
1 dsp freshly chopped tarragon leaves
squeeze of lemon juice (optional)

Melt 50g of the butter in a deep pot and lay the bacon in it. Add the garlic too and gently stew together until the bacon takes on some colour. Discard the garlic and put in the lettuce hearts. Lightly season, add the vinegar and stock and put on the lid. Very gently, braise the lettuce for around about 20 minutes or so, turning them over once (and also bringing the bacon up from beneath and draping over the lettuces) until soggy-looking and very tender indeed. Lift out both lettuces and bacon, put into a dish, cover and keep warm in a low oven.

Meanwhile, season the sweetbreads, dust with flour and gently fry in the remaining 25g of butter until golden and cooked through – about 10–15 minutes, I guess. Keep warm whilst you cook the asparagus. Place these in the lettuce juices (they will have exuded plenty of it during their cooking time) with the tarragon and gently stew for about 10 minutes until tender.

To serve, place the sweetbreads, lettuce and bacon onto two hot plates and arrange the asparagus alongside. Spoon over the tarragon-scented juices and eat at once. *Note:* If you think the juices are a little watery, reduce them slightly over a fast heat, but also make sure that they do not become too salty.

THRIFTY THREE-WAY FISH

When I saw the box of rosy red, glistening gurnard at the fishmongers, I instantly put away any thoughts of the cod and turbot that had previously caught my eye on the slab. There was nothing wrong with these other two fish, it's just that the gurnard was some of the very best and freshest I had ever seen – and cheaper too; this is partly because nobody much knows what to do with it, or thinks it only good for chopping up for fish soup, which it surely is. So, very happy with my purchase, I began to work out what I was going to do with it as I made the journey home.

I had been planning to do a fishy sort of dinner for friends anyway, as some of them did not eat meat, but I surprised even myself with the resultant three fish courses that, in essence, came about from using these spanking gurnard. The only other main ingredients that came into play were a packet of whole prawns that I already had in the freezer, some rice and a few potatoes. More about this later.

I have always been a keenly frugal cook. There is nothing more upsetting to me than seeing good food go to waste through ignorance and thoughtlessness. I once heard of a much-stellated London chef who prepares and fillets a salmon into several portions of perfectly shaped lozenges, but then chucks out the remaining unsightly pieces. Clearly these offcuts are not deemed suitable for the exacting standards that are imagined as *de rigeur* for someone obsessed with winning Michelin stars. Conversely, it is then heartening to know of a similarly well-endowed stellar French chef in the south-west of France who prepares a dish involving duck and sweetbreads, where the duck meat is collected from the fowl's neck bone. I wonder who makes the most profit here?

It is not that difficult, you know, to make food stretch. I am sure I am not alone in remembering cold meat on Monday after the family Sunday roast, followed by rissoles on Tuesday. And it is not all to do with leftovers – or really stretching for that matter; it is more to do with getting the most out of one's chosen ingredients. For instance, when I buy inexpensive chicken wings for making stock, it doesn't take more than a few minutes to lift the resultant succulent chicken meat from their spindly bones. This can be used to make wonderful chicken pies, or minced up with a little chopped boiled egg and cooked potato, Indian herbs and spices, for some savoury fried rissoles; serve with some lime pickle and cucumber raita, perhaps.

But to return to the fish dinner. The gurnard were filleted (your fishmonger can do this for you), the bones and heads from the fish, together with the shells from the prawns, made a generous quantity of fish soup. The remainder of the soup is further used to fashion a small prawn risotto as a small middle course and the fillets of gurnard briefly pan-fried and eaten with a few plainly boiled new potatoes. Here's how to do it. Each dish serves four.

main ingredients:

4 fresh gurnard, weighing approximately
500g each

400g packet of frozen, cooked, shell-on
prawns

150g carnaroli rice

700g medium-sized, well scraped,
new potatoes

for the soup:

4 tbsp olive oil

1 dsp tomato purée

4 cloves garlic, peeled and crushed

2 leeks, trimmed, chopped and washed

3 sticks celery, chopped

½ fennel bulb, thinly sliced

the fish bones and heads (see above)

the shells and heads from the defrosted
prawns (see above)

generous splash Pernod

1 glass of dry white wine

2 litres water

1 x 400g can chopped tomatoes

the peeled, pith-less zest of ½ lemon

salt and a good pinch dried chilli flakes

for the risotto:

the fishy red olive oil removed from the
surface of the fish soup (see recipe)

1 small onion, peeled and finely chopped

2 cloves garlic, peeled and finely chopped

the rice (see above)

½ glass of dry white wine

½ tsp saffron threads

500ml fish soup (see recipe)

the peeled prawns (see above)

3 ripe plum tomatoes, peeled, de-seeded
and finely chopped

1 heaped tbsp chopped flat-leaf parsley

for the fried fish:

8 fillets gurnard (see above)

salt and pepper

a little flour

olive oil

the potatoes, boiled or steamed until
tender (see above)

1 lemon, cut into 4 wedges

First make the soup. Heat the olive oil gently in a roomy pan and add the tomato purée. Fry carefully over a low heat until the purée has become rust coloured. Now add the garlic, leeks, celery and fennel. Stew gently until coloured – about 10 minutes. Tip in the fish bones and prawn shells and turn the heat up slightly. Stir around until the bones are starting to break up somewhat, turn up the heat, add the Pernod and set light to it. Once the flames have died down, pour in the wine and top up with the water. Add the chopped tomatoes and lemon zest, stir well, and season with salt and the dried chilli flakes. Slowly bring up to a simmer and then start to skim the froth from the surface, which will appear in copious amounts. Once this scum has mostly been removed, start to collect the oil that manifests itself on the surface with a tablespoon and put into a small bowl; this will be used to start the risotto. Simmer the soup gently for 1 hour, stirring occasionally, but keep spooning off the oil. Now tip the whole lot into a spacious colander, suspended over a clean pan. Allow to drip for at least 10 minutes, then press and push the mulchy mess around the colander, so that as much flavour left in the fish, can be transferred to the soup below. Discard the mulch and then pass the soup through a reasonably fine sieve into another vessel. Allow to stand for a few minutes and then remove any more oil from the surface and add to the small bowl. The soup now needs some reduction to intensify its flavour. Simmer down gently, skimming any impurities as you go, until the flavour is good and full flavoured. You want to end up with around about 1.4 litres of liquid: 900ml needed for the soup and 500ml needed for the risotto. Put 500ml of the soup into a separate pan and keep hot, ready for making the risotto.

To make the risotto, put 2–3 tbsp of the collected red fishy oil (set aside in the small bowl) in a heavy-based pot and gently fry the onion in it until golden. Add the garlic and rice and stir around over a low light until well coated with the oil. Pour in the white wine and add the saffron, and allow to bubble gently until the wine has evaporated. Now, continuing to keep the pot on a low flame, start to add the 500ml of hot soup, a ladleful at a time, allowing each addition to be fully absorbed before introducing the next, and gently stirring with a wooden spoon constantly. About three-quarters of the way through the making of the risotto, stir in the prawns and tomatoes. Check the texture of the rice as you go along, by eating a bit; it should be cooked through yet firm, but not chalky in the middle. The resultant texture should be sloppy but not soupy. Once you feel the texture and taste is right, stir in the chopped parsley.

To cook the gurnard fillets, first lightly slash the skin side with a sharp knife, only just cutting into the flesh (this will help to prevent the fish curling too much when you cook it). Season well with salt and pepper and dip the skin side into the flour. Shake off any excess and fry for about 2–3 minutes on each side in a little hot olive oil in a spacious frying pan. *Note:* It is quite a good idea to initially press down lightly on the flesh side at the beginning of the cooking process, as this helps the skin to become very crisp. Serve with the plain boiled potatoes, a little extra virgin olive oil spooned over them and the fish, and serve with the lemon wedges. As you have already had two fairly rich courses – the soup, followed by the risotto – you should not need anything more than a green salad, if that. However, this dish is particularly good when eaten with garlic mayonnaise.

THREE-STAR DRUNKS

The first time I ate this quite superb, yet simple and elegant dish I was very, very drunk. It was Paris in Springtime, about 15 years ago now, and I was with Paul, a chef-friend who was then cooking at La Tour d'Argent. Shamefully, our misbehaviour was exercised at the very smart indeed restaurant Taillevent. Well, you know, the day had drifted on a bit, and as we had not been able to secure a table before 10.30pm (as it was, booked three weeks ahead) my chum and I filled the time with rather too many Martinis…

This was to be my second visit chez Taillevent; the first and consequent visits were and have been less excitable, I'm happy to say. It is, after all, deeply impolite to turn up at a restaurant drunk, whether it be the most venerable and highly professional three-rosette establishment such as Taillevent, or a more louche affair like the bar at Fouquet's (around the corner on the Elysian Fields) where we had soberly arrived much earlier, drunk the too many Martinis and obliquely departed, delightfully ripped, towards rue Washington, just across the road and leading to our dinner. Naturally, the proprietor Jean-Claude Vrinat – one of the most polite, dignified, serious and delightful restaurateurs it has ever been my pleasure to meet – treated us scoundrels as if we were the most perfectly behaved lads he had ever entertained. Which, of course, made matters much, much worse, in the cold, morning light of *le lendemain*.

Disgracefully behaved I may have been, I can still recall this impeccable dish and, as it happens, so can my chum Paul, too. We have never forgotten the taste. Great food will always linger on the palate, however pickled be the brain. The following interpretation is a result of our combined excellent palates.

Fillets of sole
with tomatoes and basil

—

SERVES 4, AS A FIRST COURSE

75g butter

2 large shallots, peeled and finely
   chopped

4 large Dover soles, skinned, filleted
   and trimmed by the fishmonger;
   bring the bones home

4 tbsp Noilly Prat

salt and white pepper

3 ripe tomatoes, peeled, de-seeded
   and neatly diced

12 leaves of basil, snipped into strips

a small squeeze of lemon juice

75ml double cream

for the fish stock:

the sole bones, chopped and washed

1 leek, white-part only, trimmed and
   washed then finely chopped

2 sticks celery, finely chopped

1 bay leaf

2 sprigs fresh thyme

200ml dry white wine

300ml water

pinch of salt

First make the fish stock. Bring all the ingredients very slowly to a simmer and skim off any froth. Cook very gently for 20 minutes and strain through a sieve. Reduce the liquid, skimming the surface further of scum as it does so, until there is not much more than several syrupy tablespoonfuls. Strain once more through a very fine sieve, and reserve.

Pre-heat the oven to 200°C/400°F/gas mark 6.

Using 25g of the butter, grease an ovenproof dish and strew with the shallots. With a rolling pin or meat bat, gently beat the sole fillets between greaseproof paper to flatten them slightly. Fold over into a neat shape and place on top of the shallots. Spoon over the Noilly Prat and season. Cover with foil and bake in the oven for 20–25 minutes, or until just cooked. Remove and pour off the juices into a small pan. Keep the fish warm, still covered.

Add the reduced fish stock to the juices in the small pan and bring to a simmer. Reduce a little more and add the tomatoes, basil and lemon juice. Swirl in the butter until amalgamated and then add the cream. Stir all together and simmer briefly until smooth and unctuous. Check for seasoning and pour over the sole. Eat with some small, plain boiled and lightly buttered potatoes.

SWEET LAMB

Hopefully, as Easter is so very late this year, almost a whole month behind the norm, in fact, there should not – I mean *really* there should not – be any of that absurd price-hiking where spring lamb is concerned. And although the Easter festival occurs just one week from today, most lambs, as far as I know, are entirely ignorant of the occasional fluctuation within the Church calendar. I mean, last year, when Easter was three to four weeks earlier, they would surely still have been prime and up to scratch, wouldn't they?

Well we know this, butchers certainly know and supermarkets are also very much aware. However, will the tariff placed upon young lamb have significantly dropped a little in preparation for the week, this week, culminating in Good Friday 2000? Not on your life.

All, however, is not gloom and doom. For just a few weeks ago, Sid, my lovely local butcher (Olympia Butchers, 70 Blythe Road, London W14; 020 7602 4843 – who is long overdue for a fresh promotion), managed to find me some immaculate lamb's sweetbreads. So sweet and frisky these plump and pink morsels smelt, that I was moved to early summer-recipe thinking in the shaking of a woolly tail.

Roast best end of lamb
with mint and redcurrant sauce,
with gratin Dauphinois

SERVES 2

**I happen to think that a plainly roast
best end of lamb, all crisp on the
outside and pink and tender within,
together with a scoop of potatoes
cooked with cream and garlic, is almost
as good as it gets. Period. Some might
say that the accompaniment of a
slightly over-sweet sauce here is quite
out of order with the French potatoes.
Well, you know, I honestly couldn't
care less.**

1 best end of lamb, butcher trimmed
   and chined
a smear of oil
salt and pepper

for the gratin Dauphinois:
1 clove garlic, peeled and crushed
300ml whipping cream
salt and freshly milled white pepper
grated nutmeg
500g potatoes (small red Desiree, for
   preference), peeled
a scrap of softened butter

for the sauce:
4 tbsp port
1 tbsp crème de cassis
1 tbsp best redcurrant jelly
1 tbsp fine red wine vinegar (the Spanish
   brand 'Forum', a Cabernet Sauvignon
   vinegar, is especially good here)
1 level tsp arrowroot, slaked in 1 tbsp port
1 tbsp freshly chopped mint

Pre-heat the oven to 180°C/350°F/gas mark 4.

Put the garlic, cream, salt (think scant here), pepper and nutmeg into a bowl. Whisk together and leave to infuse. Now, using whichever chosen little gadget you are happy with, slice the potatoes to a thickness of a £1 pound coin – or thereabouts. Deposit the slices in a large bowl and rinse them a bit with your hands under a cold running tap. Drain them, dry in a tea-towel and tip into a roomy, shallow pan. Strain the bowl of infused cream over them and, using your fingertips (I know this is a bit messy but, frankly, it remains the most efficient method), mingle the potato slices with the cream, whilst also separating each one from the other in the process. (Be assured, this briefest of messy moments will result in a far more superior gratin Dauphinois than that of most of your other gratin Dauphinois-making chums who – until now, that is – have always considered theirs to be the very best. After all, you have hot water to wash your hands under, don't you?)

To complete the dish, slowly bring the pan of cream and potatoes to a simmer and cook for 10 minutes, or so, until the cream has visibly thickened and the potatoes are just beginning to become tender when pierced with a small knife. Lightly grease your chosen dish with the butter, tip in the contents of the pan and smooth the surface with a spatula. Clean up any dribbles and bake in the oven for about 30–40 minutes, or until the palest gold blistering is evident all over and the consistency of the contents is all a-wobble. Remove from the oven and place at the rear of the stove, where they may linger, at an ambient temperature.

Increase the oven temperature to 200°C/400°F/gas mark 6.

Smear the best end all over with oil and generously season. Place in a small roasting tin, fat side down, and roast in the oven for about 25–30 minutes, basting occasionally and also turning the joint around so that it sits bone tips uppermost, for the final 10 or so minutes. Tip out all traces of fat from the tin and leave the lamb to rest, somewhere warm on top of the stove, until ready to carve.
Note: This cooking and resting time will result in a blush of rosy-red meat. Simply roast for a little longer if this is not to your particular taste.

Meanwhile, put the port, crème de cassis, redcurrant jelly and vinegar into a small, stainless steel or enamelled pan and bring to the boil. Ignite this brew with a match, allow the flames to subside and then simmer for a further 5 minutes. Whisk in the slaked arrowroot, allow it to lightly gel the sauce for only a minute or so (any longer can sometimes cause this temperamental, though most useful thickener to suddenly break down) and then stir in the mint. Place on one side in attendance, ready to be heated through once the lamb is ready.

To serve the assembly, carve the lamb into neat cutlets, arrange upon hot plates, re-heat the sauce to spoon over them and have the dish of potatoes ready to hand.

Creamed lamb sweetbreads
with broad beans and tarragon

SERVES 2

A more seasonal combination I cannot think of just now. So I won't. I really loved cooking this one.

350–400g fresh lamb's sweetbreads
juice of ½ lemon
salt
4 full tbsp podded, small, young
  broad beans
25g butter
1 shallot, peeled and finely chopped
50ml dry white wine

2 sprigs fresh tarragon
50ml strong chicken stock
100ml whipping cream
squeeze of lemon juice
1 tsp freshly chopped tarragon
salt and freshly ground white pepper

Trim off any unsightly bits and pieces from the sweetbreads and rinse under cold running water for a few minutes. Drain, and put into a stainless steel or other non-reactive saucepan. Just cover with cold water and add the lemon juice and a little salt. Bring up to a simmer, cook for 1 minute, and drain (ditch the cooking liquor). Tip onto a plate, pick over each piece and peel off the thin membrane that covers each morsel. Put aside, somewhere cool. Bring a pan of salted water to a brisk boil and cook the broad beans for no more than 1 minute. Drain, instantly tip them into a small bowl of iced water and leave them there.

In the same (rinsed) pan, melt the butter and stew the shallot until soft but uncoloured. Pour in the wine, add the tarragon sprigs and simmer for 5 minutes until reduced to a golden, syrupy consistency. Put in the stock and bring back to the boil. Reduce over a low light until further reduced by half. Put back the sweetbreads and simmer for only 5 minutes, or so, until firm, but having a little give when poked with a finger.

Lift out the sweetbreads with a fork and keep warm in a serving dish, covered with foil. Remove the straggly tarragon sprigs and discard, add the cream to the pan, stir in and bring to a simmer. Once slightly thickened, drain the broad beans from their water and stir into the sauce, squeeze in the lemon juice, add the chopped tarragon and judiciously season. Pour the whole lot over the reserved dish of sweetbreads and stir together. Serve a bowl of correctly prepared (i.e. well scraped!), lightly buttered new potatoes alongside.

HORSEPLAY

Mr. Bill Baker, as well as being my friendly West Country wine merchant, also happens to know where are all the best spots for digging up wild horseradish anywhere along the roads that run between Wells and Weston-Super-Mare. He can pinpoint a perfect patch at 50 yards. Even the very smallest horseradish shoot, tentatively poking up out of a scrappy piece of roadside verge in mid-winter, whilst buried under a deep covering of fresh snow, is prone to a good hacking by his trusty spade – which is, at all times at the ready, in the boot of his mud-splattered motor car.

But, of course, he is absolutely right and cares deeply about finding fresh roots of horseradish whenever there is a joint of beef waiting to be roasted.

It is something that comes naturally to the intelligent cook and so I salute this most worthy of escapades. Whilst other passing motorists may well stare at this big man as he digs up great clods of earth by the side of the road with both fear and bewilderment, they most definitely put their foot firmly on the accelerator when he finally holds on high several gnarled roots and exclaims with loud joy. They probably think he's some kind of organic drug dealer.

As one aspect amongst many good cookery practices, the ingredients are out there if you care to find them. Naturally, they don't all come for free from the side of the A38, but the freshest and best will always reap huge dividends once the time comes to eat the results.

Homemade horseradish concentrate

MAKES ENOUGH TO FILL A SMALL KILNER JAR

The basis upon which all the following recipes are based. To make it is an elementary task and – if you adore the smell of fresh horseradish as much as I do – this can be really quite an exciting kitchen event. You only have to wave a freshly grated bowlful under the nose of unwanted neighbours or unruly children and... well, it's the next best thing after nerve gas, that's all I'm saying.

Some folk bang on about how distressing it is to grate your own horseradish: the tears, the huge amount of labour involved and, perhaps more importantly, actually laying your hands on a stick of the same in the first place. In London, I buy my roots from Selfridges Food Hall, but I reckon that if you ask your local greengrocer nicely, I am sure they will be able to find some. Although it is no trouble to purchase a nice and sturdy, thick, foot-long length of it in London W1, it is clear that this is not a local crop. (Great groves of it growing in and around the allotments of Bond Street or Berkeley Square? I don't think so.) These giant roots, I assure you, are imported from nether climes. Spooky old Scandinavia, I reckon and most certainly nowhere near the A38.

To have something so delicious to hand in the fridge is worth a few salty drips from *my* tear ducts. And as for the labour involved? This has become a piece of cake now we have the amazingly efficient Microplane® grater (available from all good kitchen shops), whose razor-sharp teeth make light work of this tough root.

A word of warning regarding the grating of horseradish. It *must* be grated by hand before further puréeing; if you are tempted to take the short cut of dicing the root and then pulverising it in a food processor, the result will be an inedible, deeply bitter mass fit only for the dustbin. And it must be grated *across* the grain of the root. Some cook on *Woman's Hour*, recently, gave the impression horseradish could be grated along the sides of the root. This, of course, is poppycock. The result of such shoddy grating will only result in fibrous strands, minimum punch and, once again, unwanted bitterness.

200g horseradish root, peeled and finely grated

5 tbsp water

2 tsp Maldon salt

1½ tbsp caster sugar

5 tbsp lemon juice – or half lemon juice and half white wine vinegar for a sharper taste

Place all the ingredients in a food processor and purée until smooth. Tip into a Kilner jar or similar, and place in the fridge, where it will keep quite happily for up to two weeks, though its pungency will quietly fade day by day. The acidity is the key to longevity.

Creamed horseradish sauce

MAKES 4 SERVINGS

Smoked eel and trout favour a spoonful of creamed horseradish, as does an occasional poached chicken, carved up and served warm with spring vegetables. Boiled salt beef and tongue like it too, though these two like it even better when puréed with beetroot (see later). But don't be fooled by the idea of 'horseradish dumplings'; like mustard, all the pungency of horseradish becomes severely diminished when heated.

Of course, it is roast beef and Yorkshire pudding that horseradish was expressly created for. Moreover, I find the dish almost inedible if there is not a large bowl of horseradish to hand. And it is not just the beef: the Yorkshires are delicious with it, as too are the roast potatoes and burnished parsnips. Left-over cold roast potatoes with horseradish? Words simply cannot describe this ultimate gourmet snack... Then again, I am now not so sure whether a sandwich filled with thinly sliced rare-roast beef and fresh horseradish is not one of the very finest things it is possible to eat. And it is important that the bread should be soft and white – none of that sourdough-Italian-rustic-country-full-of-holes-hippy-nonsense – and well buttered with good and salty, yellow butter.

4 tbsp horseradish concentrate

200ml double cream

maybe a little extra salt and sugar to taste

Using a whisk, beat all the ingredients together in a small bowl for a minute or so until loosely thickened. Serve alongside slices of cold rare-roast beef this very summer.

Chrain
to serve with
boiled calf's tongue,
for example...

———

MAKES ENOUGH FOR 4 SERVINGS

I know that I have offered up this devilishly ruby paste to you before on these pages, but when writing of horseradish it simply cannot be omitted. But a word of warning: of all horseradish preparations, this is the most powerfully pungent. Once whizzed up in the processor, this particular brew might well kill granny stone dead if you offer up the mixing bowl to her pinkly powdered nose.

3 medium-sized cooked beetroots, peeled and cut into chunks
3–4 tbsp horseradish concentrate
1 tbsp balsamic vinegar
1 level tbsp caster sugar
salt to taste

Place all the ingredients in a food processor and whiz until smooth. Serve alongside slices of freshly boiled calf's tongue or salt beef.

Horseradish-flavoured homemade tomato juice
for the making of
Bloody Marys

———

MAKES A SCANT LITRE

I am really very excited indeed that I have finally come up with a homemade tomato juice that seems to work.

1kg-plus very ripe tomatoes, cored and cut into quarters
1 heaped tsp Maldon sea salt
1 tbsp caster sugar
125ml water
1 tbsp horseradish concentrate

Place the first four ingredients in a stainless steel pan, cover and gently warm over a low heat until the tomatoes are completely collapsed and much juice from the fruit has been released; about 20 minutes cooking time, I guess. Tip the entire contents of the pan into the mouth of a vegetable mill (*mouli-légumes*) fitted with the finest blade, grind the mulch until only the very last seeds and skin remain. Leave to cool completely and then stir in the horseradish concentrate. Leave to infuse for 10 minutes or so and then pass through a fine sieve using a small ladle to press down upon all solids, so extracting every last vestige of flavour. Pour into a glass bottle and chill in the fridge until ready for use.

Horseplay

107

Homemade horseradish and tomato ketchup relish
for clams or rock oysters

———

In the Oyster Bar at Grand Central Station in New York City, along with lemon and Tabasco sauce, they serve up a little paper cup of ketchup mixed with grated horseradish. This is not particular to the Oyster Bar. Moreover, I now reckon it is the American alternative to that little bowl of French shallot vinegar. However, I really quite like this stuff, especially with clams. Here is my homemade version. *Note:* **As the reduction process will almost obliterate the original infusion of horseradish (due to heat), it is necessary to add more at the end.**

300ml homemade tomato juice (see page 106)

2 tbsp horseradish concentrate

Place the tomato juice in a small stainless steel pan and quietly reduce over a very moderate heat until almost sauce-like. Remove from the heat, cool for about 20 minutes and then stir in the horseradish. Chill in the fridge until ready to use

Horseradish mousse
to accompany cured herrings and/or gravadlax

———

MAKES 4 MOUSSES

The simplest of savoury mousses. *Note:* **The horseradish juice may be extracted from the horseradish concentrate by pressing an amount of the concentrate through a very fine sieve – with the aid of a small ladle – into a bowl.**

150ml double cream
1 tbsp freshly chopped dill
1 tsp caster sugar
1 leaf gelatine, softened in a cup of cold water

1 dsp lemon juice
4 dsp horseradish juice (extracted from a jar of horseradish concentrate)

Lightly whip the cream with the dill and sugar. Melt the gelatine leaf with the lemon juice over a low heat, cool slightly and then fold into the cream/dill mixture with the horseradish juice. Oil four small dariole moulds and pour in the mousse mixture. Cover the surfaces with a small piece of clingfilm and allow to set in the fridge for at least 4 hours. Turn out to garnish one's chosen fish.

SPUD-U-LIKE

The celebrated Mr. George Trenouth of Trevone Farm near Padstow, Cornwall, first came to my attention via the table of restaurateur and telly lovely, Rick Stein, several years ago now. A very proper Cornish farmer of a certain number of years (perhaps just a shade over 60 of them), Mr. Trenouth grows the very finest potatoes I have ever had the pleasure to cook and eat. So much so that I now feel a little embarrassed over quite how many pounds of them returned to London with me – the exact quantity remains a bit of a blur.

There were seven of us eating, as I recall, and it was lobsters all round. None of that 'Would you all like a selection of vegetables for the table?' nonsense here. Oh no. Just one enormous bowlful of marble-size, scrupulously scraped, buttered and mint-flecked Trevone new potatoes was simply plonked upon the table. Never had the spud been presented with so much pride and flourish as they were that night.

Ignoring the lobster entirely, we set upon them as if possessed. Thinking back now, in themselves they would have made the most splendid first course. The lobster was merely adequate. A garnish, perhaps. Nothing we ate compared with those first, early Cornish nuggets, served in such luxurious quantity, so easily spooned from their capacious bowl, so tender and sweet… Oh, all right then, the lobster was utterly sensational, too.

Mr. Trenouth senior (my invoice says 'W.E.G. Trenouth and Son') also sold me some early Cornish strawberries (this was the May bank holiday), several pots of extraordinarily good clotted cream and a few sprigs of fragrant mint for the simmering of my farinaceous jewels. I will now cease these endless and flowery superlatives. Enough! Then again, I should also say that an entire shed of premature, blowsy basil plants ready to be planted out in the up and coming Cornish summer sun smelt gorgeously fragrant as I reluctantly drove off through the farm-shop gates…

2007 – Sadly, the great George Trenouth died in 2005.

Tiny new potatoes
with caviar and chives

—

SERVES 4, AS A LUXURIOUS SNACK

WITH A GLASS OF CHAMPAGNE

OR ICED VODKA

**Possibly the finest accompaniment to
caviar that I can think of.**

20 equal-sized tiny new potatoes,   caviar
   scrupulously scraped   snipped chives
butter

Prepare and cook the potatoes in exactly the same way as for the 'simply boiled'
recipe on page 114. Drain and keep warm. Now, using a teaspoon or – even better
– a melon baller, cut out a small cavity in the surface of each potato and add a flake
of butter. Over-fill with caviar and sprinkle with chives. Eat with joy.

Warm new potato and asparagus soup
with cucumber, mint and yoghurt

—

SERVES 4

The way of cooking this soup is based upon a favourite one that I have been using for many years now. I should admit that this recipe singularly goes against my constant, almost Draconian opinion that all soups – whether vegetable-based or not – are so much better when made with a light poultry stock.

The original recipe (using tomatoes and new potatoes) comes from *The Greens Cookbook* by Deborah Madison (first published by Bantam Books, 1987), the founding cook of the ground-breaking vegetarian restaurant of the same name in San Francisco, which she opened towards

the close of the 1970s. It is, without doubt, the most intelligent and thoughtful cookery book ever published with regard to this specialist culinary subject. I would, in fact, go further to say that there does not seem to be a duff recipe within the entire volume.

40g butter

1 onion, chopped

2 tbsps white wine vinegar

750ml water

3–4 sprigs fresh mint

400g asparagus spears (the cheaper English 'sprue' is perfect here), trimmed, roughly chopped and washed

300g new potatoes, scraped and roughly chopped

250ml milk

to finish the soup:

½ small cucumber, peeled, de-seeded and diced small

salt and pepper

1 tbsp freshly chopped mint, plus a little extra for sprinkling

2 heaped tbsp yoghurt

a little paprika

Melt the butter in a stainless steel or enamelled pan and fry the onion until soft. Add the vinegar, 100ml of the water and the mint sprigs and allow to reduce to almost nothing. Fish out the mint sprigs, introduce the rest of the water and then the asparagus, potatoes and milk.

Simmer gently until the vegetables are very tender indeed. Pass through the finest blade of a vegetable mill (*mouli-légumes*). Mix the cucumber, seasoning, mint and yoghurt together in a small bowl. Ladle the soup into warmed bowls and spoon a little of the yoghurt mixture into each serving. Sprinkle with paprika and a little more mint.

Purée of new potatoes
with olive oil

———

SERVES 4

Yet another recipe from someone else. Call me unoriginal. But, you know something, this particular way with new potatoes paved the way for what was soon to be a veritable tidal wave of slickly dressed potato purées. So, we may blame the Swiss chef Frédy Girardet this time. However, this original is absolutely delicious.

Note: **It is best to use mids here (larger and later, seasonally, than early new potatoes).**

300g new potatoes, scraped	salt, freshly ground white pepper
120ml whipping cream	and a touch of cayenne pepper
120ml finest and fruitiest olive oil	

Boil the potatoes in salted water until very tender. Drain and pass through the finest blade of a vegetable mill (*mouli-légumes*) into a pan. Over a gentle heat, quickly incorporate the cream using a whisk, until fully incorporated. Continuing over the same heat, now stir in the olive oil with a wooden spoon and beat together until slick and smooth. Season and serve. Very good eaten with simple roast rabbit (see page 226).

Simply boiled new potatoes
with mint butter

———

SERVES 2

This is how we ate the Trevone farm new potatoes at The Seafood restaurant. This almost doesn't need a recipe, but as you know full well, there are always words from me when it comes to the exacting preparation of new potatoes. Firstly, though, a word or two about this year's crop of Jersey Royals…

Well, they are a little better than the last few years is all I have to say, but still a long way away from how they used to taste. The over-forced early Jerseys grown under glass or polytunnels I now see as nothing more than a joke; I have seen these for sale as early as February in some London greengrocers. Well, shame on both parties, frankly.

Some examples that I have recently fondled are not only sporting a pale green hue just beneath the skin (difficult to remove with the thumb, which is always a bad sign at any time) but are worryingly spongy when squeezed. Let's be honest, a stored 'new' potato becomes an 'old' stored potato after just a few days. I reckon, in fact, that there have been some Jersey potatoes I have seen for sale over the last few years that have been three weeks or more old rather than three days.

Perhaps such worrying moments as this are more to do with wholesalers over-buying than anything to do with the island's growers; i.e.: those who choose to store and stockpile without any consideration whatsoever for those who eventually go home with them wrapped up in a brown paper bag.

And, furthermore, when was the last time that most of you took home a pound or two of Jersey potatoes in a brown paper bag? Supermarkets don't *do* brown paper bags. Brown paper bags don't work at the checkout, do they. Actually, come to think about it they do, curiously enough, for mushrooms. But the bags are white and they say 'mushrooms' on the outside together with a picture of a mushroom too, just to make sure. Geddaway.

Shall we do the recipe for simply boiled new potatoes with mint butter now?

3 big handfuls of tiny new potatoes
water
salt
butter
pepper
freshly chopped mint

Put the potatoes in a big bowl in the sink, run a tepid tap over them for a few minutes and rumble them about with your hands a bit. Once most of the dirt has been rinsed away only then begin to scrape them. The most efficient way to achieve this imperative early stage is to now also have another pan at the ready, also in the sink, to then accommodate the cleaned potatoes. This new pan should have a constant stream of cold water running into and over it, so washing, in the process, any clinging bits of flimsy skin missed during the scraping process.

This scraping should always be done with a small sharp knife. It cannot be emphasised enough that this should be the easiest of tasks; if it is difficult, it is clear that the potatoes are anything but new. There truly is nothing worse than a new potato cooked with its skin intact. Just go away all of you who say 'But all the goodness and vitamins of a potato lie just beneath its skin!' This does not mean you have to leave it there to get to it.

Incidentally, two years ago, around about this time of year, I sat all alone for lunch in the grill room of the Savoy hotel, London (I regularly enjoy a solitary lunch but, on this particular occasion I had been stood up) patiently removing the skin from a plateful of cooked new potatoes with my table knife – and they were imported! The single pleasure of completing this task – apart from for my own pleasure, eventually – was to look upon the faces of passing waiters as they watched me doing it. I guess it would have been quite nice if just one of them had suggested that the kitchen could manage this rather than me, but because the kitchen were a lazy bunch, it was all flummox and bewilderment for them over my careful activity.

But I digress. Simply boil the potatoes in salted water until just tender, drain and return to the pan with much butter, pepper and chopped mint. Turn around with a wooden spoon until well coated with the butter and mint. Serve at once.

COFFEE AND CREAM

One would surely think that, what with almost every single high street up and down the land lately sporting many more coffee shops than there are butchers, bakers, greengrocers and mongers of both fish and iron (there exists, curiously enough, a fine candle-maker at the bottom of my street; as to whether they make sticks to go with them, I am unsure), it seems curious to me that this madness — for that is what it most surely is — hasn't, consequently, further spurned all manner of delicious coffee desserts and puddings as a direct result.

The one exception here, of course, is the ubiquitous tiramisù. The very first one that I remember eating was at Le Caprice, around about the early-to-mid 1980s — and had never seen it anywhere else before that. The standard London Italian of the time, after all, was quite content to continue serving up oranges in caramel, zuppa Inglese, crème caramel, the occasional zabaglione and — it must be said — a bought-in cheesecake of such consistent quality (very

light, very cheesy and utterly delicious) that were they to have made their own, it would surely have disappointed the majority of their loyal clientele.

Particularly renowned these days is the tiramisù made by one Francesco Zanchetta, the long-standing, good-looking chef of the Italian restaurant Riva in Barnes, West London. Without doubt, his rendition remains the best in town — and possibly everywhere else, come to that. Francesco has been making his tiramisù in exactly the same way, in his impossibly compact *cucina*, ever since the emphatically chic Andrea Riva first opened his eponymous and deeply personal establishment almost eleven years ago now.

2007 — As far as I know, Francesco Zanchetta left the kitchens of Riva about two years ago. He had been there since the earliest days, if not right at the very beginning — the summer of 1990. Over the years since, I have probably eaten at Riva more than any other restaurant anywhere.

Francesco Zanchetta's Tiramisù

Here is Francesco's recipe, almost to the letter.

for the creamy bit:

3 egg yolks

1 egg

50ml white wine

50ml Marsala

2 tbsp Amaretto

100g caster sugar

250g mascarpone, at room temperature

1 tsp espresso coffee powder

for the biscuit bit:

3 full cups of espresso coffee (single
   espresso size)

1½ tbsp caster sugar

2 tbsp Marsala

175g Italian savoiardi biscuits (or good
   quality sponge fingers)

2 level tbsps of cocoa powder for dusting the
   surface – and dust it nice and thick, please

Note: Tiramisù is best prepared the night before, so that the 'cream' binds better with the biscuits.

Make a zabaglione (or sabayon) by whisking the egg yolks and whole egg, white wine, Marsala and Amaretto in a stainless steel bowl suspended over a pot of simmering water, kept ticking over a low heat. Continue whisking in this fashion until the mixture starts to become very thick. Once it is firm and fluffy, remove the bowl from the pan but continue whisking regardless for a few more minutes. Now add the sugar, which should melt very quickly, thus cooling the zabaglione before incorporating the mascarpone. Gently fold in the cheese with the espresso powder, and then finally beat everything together fast for a minute or so, to both lighten and fully smooth the 'cream'. Keep the mixture cool.

For dipping the biscuits, first mix together the espresso coffees, the sugar and Marsala in a bowl large enough to soak the biscuits. Dip a couple of them in at a time until they are moist but not breaking up; this is best achieved by having the coffee good and hot, so it soaks in more quickly. The biscuits should be soft, rather than sodden. Cover the base of a large and shallow, rectangular dish or Tupperware container with a layer of biscuits, all placed tightly together and in the same direction. Pour over half of the 'cream' and then add a second layer of biscuits, but this time place them at right angles to those underneath (this helps to prevent the tiramisù falling apart when serving up). Cover with the remaining 'cream' and dust thickly with cocoa powder. Cover and chill overnight in the fridge.

Coffee bavarois

SERVES 4

A lovely, subtle flavour of coffee, here, as the custard is infused with whole beans rather than having been ground.

250ml full cream milk
100g high roast, best quality
    coffee beans
100g caster sugar
4 large egg yolks

1 tbsp Tia Maria
2 leaves gelatine, soaked in cold water
    until soft
200ml double cream, very cold

Note: Have ready four metal dariole molds (approximately 150–160ml capacity) very lightly smeared with a flavourless oil and kept chilled in the fridge. Also have some ice cubes at hand, ready to tip into a large bowl of water for arresting the cooking of the coffee custard once decanted from pan to bowl; the latter should be previously placed in the freezer compartment.

Put the milk onto a low heat and tip in the coffee beans together with only 50g of the caster sugar. Stir well, and bring up to the boil. Allow the milk to seethe up over the coffee beans once, remove from the heat, give it a brief whisk and pour into a glass or stainless steel bowl. Cover the bowl with some sort of lid and suspend over a pan containing hot (not boiling) water for 1 hour; the idea is to keep the milk hot and, therefore, continuing to extract flavour from the coffee beans by sustained heat. What I tend to do is decant tepid water and then top up with water boiled up in a kettle – and do this about every quarter of an hour.

Now strain the coffee-flavoured milk through a fine sieve into a clean bowl and set aside. Discard the coffee beans. Briefly beat together the egg yolks and the remaining 50g of caster sugar until thick and yellow, then add the coffee-flavoured milk to them. Gently whisk together and then pour straight back into the used milk/coffee bean pan. Make a thinly textured custard with this mixture, being careful not to allow it to boil but be assured that it does, actually, lightly thicken. Quickly decant into the (previously chilled) bowl, using a spatula to collect every scrap and whisk the mixture to disperse hotter spots amongst the cooler ones. Now immerse this into a large bowl of iced water.

Put the Tia Maria into a small pan and add the softened gelatine leaves. Warm through very gently whilst stirring together with a wooden spoon. Once the gelatine has fully melted into the liqueur, whisk it into the cooling coffee custard, being sure to collect every last gelatinous smear from the pan. Now pass the custard through a fine sieve into a clean bowl. Return to the icy water or, depending on your schedule, simply place in the fridge, so allowing the setting process to begin.

Once the custard has partially set (still quite wobbly in the middle), whisk energetically until very smooth once more. Beat the cream in another bowl until loosely, softly whipped (on no account continue beating until stiff, as the cream can easily split as it is folded into the coffee custard). Begin by folding just one or two tablespoons of cream into the custard before adding the rest. Deftly combine until all the white streaks of cream have disappeared. Spoon into the pre-prepared moulds exactly up to their rims, press a tiny piece of clingfilm upon the surfaces and put to chill in the fridge for at least 5 hours, preferably overnight.

To serve, run a small knife around the inside of each bavarois and upend onto small, chilled plates. Very good eaten with more loosely beaten cream flavoured with a little more Tia Maria or, as illustrated here, with a freshly made hot espresso poured over at the last minute.

Coffee ice cream

SERVES 4—5

An ice cream made with coffee always causes me to realise quite how extraordinary is its unique taste. Not the creamy capped espresso, the frothy filled thick cup of cappuccino, or even the luke-warm, tall glass of Venetian latte; just why is it always *molto tepido*? But once these crushed beans infuse milk, cream, eggs and sugar with their aromatic oils and deeply roasted flavour, the result astonishes me each and every time.

Coffee ice cream also happens to be one of the simplest to make, so that's nice, too: a milky infusion, a little whip of egg yolks and sugar, a stir and a coolant of cream. A machine to ice, smooth and thicken the cream is a luxury so worth investing in; I find it incomprehensible that all but the lowliest bedsit does not have one. I know they are expensive to buy, but I would rather save for one of these than squander my money on electric woks, electric steamers, microwave ovens, and slow-cookers (does anyone really use these?), with the smug knowledge that I can make ice cream all year round. With an ice-cream maker in the corner of the thinnest galley kitchen, and a few ingredients from the most basic of corner shops, one of the finest desserts is always there at the flick of a switch.

600ml full-cream milk
75g coarsely ground coffee
5 egg yolks
125g golden caster sugar
400ml double cream
1—2 tbsp Tia Maria (optional)

Put the milk onto a low heat and tip in the coffee. Stir well, and bring up to the boil. Allow the milk to seethe up over the coffee once, remove from the heat, give it a brief whisk and cover. Leave to infuse for at least 30 minutes. Strain through muslin into a bowl. Beat together the egg yolks and sugar until thick and pale yellow, then add the coffee 'milk' to them. Gently whisk together and pour back into the (rinsed out) milk pan. Make custard with this mixture, being careful not to allow it to boil, but be assured that it does actually slightly thicken. Pour into a chilled bowl and whisk in the cream and Tia Maria, if using. Leave to cool completely and remove any surface froth with a spoon. Churn in an ice-cream machine.

Note: Apart from flavour, another advantage of adding the liqueur is that it keeps the texture of the ice cream softer than is usual, as alcohol does not freeze solid. This is good news if you go the manual route, freezing the mixture in trays and doing the intermittent whisking thing.

SHARP PRACTICE

The first recipe this week is a variation on something called a lemon posset. It is a magical mousse, of sorts, where the acidity which is added to boiled cream and sugar sets the mixture without the need of eggs or gelatine. Fantastic, really, and so easy to make. The addition of orange jelly on top creates a swish finish to the thing. 'Oranges and lemons say the bells of St. Clement's', so the song goes…

2007 – This is one of only two recipes in this book which have appeared in others I have written. The simple reason is that in each case the photograph taken by Jason was so marvellous, it seemed a shame not to include it. This one appears in *Second Helpings of Roast Chicken* (Ebury Press, 2006).

Then there are these two refreshing fruit granitas, each reinforced by fragrant alcohols: Campari in the red grapefruit and Angostura bitters in the pink one. Apart from adding elusive undertones, they also brighten up their pale blushes.

And finally… The name 'Angel Pie' once more refers to a recipe from my old favourite *The Good Food Guide Dinner Party Book* (published in 1971, now out of print). One Wolfgang Stichler was the chef responsible for this delicious confection, and it would have then been found at the Square and Compass Inn, North Rigton, Yorkshire. A really lovely way with meringue, I think, being all at once creamy, sweet, tart and crumbly. The passionfruit is a later addition which, although it might not be exactly citrus, is possessed of similar, sharp-ish notes. I also see it as a gentle nod to the delicious pavlova, upon which the meringue mixture is based.

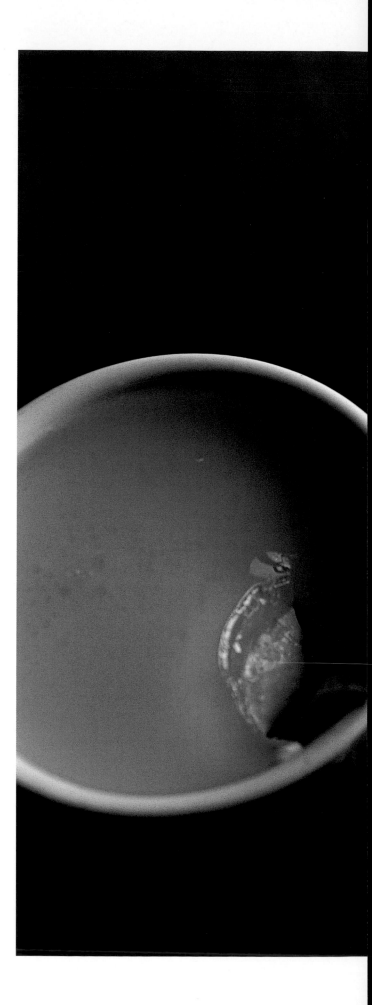

St. Clement's cream

MAKES ENOUGH TO FILL 6 LARGE RAMEKINS

for the creams:
juice of 2 large oranges
500ml double cream
100g caster sugar
grated rind of 2 lemons
grated rind of 1 large orange
juice of 2 lemons

for the orange jelly:
1 leaf gelatine
150ml freshly squeezed orange juice
juice of ½ lemon
1 tbsp Grand Marnier (optional, but it
    does give the orange jelly a better
    flavour, not to mention colour!)

Put the orange juice into a small pan and, over a low heat, reduce until syrupy – by about three-quarters, I guess. Put to one side. Bring the cream, sugar and rinds of the two fruits to the boil in a large pan (the size of the pan is important here, to allow for the expansion of the cream as it boils). Boil all together for exactly 2 minutes. Take off the heat and whisk in the lemon juice and reduced orange juice. Leave to infuse for 15 minutes. Now strain everything through a fine sieve into a bowl and then ladle into the ramekins. Chill for at least 4 hours.

To make the jelly, first soften the gelatine in cold water until soft and spongy. Bring the orange and lemon juice *just* to the boil, noted particularly by the moment when a scum forms on the surface. Immediately strain through a piece of muslin into a clean pan and stir in the softened gelatine whilst the juice is still hot. Add the Grand Marnier. Leave to cool to room temperature and then carefully spoon about a tablespoonful over the surface of each 'cream'. Return to the fridge to chill for a further 1 hour, before serving.

Angel pie
with passionfruit

MAKES 6 MERINGUE CAKES

for the meringue:

3 egg whites

pinch of salt

¼ tsp cream of tartar

125g caster sugar

1 tsp cornflour

1 scant dsp white wine or cider vinegar

a little extra caster sugar, for sprinkling

for the lemon curd:

grated rind and juice of 2 unwaxed lemons

90g unsalted butter

75g caster sugar

2 large eggs, beaten

300ml double cream

1 tbsp caster sugar

3 passionfruit

Pre-heat the oven to 140°C/275°F/gas mark 1.

Using a scrupulously clean mixing bowl, whip the egg whites with the salt and cream of tartar until soft but able to hold a peak. Beat in half the sugar, a tablespoon at time, until glossy and stiff. Now fold in the rest of the sugar, the cornflour and the vinegar using a large spatula, with authoritative scoops rather than mimsy movements; the air must be contained, sure, but the sugar does also need to be thoroughly mixed in.

Lightly grease six individual tart tins with butter and sift over a spoonful of flour into one of them. Shake it around a bit to disperse the flour in an even coating and then tap off the excess into the next one. Continue with the remaining five tins. Spoon the meringue mixture into each tin, shaping the meringue into shallow 'nests'. Sprinkle with a little extra caster sugar, slide into the oven and bake for about 1 hour, or until pale golden, and with their surfaces lightly crusted. Leave to cool in their tins before removing and placing on a cake rack.

Meanwhile, make the lemon curd. Place the rind and juice of the lemons, the butter and sugar in a bowl. Place over a pan of simmering water and allow to melt. Whisk in the beaten eggs until everything is smooth. Stirring slowly and continuously, cook together until the mixture is really good and thick. Scrape out into a bowl, give it a final whisk and leave to cool. Cover and place in the fridge until needed.

To serve, place each meringue 'nest' (I hate this word, but it is descriptively useful here) on an individual plate. Fill each one with lemon curd. Whip the cream with the sugar until thick and then either pipe or spoon it decoratively over the curd. Cut each passionfruit in half and scoop its contents over the cream and meringue.

Two grapefruit granitas

SERVES 4

for the red granita:
500ml freshly squeezed red grapefruit juice
100g caster sugar
2 scant tbsp Campari

for the pink granita:
500ml freshly squeezed pink grapefruit juice
100g caster sugar
2–3tsp Angostura bitters

Note: Place two shallow metal trays in the freezer before you start the recipe.

Put the three ingredients for each granita into two bowls, then whisk together to dissolve the sugar. Carefully pour into the trays in the freezer and leave there for about 20 minutes before having a look. What you are looking for is ice crystals forming around the edge of the trays (completely opposite to sorbets, as the ice crystals here are part of their essential charm). Once the crystals have started to form around the edges, gently lift them with a fork into the not-so-frozen middle part. Return to the freezer. Have another look in a further 20 minutes and repeat the forking. Continue this procedure until the mixtures have formed crystals; this process may take anything up to 1–2 hours. Once fully crystallised, tip into a suitable, lidded plastic containers and store in the freezer until ready to use. The granitas should keep their granular texture for a few days, but kept for much longer, they will begin to firm up into blocks. Very good eaten with syllabub.

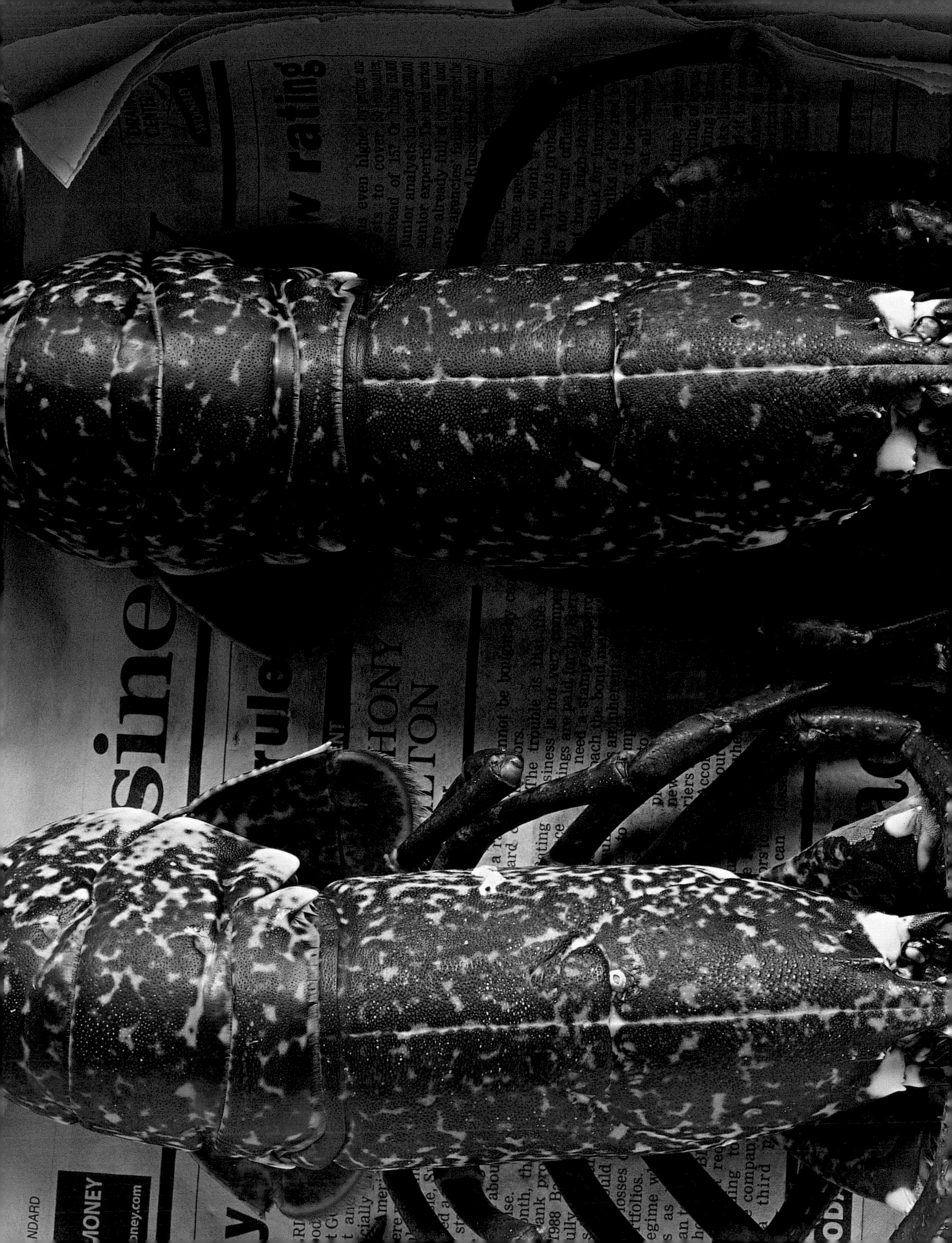

YOU SAY TOMATO, I SAY…?

It is a sad fact in these modern times that a simple, ripe, heavy-with-juice tomato continues to remain elusive for most of us in the UK. We are pathetically informed, you see, that a box of naturally ripe tomatoes is supposed not to travel well. And even though the flight time or length of a lorry's journey from Nice to Notting Hill is surely not *that* long, the tomatoes that are sent to us never seem to be how we remember them at source, where we last ate them in the shade of a plane tree or were overwhelmed by great piles of them on a market stall in, say, Avignon.

I mean, *I* have brought a few trays of tomatoes back with me from Provence in the boot of a motor car and spent a couple of days doing so – and in the middle of summer. Quite perfect when unloaded in Shepherd's Bush, thank you very much. So why cannot some inspired folk do the same with the use of a nicely refrigerated van? And yet we eat frozen, green-lipped mussels all the way from New Zealand. Just what is wrong with us?

At the beginning of this month I slipped over to Dieppe to stay with English friends who have a house near that town. Even in their local village, which does not sport the most inspired collection of shops – apart from the garage (whose extremely helpful owner Monsieur Leconte fixed my car following a minor *contretemps* with a gatepost) and the *boulangerie* – it was no trouble at all to find a couple of kilos of perfectly ripe, red and tasty tomatoes in their equivalent of our Costcutter or Londis. This is surely madness, when we know perfectly well that Dieppe is not that far from Newhaven, just another few miles of sea…

Naturally, as always, it just depends on how much anyone cares about such things. The very fact that Dieppe has a magnificent twice-weekly market, fresh fish from the quayside almost every day and diverse seafood cafés, bars and restaurants, whereas Newhaven has next to nothing, just might have something to do with it.

Edouard de Pomiane's tomates à la crème

SERVES 2

4 medium-sized ripe tomatoes
a large knob of butter
salt and pepper

3 heaped tbsp crème fraîche or
double cream
a few fresh mint leaves, chopped
(optional)

Apart from Edouard de Pomiane's brevity of description – a talent to amuse as well as to instruct precisely – the recipes in his book *Cooking in Ten Minutes* are themselves nothing less than inspired. And by inspired, I also mean intelligent, practical and interesting to read. To compare a ridiculous clown, demonstrating on television how to (supposedly) 'cook in 10 minutes' – to use the original and *genuine* words of Pomiane – would do a grave disservice to this witty and sparkling original. Incidentally, would it not be a refreshing change, for once, for a good cookery book to sell extremely well without the boost of an absurd television series behind it. However, it *is* heartening to know that Pomiane's book (now re-published by Serif) is still selling, 50 odd years on.

Note: I have taken the liberty of adding a few leaves of coarsely chopped mint to the dish, simply because I like it there. You could also add basil if you like, but not the two together.

Cut the tomatoes in half through their circumference. Heat a frying pan over a medium heat, melt the butter in it and lay out the tomatoes, cut side down. Cook for 5 minutes during which time you puncture, here and there, the rounded sides with a sharply pointed knife.

Carefully turn the tomatoes with a palette knife and cook for a further 10 minutes. Turn them again, and after a couple of minutes, when their juices have started to run, turn them back so that the cut sides are uppermost. Season with salt and pepper. Spoon the cream between the tomatoes (add the mint or basil now) and mix it lightly with the juices. As soon as it bubbles, slip the tomatoes and their sauce onto hot plates. Serve immediately.

Tomato jelly
with tomato cream

———

SERVES 4

I was inspired to make this luscious and cooling combo after eating at the restaurant of Michel Guérard earlier this year, way down in the southwest of France, in that heavily wooded region called Les Landes. The dish in question consisted of a deliciously light and jellied poultry consommé with tiny vegetables and soft herbs, all set into a shallow soup plate. A waiter, tableside, and using a large silver tablespoon, carefully cloaked the jelly with a 'vichyssoise' of celery, scented with truffle juice. The contrast between the trembling jelly and the unctuous celery cream was astonishingly fine. A unique epicurean moment of my life, if you really want to know.

for the jelly:

2kg very ripe tomatoes – it is not
   worth making the jelly if they are not
2 cloves garlic, peeled and sliced
salt
pinch of dried red chilli flakes
1 large bunch of basil (reserve a dozen
   or so small leaves)
2 leaves of gelatine

for the cream:

4–5 tbsp of the tomato pulp
1–2 tsp sugar, to taste
salt and a few shakes of Tabasco
200ml double cream

Note: It is essential to use a stainless steel or other non-reactive saucepan here.

Plunge the tomatoes into boiling water for 10 seconds, immediately drain and then peel them. Using a sharp knife, cut and slice them, anyhow, directly into the pan, so as not to waste any precious juices. Put in the garlic, salt and chilli and set on a low light. Bring up to a simmer, stir and put on a lid. The liquid that forms comes purely from the tomatoes. Cook for 40 minutes. Tear in the basil leaves and continue simmering for a further 10 minutes. Strain through a colander into a clean bowl or other pan. Leave to drip for a good hour, but do not force through any of the pulp or you will unnecessarily cloud the jelly. *Do not discard this pulp.* Soften the gelatine leaves in cold water. Squeeze dry and warm through in a small pan with a little of the tomato liquid, to melt it, then stir back into the strained liquid. Tip the pulp into a bowl and put aside.

Now, either using a damp tea-towel or jelly bag, further strain the tomato liquid into another scrupulously clean bowl. It is best to support the towel/bag well above the bowl (jelly bags usually have strings attached so that they can be hooked up). Allow to drip until it stops completely. The liquid should settle into the bowl and be clear; do not panic unduly if it is not, as it will still taste jolly good. However, if there is a little sediment at the bottom, simply pour off the clear liquid into another container. Pour enough jelly into individual soup dishes to fill them by three-quarters, drop a few basil leaves into each and then put into the fridge to set.

To make the cream, liquidise the (reserved) tomato pulp and sugar until as smooth as possible. Push through a fine sieve into a bowl, season boldly with salt (the addition of the cream will mollify the mixture and you will not be able to add seasoning later for fear of curdling by further stirring) and add a little Tabasco to taste. Loosely whip the cream by hand until showing soft peaks and gently fold into the tomato until all is pale pink and without streaks. Once the jelly has set, carefully spoon over the tomato cream and serve at once.

SALAD DAYS

It sounds so dull, doesn't it, chicken salad? Well, meaningless, in fact, in that it rarely conveys any accuracy as to its actual composition. For it could be a slime of leftover roast chicken shreds and salad cream, a single anaemic white sliced breast with frills of lollo-rosso and little else, or a selection from the 'eat as much as you want for £4.95' buffet.

Yet a carefully constructed cold chicken salad is a lovely thing to eat in warm weather – though, truthfully, I could eat it at any time of the year, rain or shine. Now it *may* be made from a leftover roast (assuming the roast was a fine one to start with), but only so long as there are enough good bits left to play with. Ultimately, however, I believe it should be made from scratch. 'Excuse me?', I hear you say. 'Roast a chicken especially to make a salad? Just a salad? You must be mad!'

Italian cooks think nothing of roasting a whole piece of veal to make one of their favourite summer dishes, *vitello tonnato*. Similarly, amongst a dish of Imperial Pekinese hors d'œuvre, there will always be an array of cold sliced pork of some sort, often pressed and preserved, especially cooked for the occasion. Cold chicken with sesame sauce – the original Bang-Bang Chicken – is another contender here.

Within these shores, however, cold meat and fish assemblies – apart from the ubiquitous cold buffet selection of salmon, rare (rarely) beef and cold ham – are almost never considered as being composed or intentional, remaining as afterthoughts in the domestic scheme of things. Now, I am as fond of leftovers as anyone else, it is just that the fresh taste of a premeditated cold meat or fish salad makes you realise how stunningly good something like this can be when due care is generously lavished over its preparation.

A cold fish salad, too, is something that many might turn up their noses to. Yet, served warm – or the *salade tiède* to incurable fluffy gourmets – it gives off that aura of something really quite special and different. Both the above examples are delicious if done well; equally appalling when done badly. That is all there is to it, of course: good cooking and bad cooking.

I find it difficult to wrench myself away from the egg yolk and oil emulsion when it comes to dressing a substantial salad; the simple vinaigrette, whatever the additional flavourings, just doesn't seem to perform as well as the lotion that is mayonnaise. In the following recipes, this is transformed into as thin or thick a coating as suits the salad's composition.

Salad of cold roast chicken

with watercress and
sweet-mustard
dressing

———

SERVES 6

Watercress with chicken and mayonnaise is my favourite sandwich. The peppery bite of the leaves, together with a smear of cooling mayonnaise and moist slices of white breast meat is a winning combination. Nowadays, of course, one finds that our very own watercress leaves have now been flung aside in favour of the more bullying rocket, which is sad. I don't think rocket lies comfortably in a British sandwich, do you?

Regular readers may be familiar with my dislike of honey. However here, its cloying flavour seems to evaporate during the roasting process, but does give a wonderful mahogany sheen to the bird's skin and a subtle sweetness to the cooking juices.

1 x 2kg free-range chicken
juice of 2 lemons; pared rind of one
salt and pepper
2 dsp clear honey, warmed
200ml white wine
1 dsp best Dijon mustard

3–4 heaped tbsp thick mayonnaise
2 healthy thick bunches of beautiful
   watercress, trimmed of stalks,
   washed and dried
2–3 tbsp light olive oil
2 small shallots, very finely chopped

Preheat the oven to 200°C/400°F/gas mark 6.

Put the chicken into a suitable roasting dish and pour over the lemon juice. Season, and deposit the bits of lemon rind around the bird. Spoon over the honey and add the wine. Roast the bird breast side uppermost for 30 minutes. Remove, turn the temperature down to 170°C/325°F/gas mark 3 and continue to roast the bird, but this time turned onto one side for 15 minutes and then a further 15 minutes on the other. Revert the chicken to its initial posture and cook for a further 30 minutes at 140°C/275°F/gas mark 1, basting occasionally. This attentive, gentle cooking method ensures a uniformly burnished skin and much succulence within the flesh; perfect for the cold cut. Lift out the chicken onto a dish and leave to cool thoroughly. Strain the juices through a fine sieve into a small pan.

Reduce this liquid by one-third, or until well flavoured, skimming off any scum that may form during the process. Add the mustard to the mayonnaise and loosen with enough of the chicken juices to achieve a thin, cream dressing. Check for seasoning. Simply shine the watercress with enough olive oil using your hands, deftly done in a salad bowl. Arrange onto a grand platter or individual plates. Sprinkle with the chopped shallots. Carve the chicken into small pieces in whichever way you see fit, and arrange over the leaves. Apply the dressing with affection.

Salad of steamed cod
with capers and thinned mayonnaise

SERVES 4

Making the cod taste good as it steams is the trick here. The suggested flavourings are only a guide, so you can fiddle about to your heart's content once you are happy with the basic system. But first of all, naturally, one needs a steamer. I use the dirt-cheap stacking ones that can be found in Chinatown, here in London (or in the better Asian supermarkets in the bigger provincial cities). They are fashioned from spun aluminium, usually offer two perforated layers, together with a domed lid and capacious base pan where the water goes. The smallest of these will not set you back much more than a tenner and, with care, will last for years (they also double as a really useful straining implement, using one of the layers suspended over the base pan, as you might a colander over a cooking pot).

500g piece of thick cod fillet, skin intact, bones removed
salt and cayenne pepper
1 scant tbsp sherry vinegar
2–3 tbsp fruity olive oil
a few sprigs of dill or, even better, wild fennel
1 small shallot, peeled and finely chopped

3–4 tbsp thick mayonnaise
a squeeze of lemon juice (optional)
the most inner hearts of 3 round lettuces, leaves separated, washed and dried
a few sprigs of flat-leaf parsley, leaves only, roughly chopped
1 heaped tbsp capers, drained and lightly squeezed in the hand
a little extra olive oil

Put the cod (skin side up) into a suitable dish that will fit in your steamer. Season with the salt and cayenne and then spoon over the vinegar and oil. Lay over the chosen herb and sprinkle the shallot around the fish. Have the water in the steamer boiling, cover the dish tightly with foil, put onto one of the perforated layers and attach the lid tightly. Leave to boil at full pelt for 5 minutes and then switch off the heat. *Do not remove the lid for 20 minutes.* Once the time is up, remove the dish from the steamer and remove the foil. The cod will now be cooked, its juices having mingled nicely with the oil and vinegar.

Remove the herb and discard. Now, holding the cod with the back of a fish slice, strain off all the juices into a bowl. Remove the skin from the fish (it should peel off in one neat piece), cover the dish with a plate and keep warm. Pass the juices through a sieve and whisk together. Add enough of this mixture to the mayonnaise to achieve a loose, coating consistency. Check for seasoning and add a little lemon juice if you think it necessary. Briefly dip the lettuce leaves into some of the juices and dress four plates with them, laid flat. Flake the cod over these, scatter with the parsley and spoon over the sauce in dribs and drabs. Distribute the capers willy-nilly and splash with a little extra olive oil.

FISH SHOP

The inspiration for this week's fishy feast came about by meeting up with the exemplary Clive Davis early one morning a few weeks ago. He runs the (new-ish) Fish Shop at Kensington Place, neatly tethered to the most southerly corner of Kensington Place (the restaurant) and which is, in fact, also on the corner of Kensington Place (the street). And all of this is situated at the Notting Hill Gate end of Kensington Church Street, London W8 – at number 199, to be precise.

At around about 07.45 hours I turned up at the shop to find Clive deeply hemmed in amongst three dozen or so polystyrene boxes stacked up in piles all around him, attempting to sort out in which box were the fish I had asked that he might find for me from a telephone conversation the day before. So it was, as he rummaged around displaying further wonderful species, that I then began to buy other fish too… 'Oh, yes, can I have some of those too, please?'

Hence more fish, more recipes, less preliminary chat this week. Do talk to Clive. He will sell you the best fish you will ever eat. All the fish featured seem to be seasonally ripe, just now.

2007 – The lovely Clive has long departed for pastures new – or shores, perhaps. However, this remains as one of the very finest fish shops in London. Apart, that is, from a rather splendid one that opened last year a five minute walk away from my front door. It is called Cape Clear and is situated on the Shepherd's Bush Road, just around the corner from Brook Green. We all feel blessed around these parts, we really do.

Baked John Dory
with orange butter sauce

—

SERVES 2

The taste of orange with certain fish is very fine indeed, particularly so with a piece of poached wild salmon sauced with the hollandaise derivative known as sauce Maltaise (this is also very good with asparagus, too). Twenty odd years ago I remember eating John Dory with sauce Maltaise at The Carved Angel restaurant in Dartmouth, Devon, and it was simply marvellous. This orange butter sauce is equally delicious and coats the fillets of fish in the most agreeable fashion.

2 medium-sized John Dory, trimmed by the
    fishmonger of both head and fins (I only
    used the un-trimmed fish in the
    photograph because it looked so fine)
a little oil
salt and pepper
a squeeze of lemon juice
a knob of butter
a splash of white wine

for the butter sauce:
1 large orange
juice of ½ lemon
150–175g best, unsalted butter
salt and a touch of cayenne pepper

Preheat the oven to 200°C/400°F/gas mark 6.

First make the sauce. Remove 3–4 strips of skin from the orange using a potato peeler (without pith) and place in a small, stainless steel pan. Juice the orange and add to the pan with the lemon juice. Simmer until there is only a tiny amount of liquid left. Now, over a very low heat, introduce the butter in small pieces using a small whisk, making sure that you allow each piece to emulsify before incorporating the next one. Once all the butter has been used up, and the seasoning and texture pleases you, strain through a fine sieve into a warm bowl or sauce boat. *Note:* If you think the sauce is too thick, simply add a little warm water to thin it.

Rub a light film of oil over each side of the fish and season liberally. Place them in a roasting tin and add the lemon juice, butter and white wine. Cover with foil and bake for 15 minutes. Remove, turn the fish over, re-cover and cook for a further 10 minutes. Lift the fish out from the tin onto a hot serving dish, spoon over any juices and serve up with sauce handed separately at table. *Note:* The filleting of a John Dory is possibly the easiest I know. After scraping off the skin (although this is not entirely necessary) the fillets lift off from both sides as if designed for the job in hand.

Sea trout
in Champagne sauce

SERVES 4

When I was working at La Normandie restaurant in my youth, we used to make this dish using rainbow trout. Even now, I can never forget my first taste of the intense cream sauce that resulted from the *cuisson* (cooking juices and discarded debris of the fish) from these simple farmed fish. And it occurs to me still today, that no matter how carefully one makes a delicate fish stock, the particular fashioning of this cream fish sauce remains unmatched in culinary sorcery – and, what's more, almost any fish will manage it for you. In case you are wondering, Champagne is not entirely necessary. However, the wine used should be good. But, why not invest in a whole bottle of relatively good fizz and then drink the remainder whilst you eat it.

50g softened butter
5 shallots, peeled and chopped
1kg sea trout beheaded, gutted,
    well cleaned out and rinsed
thyme and bay leaf or ½ tsp of
    mixed herbs
salt and pepper
½ bottle Champagne or other good
    quality dry white wine
275–300ml double cream (or
    whipping cream for a lighter sauce)
squeeze of lemon juice, to taste

Preheat the oven to 400°F/gas mark 6.

Using half the butter, grease a deep roasting tin that will accommodate the fish snugly. Sprinkle with the shallots and smear the remaining butter over the fish. Add the herbs and season the fish inside and out. Pour over Champagne or wine. Tightly cover with foil and bake in the oven for 20 minutes. Remove, uncover and carefully turn the fish over. Bake for a further 15–20 minutes, or so. Remove once more and leave covered for a further 15 minutes, or so. Flick off any clinging bits of shallot, lift out the fish and place on a chopping board to cool slightly. Using a spatula now transfer everything left in the roasting tin to a saucepan.

Remove the skin from the fish with a small knife, lift off the fillets (most of the bones will remain attached to the frame) and lay them back into the (rinsed out) roasting tin. Reserve. Put all the skin and bones (broken up slightly) from the fish into the saucepan and set over a moderate heat. Allow to reduce until most of the liquid has been driven off and the mixture is sticky. Add the cream and stir together. Bring to a simmer and cook gently for 20 minutes, or so, until the consistency is custard-like and sporting a nice ivory colour. Strain through a fine sieve into another pan, pushing down hard on the solids to extract every last vestige of flavour. Taste for seasoning and add a touch of lemon juice to sharpen it up a bit. Warm the fillets of fish through by placing them under a moderate grill for a few minutes, but without colouring them. Place portions of the fish onto hot plates and spoon the sauce over.

Note: The fish may be garnished with the traditional *fleuron*. These are crescents of puff pastry that have been cut out with a fluted cutter, brushed with egg-wash and baked in a hot oven until puffed and golden. If you enjoy doing these sort of things, feel free; if not, don't bother.

Lightly soused herring fillets

SERVES 4

This recipe is based upon a Jane Grigson recipe from her exhaustive and brilliant *Fish Book* (Michael Joseph, 1993). Next week I will be offering up a recipe which utilises these herrings admirably: an assembly that includes gravadlax, soused herring, pickled cucumber and a dill and horseradish mousse to set the whole thing off. The premise of the piece is horseradish; the perky assembly is one that I created for the menu of Hilaire, the restaurant I once cooked in on London's Old Brompton Road, nearly 20 years ago now. Sir Terence Conran rarely ate anything else – and he sometimes ate at Hilaire three times a week.

2007 – Please refer to 'Horseplay' (pages 104–109) for a recipe for the horseradish mousse mentioned above – and all kinds of other horseradish ideas, too!

40g Maldon sea salt

400ml warm water

4 very fresh herrings, gutted and filleted (ask your fishmonger to do this)

for the sousing:

250ml white wine vinegar

150ml sweet cider

3–4 small dried chillies

2 bay leaves

1 small white onion, peeled and thinly sliced

a coarse grinding of black pepper

Mix together the salt and water and leave to cool. Put the herrings in a shallow china dish and pour over the saline solution. Leave to soak for 2 hours. Drain them and ditch the solution. Pat the fillets dry and return them to the dish.

Whilst the herring fillets are reclining in their brine, prepare the sousing mixture. Briefly boil together the vinegar, cider, chillies and bay. Leave to cool. Strew the onion over the herring fillets, pour over the cooled sousing liquid and grind over the black pepper. Cover with clingfilm and leave to marinate in the fridge for at least three days – or a little longer, preferably; preferably as long as until next week, in fact…

Fresh anchovies
with garlic and breadcrumbs

SERVES 2, AS A FIRST COURSE

The first time I ate fresh anchovies prepared in this fashion was at the tiny La Merenda, in Nice. The minuscule kitchen being open for all to view, I once noticed that it was the genial fellow who helps with the washing up who was also responsible for both preparing and cooking these superb anchovies. And, do you know, it will forever be one of my fondest memories of the professional kitchen as to when someone who initially starts out as a washer-up will occasionally, in time, become the most accomplished and passionate of cooks – and which happens more often than you would ever think.

10 fresh anchovies, filleted and gutted (if you lightly squeeze the fillets away from the central bone with your thumb, you will be amazed how very easily they fall away)

2007 – Both the Kensington Place Fish Shop and Cape Clear will be able to furnish you with fresh anchovies in season.

a little olive oil
3 heaped tbsp fresh white breadcrumbs
2 cloves garlic, peeled and finely chopped
2 heaped tbsp freshly chopped parsley
salt and pepper
lemon quarters

Smear an oven tray with olive oil and then lay out the flattened anchovies skin side down. Mix together the breadcrumbs, garlic, parsley and seasoning and carefully cover the anchovies with this mixture, lightly pressing it down with your fingers onto the fish. Lubricate with a little more olive oil and bake on the top shelf of a hot oven for 5–7 minutes, or so, until pale golden brown – and not a little toasted in parts. Serve with lemon quarters to squeeze over.

Monkfish liver

SERVES 2

Now, a rare delicacy to finish up with. Clive's gift to me for spending so well, I guess – but then he knew I would love some, being the sporty cook that I am.

Monkfish is fish foie gras. I don't know of any London fishmonger that might offer it other than The Fish Shop at KP. But then you could always enquire of any monger; I mean, let's be honest, most of them offer monkfish tails themselves, so why should they not go out of their way to find you some of their astonishingly delicious inner delicacies too?

1 monkfish liver
salt and pepper
flour

butter
lemon juice or red wine vinegar

Slice the monkfish liver into moderately thick slices. Season. Dust with flour. Fry in butter until lightly crusted and golden on each side. Add a little lemon juice or vinegar to the pan and then transfer onto hot plates. Eat quickly, with tearings from a crusty baguette or with plainly boiled potatoes.

COLD CUTS
AND
RAW BITS

Two rather long recipes this week to start off with and a very short one to finish. Unusually, for me, I decided to write the recipes before I began the introduction this time, so must therefore slightly curtail my usual preliminary natter. As I often venture way past my requested allotment of words anyway, it would seem the daftest think imaginable to then have to lose a recipe simply as a result of overzealous wittering now.

So, with that, here is today's brief: two cold cuts, easily workable if you have the inclination, into intensely savoury offerings by means of a little fore-thought and those with time on their hands; think weekend lunch in the garden. Personally speaking, delicious cold food, mindfully prepared, will often delight me more than hot dishes, given the opportunity. There is also a classic steak tartare for you to get to grips with. This, conversely, takes a matter of minutes to prepare. But promise me you will leave the food processor or mincer in the cupboard, just this once.

It may not immediately occur to most folk, but thin cold slices of crisp belly pork are one of the very nicest things to eat. But, then, roast belly pork, even when eaten hot, is not the most common of British joints in the first place. The Chinese, however, have been roasting belly pork for hundreds of years and with more success than anyone else at all. Moreover, I would further advocate that Chinese cooks are possibly the finest roasters, period.

Even though the preparation of the following cold dishes may sound time consuming and a bit of a fiddle, believe me, the results are well worth the effort involved. And talking of effort, some of you may think that there is a great deal of this palaver involved in some of my recipes. Now here, I cannot really help you. All I *can* say is that the results of a little exertion often produces something unusually special. Failing that, there are always supermarket ready-meals, Chinese takeaways and more restaurants and cafés out there than anyone could possibly need. The choice, my dears, as always, is yours.

Crisp belly pork salad

—

SERVES 4

1.5kg fatty belly pork with ribs, the skin thinly
    scored with a sharp knife (I use a Stanley
    knife to do this; your butcher's knife will be
    almost as sharp – and possibly safer)
1 tbsp Chinese five spice mixture
2 tsp ground white pepper
1 tbsp Maldon sea salt

for the stock:
1 litre water
75ml soy sauce (Kikkoman for preference)
75ml dry sherry
1 small bunch spring onions, chopped
3 cloves garlic, peeled and crushed
1 tsp dried chilli flakes
4 strips orange rind
1 pig's trotter, split in two and then chopped up
    (definitely ask the butcher to do this)

for the dressing:
1 dsp made English mustard
1 tsp sugar
1 clove garlic, peeled and crushed to a paste with
    a pinch of salt
1½ tbsp smooth peanut butter
½ tbsp sesame paste (tahini)
1 tbsp toasted sesame seeds (keep a few back
    for garnish)
1 dsp bottled chilli sauce
3 tbsp salad cream (yes, Heinz salad cream!)
a little of the pork stock

for the salad:
1 small cucumber, peeled, de-seeded and cut
    into strips
1 bunch of spring onions, trimmed, washed and
    shredded
1 bunch of watercress, washed and trimmed
1 large, mild green chilli, sliced
toasted sesame seeds (see above)
a handful of fresh coriander and mint leaves –
    about half and half – torn up a bit

Start the recipe the day before you want to eat it.

Fill the kettle and boil. Lay the belly pork on a cooling rack over a deep tray, skin side uppermost. Slowly pour boiling water over the skin until the kettle is empty and the lines of scored skin have become visibly separate. Discard the water. Turn the belly pork over onto a large tray and rub the meat with the five spice mixture and pepper, working them in well with the tips of your fingers. Now turn over once more and rub the coarse salt into the skin. Hang the meat up to dry, in a cool and draughty place, preferably overnight.

Preheat the oven to 230°C/450°F/gas mark 8.

Mix together all the stock ingredients in a bowl and then pour into a deep roasting tin. Over this, suspend the same cooling rack as you used the day before and place the pork upon it, skin side up. Slide into the oven (top shelf) and roast for 15 minutes. Now turn the temperature down to 180°C/350°F/gas mark 4 and cook for a further 40 minutes. Take the pork out, top up the stock with water if it seems to have reduced too much, and then turn the oven back up to the previous temperature. Once the oven has come back up to temperature, return the pork to the oven and roast for a final 10 minutes, or so.

Note: Although this diversity of temperature may initially sound a little unorthodox, it does seem to help effect the best crackling I know; the preliminary dousing with boiling water and drying out overnight, nonetheless, also remains an important key step.

Whilst allowing the pork to cool, pour the stock from beneath it into a clean pan. Remove the rib bones from the belly pork (they should wiggle out quite easily from the meat, now cooked) and add them to the stock. Keep the belly somewhere cool, until ready to slice. Now put the stock to simmer for 40 minutes, whilst also skimming off any scum that forms on the surface. Strain through a colander into a bowl and leave to drain. Discard all solids and remove all excess fat with several sheets of kitchen paper. Now carefully pass this liquid through a sieve lined with folded muslin into a bowl. Taste for seasoning, though it should not need much – if any. Place in the fridge, to cool and set until lightly jellied.

Place all the dressing ingredients in a liquidiser (best) or food processor and purée until very smooth. Add a little of the jellied stock to thin slightly, as the consistency should emerge as something similar to pouring cream. Decant into another bowl. Toss together the cucumber, spring onions and watercress, arrange onto four plates and spoon the dressing judiciously over each serving. Using a sharp serrated knife, cut the pork as thinly as you dare and drape the slices across the salad. Now take the lightly jellied stock and, using a pastry brush, paint each slice of pork with it until glistening. Finally, strew with sliced green chilli, toasted sesame seeds, coriander and mint – and then give yourself a jolly good pat on the back.

Cold veal
with sliced egg
and anchovy sauce

—

SERVES 4

for the veal:

1kg (approximate weight) joint of
   lean-ish veal
olive oil
salt and freshly ground white pepper
a handful of cheap pie veal pieces
   (or scraps of veal trimmed from
   the joint)
1 small onion, peeled and
   roughly chopped
2 sticks celery, chopped
100g button mushrooms, sliced
1 large tomato, roughly chopped
2–3 leaves fresh sage
1 glass of white wine

for the sauce:

1 tsp white wine vinegar
1 dsp Dijon mustard
3–4 salt anchovies, to taste
5–6 tbsp stiff mayonnaise
some of the veal juices (see
   method below)

to garnish:

4 hard-boiled eggs, sliced
a few capers
a trickle of olive oil (optional)

Preheat the oven to 180°C/350°F/gas mark 4.

Rub the joint with olive oil and season lightly (there are anchovies, later, remember). Take a solid-bottomed, cast-iron roasting dish that will happily sit upon a flame as well as go into the oven and add a spoonful or two of olive oil to it. Heat the oil and introduce the joint. Gently fry the meat on a low heat over a period of about 15 minutes, or so, turning it through the oil until all surfaces are lightly gilded. Lift out the veal and rest it on a plate or tray.

Now add the veal scraps, vegetables and sage to the roasting dish, turn up the heat a little and toss them around until softened. Pour in the wine, allow to bubble up and then reintroduce the veal joint. Baste with the winey liquid for a minute or two, cover with foil and further cook in the oven for about 25–30 minutes more, by which time the meat will have cooked to a pleasing rosy-pink within. Lift out from the oven, remove the foil and loosely wrap the meat inside it. Transfer to the same plate or tray you used before and leave to cool completely.

Tip the contents of the roasting dish into a fine sieve suspended over a small bowl and extract all the juices by pressing down upon them with the back of a ladle. Place the bowl in the fridge to cool completely, and until the fat has set upon the surface to such a degree that it may easily be lifted off with a spoon. Hopefully, it should be slightly jellied. Tip into the bowl of a liquidiser or food processor and add all the other ingredients listed for making the sauce. Process until very smooth and then strain, once more (sorry!), through a fine sieve back into the (wiped clean) bowl. Return this to the fridge for at least 30 minutes.

To serve (finally!), thinly slice the veal and arrange it, slightly overlapping, onto a large and handsome, white (for preference) oval platter. Whisk the sauce to loosen it a little and spoon carefully over the veal, whilst also allowing some of the pink qualities of the meat to remain visible. Decorate each piece of veal with a slice of egg and then dot each of these with a single caper. Trickle with a little olive oil, if liked. Perfect eaten with warm potato salad: waxy potatoes steamed or boiled, then peeled, sliced and dressed whilst still warm, with a little red wine vinegar, olive oil and snipped chives.

Steak tartare

SERVES 1

125g tender, sinew and fat-free
    steak (rump, fillet or sirloin),
    well chilled
1 scant tbsp finely chopped gherkins
1 scant tbsp finely chopped (lightly
    squeezed dry) capers in vinegar
1 scant tbsp finely chopped onion

3 good quality (packed in olive oil)
    salt anchovies, finely chopped
1 tsp Dijon mustard
a few shakes of Worcestershire sauce
freshly ground pepper
1 dsp finely chopped parsley
1 small egg yolk

Using a favourite, flexible sharp knife, first cut thin slivers from your chosen
piece of steak – it matters not from which part of the meat you begin cutting.
Then take up your heaviest, strongest blade and firmly set about chopping these
slivers into swift submission. The accompanying picture, more than any words,
better illustrates the general gist of things here.

Place all the ingredients together in a previously chilled, roomy bowl and mulch
together with clean hands until fully amalgamated. Form into a patty and serve
without delay (to prevent discoloration and leaching from the acidic garnishes) –
and not without a bowl of crisp chips alongside. For I do, most definitely, think
that a freshly made steak tartare eaten with hot chips is a gastronomic marriage of
epic proportions.

COMFORT AND JOY

I endured a particularly nasty tummy bug recently. Once I had started to feel marginally better, the only things I felt inclined to restore myself with were the inevitable cups of sweet tea, a steaming mug of Bovril, ice-cold Ribena and, gingerly, the thought of a dish of boiled chicken and potatoes. (My mother's favourite when ailing was always a tomato sandwich made with white bread and no butter, the damp slices turning a blotchy pale pink as a result.)

Of course, boiled chicken need not be thought of as invalid food alone. It has always been – after roasting – one of my favourite ways to eat a tasty fowl. I tend towards the word 'poach' rather than boil, but then poached chicken doesn't quite have the same ring to it in English culinary language – although it sounds absolutely bang on to say *poulet poché à la crème*. Perhaps it is the alliterative French that makes it sound better.)

Literally 'boiling' any sort of meat or fowl is going to render the meat tough, stringy, eventually tasteless and – however much cooking liquor surrounds it – dry and dull. A gorgeous slab of salt beef brisket should languish and float in a carroty broth that merely shudders for a couple of hours, with two clove-studded onions bouncing alongside resembling menacing mines. Ham hocks, an ox tongue and continental boiling sausages would, respectively, shrink, shrivel and possibly burst out of their skins, if the liquid were left to recklessly roll, when making something akin to the Italian *bollito misto*.

The other very important point to consider when poaching is the stock or broth the meat is cooked in.

Once again, if left to rage rather than simper, any fats or vegetable solids will agitate themselves into the broth and cloud it up a treat. Not something you really want at all. If my butcher has a spare pig's trotter, I'll ask to have it swiftly cleaved, and then it's into the pot with the chicken. This will help the resultant broth to set if you then wish to clarify it and make a shimmering pot of chicken jelly.

I will certainly make that jelly, because I am eager to serve it with the truly delicious and simple chicken terrine (this follows the poached chicken recipe). This is something I recently came across from a restaurant called écco, in Brisbane, which last year (1997) won the Australian Gourmet Traveller Restaurant of the Year Award. The judge was Rick Stein and I suspect that if this especially good terrine was one of the dishes he tried when he ate there, it would have secured the award on the merits of this alone.

It is worth searching out a pedigree chicken for the terrine, even though the creature has been skinned, dissected, boned and packed away into an oval lidded porcelain vessel (which is the one I used in my kitchen); it no longer resembles a chicken, is what I'm trying to say. écco published the recipe in their very nice spiral bound *écco 1998 diary, with some of our most requested recipes*, which I found for sale in an upmarket delicatessen in Sydney. This book appears to be a jolly idea: serviceable, handsomely put together and very user-friendly. Unusually, a diary one would like to keep for years to come.

Poached chicken
with vegetables
and potato slurry
with parsley

—

SERVES 4

Slurry is not the first word one thinks of in terms of dinner, but it is an accurate description here. Once again, try to get a decent chicken.

1.5kg free-range chicken

½ chicken stock cube

1 pig's trotter, split in two lengthways by the butcher (only use if you wish to make a jelly from the resultant stock)

2 celery hearts, the outside ribs trimmed with a potato peeler

4 medium leeks, trimmed of most of the green parts and well washed, left whole

4 medium carrots, peeled and split lengthways

2 medium onions, peeled, left whole, and each pierced with 2 or 3 cloves

a bouquet garni, consisting of a fat bunch parsley stalks, 2 bay leaves, 3 branches thyme and a length of string to tie them together

200ml white wine

for the potato slurry:

4 large floury potatoes, peeled and cut in half

1 large bunch flat-leaf parsley, leaves only (the stalks used for the 'fat bunch' mentioned earlier, in the bouquet garni)

50g butter

salt and pepper

Put the chicken and halved stock cube in a suitably large pot (with trotter if using) and cover with water. Gently bring up to a shuddering simmer until much scum settles on the surface. When this resembles river effluent, methodically remove with a large spoon and put it down the sink. Once the surface is clean, push the four vegetables under the surface, together with the bouquet garni and wine. Return to a simmer, skim again when necessary, and poach quietly for about 1 hour.

Cautiously lift out the chicken and vegetables and keep hot, ticking away inside a steamer, for instance. Discard the exhausted bouquet garni and the trotter, if used.

Now put the potatoes in a small pan and just cover them with some of the chicken stock. Cook the potatoes gently in this, until tender and beginning to collapse. Drain well, using a sieve, but keep the delicious starchy broth hot on a low flame until later. Force the potatoes through the coarse blade of a vegetable mill (*mouli-légumes*) or crush with a hand-masher; it is imperative that the potatoes do not become a smooth purée. Finely chop the parsley leaves and stir into the potatoes with the butter. Adjust seasoning.

Joint the chicken into convenient pieces and arrange onto a hot serving dish with the vegetables. Spoon over some of the reserved potato broth and offer the pale green, parsley-flecked slurry in a separate dish.

Terrine of chicken
with lemon, basil and garlic

SERVES 6

Philip Johnson, chef/proprietor of écco, asks that you remove the skin from the chicken, using it to line the terrine mould before packing the chicken morsels within. It really does make a difference if you do this fairly simple task, so please have a bash.

Start by cutting away the skin with the bird placed upside down, breasts resting on a chopping board, making a lengthy initial incision along its backbone. As you start to cut the skin away, it will soon begin to separate itself from the flesh quite naturally, slipping away from the pink meat as you explore beneath the skin. Surprisingly, the skin is more resilient to the occasional rupture than you might imagine. As you work your way around the contours of the bird, before you realise where you are, you will soon be left with a huge rectangular flap of chicken skin.

Note: The reference to making a delicious chicken jelly in the previous recipe is easily made here too. Use the chicken carcasse for a good stock, once divested of its meat and, again, add a trotter to ensure a quality stiffness to the jelly. The details of the fabrication of a simple chicken stock, into a delectable savoury jelly is, here, given in full – particularly as the finished dish will then have used up skin, bone, cartilage, flesh, giblets, etc. Nothing left. All used up. Isn't that just terrific?

1 x 2.3kg free-range chicken with giblets
(approximate weight, but varying only by
the odd 100–150g or so either side as this
recipe needs to be fairly exact)
20g basil leaves
50g peeled cloves garlic (new season's
when possible)
grated zest of 1 large lemon
20g Maldon sea salt
about 1 rounded tsp finely milled white
peppercorns
a few scrapings from a nutmeg

for the jelly:
1.5 litres water
chicken giblets, chopped
1 pig's trotter, cleaved lengthways
½ chicken stock cube
300ml white wine
1 large carrot, peeled and coarsely chopped
3 sticks celery, coarsely chopped
1 large onion, peeled and chopped
1 bay leaf
3 sprigs fresh thyme
12 peppercorns
some fresh parsley stalks

Remove the skin of the chicken with your favourite small sharp knife, as described above. Once you have the flat piece of chicken skin, place it on a work surface, the familiar side of chicken skin face down, and trim off any fatty or unnecessary bits.

Preheat the oven to 180ºC/350ºF/gas mark 4.

Remove all the flesh from the breast, thigh and drumstick and cut into 2cm pieces. Put into a roomy bowl and mix in the basil, garlic, lemon, salt, pepper and nutmeg. Use your hands here, mulching everything together, until all seems well blended. Pile this muddle into the middle of the chicken skin, fold over the flaps to form a loose parcel and then fit neatly into a suitably sized terrine mould or a dish that you regularly use to make pâté in. It matters not a jot as to the dimensions here, just choose a container you feel happy with.

Put the terrine dish into a deep tray and fill with boiling water from the kettle, so that it reaches three-quarters of the way up the sides of the dish. Cover with a lid or foil and bake for 1 hour and 20 minutes on the middle shelf of the oven. *Note:* The skin and contents will naturally do their own thing as they cook: the skin will shrink back, the meat will contract, juices and fat will exude and coagulate. This is meant to be.

Once cooked, remove the terrine dish from the water, tip the water away and return the terrine to the tray. Leave to cool and settle for 15 minutes. Compress the surface of the terrine with a board or lid, weighted down with something such as a couple of family size tins of baked beans, for about 1 hour. Fat and juices will have welled up during this time, maybe flooded over the lip of the dish; collect these and re-introduce them back into the dish. Cover with clingfilm and put into the fridge for at least 12 hours to cool and set.

To make the jelly, chop up the carcasse into small pieces and put into a roomy pan with all the other ingredients listed for making the jelly. Slowly bring up to the boil, allowing an unsightly scum to form on the surface. Just before little boiling points appear on the surface of the stock, start to remove this scum with a large serving spoon and jettison down the sink. The liquid will already start to look quite clear underneath. (The natural albumen within the poultry carcasse is a natural clarifier; there should be no need to further clear the broth with egg white etc if you are diligent with your skills over despumation.) Also, make sure that you do not allow the broth to emit much more than a quiet shudder as it cooks, for about 2 hours.

Strain through a colander into a pan or bowl. Allow to drip for 15 minutes. Then, once more, strain the resultant liquid through a sieve lined with a clean, fine tea-towel into another vessel. Leave to cool, remove any unsightly globules of fat from the surface, and put into the fridge to set. Both terrine and jelly should hopefully mature to readiness at one and the same time.

To serve, slice the chicken terrine thickly, directly from the dish, making sure that you use careful sawing motions as you cut, so as not to tear the pressed chicken meat as you go. Tip spoonfuls of the jelly onto a chopping board and mince with a knife into a glistening mass. Pile onto the plate – or plates – on which you wish to present the terrine. Eat with hot buttered toast.

I KNOW WHAT I LIKE

As is so often the case in London with me these days, whenever I visit Paris I similarly tend to drift back towards the same old favourite eating places — be it brasserie, bistro or full-blown restaurant. As I think I may have mentioned here before, regularity and familiarity are, for me, the key to eating well anywhere. Those who choose to flit around from new place to new place — and, as we well know, there are far too many of those just now — might garner the minutest frisson from actually being blessed with a table and clock a handful of minor celebrities, but they will also wait hours for the food to appear because the kitchen has not quite settled in yet (it is, in fact, in utter turmoil because there are most probably kitchen-fitters and chefs working in tandem). This sort of carry on is not for me.

But, you know, even when such a joint has finally settled down I rarely find myself having the urge to go; too much of a dull creature of habit, that's me. And I rarely book in Paris, either. There will always be somewhere else to go if the chosen place is full or if there is a wait. But then I also don't mind waiting. After all, there is no more congenial place to sit and linger with a glass of something than a Parisian café or bar across the street or round the corner. This scenario hardly exists at all, in London.

So, it was back to brasserie Lipp in Saint Germain (twice), Chez Georges just off the place de Victoires (once), the Italian l'Osteria in the Marais (twice — and I wish it could have been three times so much do I adore this place), the very grand Taillevent near the Etoile (once) and the much loved bistro L'Ami Louis, just a short walk down from the place de la République (once). Here are a couple of recipes inspired by two of them and a third resulting from some judicious shopping.

Quails with peas

———

SERVES 2

I was always convinced that the only problem – in relative terms, that is – of eating chez l'Ami Louis on one's own was that some of the main course dishes that I have most enjoyed are intended for two or more people: the fine roast chicken, the blackened and crusted *côte de boeuf* or, in season, the small gigot of spring lamb.

However, having recently experienced two singular lunches there, I finally had the opportunity to try other dishes – namely, the duck confit with pommes béarnaises (a crusted cake of magisterial proportions made from lumps of crushed potatoes fried in goose fat and then showered with chopped garlic and parsley) and the pigeon with peas.

As it is difficult to find French pigeons (*pigeonneau*) in Britain, I have opted to offer an alternative recipe for quails treated in a similar fashion. I know that the methods here are different to those of the kitchens of L'Ami Louis, but at least the inspiration is behind it.

1 thick slice of pancetta or streaky bacon, un-skinned and cut into 1cm cubes
25g butter
4 quails
salt and pepper
12 small button onions, peeled
4–5 cloves garlic
1 glass of white wine
2 tbsp strong, jellied poultry stock
1 or 2 sprigs fresh sage
1kg fresh peas, podded (use tinned peas – drained – rather than frozen, if you decide not to use fresh)

Preheat the oven to 180°C/350°F/gas mark 4.

Using a shallow, ovenproof pan or dish, gently fry the pancetta in the butter until golden brown. Remove the pancetta to a plate and reserve. Season the quails and, in the resultant fat, colour them on all sides. Also remove these and put with the pancetta. Now add the onions and garlic and gently gild these too. Pour in the wine and allow to reduce by one-third before adding the stock. Stir in the sage, tip in the peas and reintroduce the quails and pancetta. Bring to a simmer, check for seasoning and place in the oven, covered, for 30–40 minutes. If you wish, remove the cover for the final 10 minutes to give a final browning to the birds.

Caponata

SERVES 4

Toni Vianello's tiny l'Osteria continues to amaze me each and every time I go to Paris, so much so that to only go once is now simply not enough. This time I enjoyed some home cured ham (sent from a friend in Vianello's home region in northern Italy), his quite astonishingly light and bouncy gnocchi (on this occasion with the classic lubrication of butter and sage), some enormous white, deeply flavoured asparagus with olive oil, parmesan and a poached egg, a dish of *baccala* (a speciality of Vicenza) that I now consider the pinnacle of all variations around the preparation of salt cod and, finally, a simple, fragrantly sweet and sour plate of that Sicilian speciality, caponata. And there were, of course, two more hits at Vianello's exceptional tiramisu.

One might say that frequenting an Italian restaurant in Paris so often may be seen as perverse in the extreme, but when cooking is as uniquely special as this it would be equally perverse to ignore such a find. Here is my take on his caponata. I was surprised to find peppers in it, but have since found out that there is more than one rendition of this famously good dish of stewed aubergine. I don't think my finished dish was as good as that of l'Osteria's, but hope you will enjoy it all the same.

2007 – I understand that the great Tony Vianello may have since retired from the stove, but that one of his former chefs is now cooking and running the place – and apparently it is still very good indeed.

2 large aubergines (preferably those fat, purple and white Sicilian ones if possible), peeled and thickly sliced into half rounds

salt

1 large red onion, peeled, halved and thickly sliced

4 sticks celery, peeled, halved lengthways and sliced into small lengths

1 small yellow pepper, halved lengthways, de-seeded and thickly sliced

1 small red pepper, halved lengthways, de-seeded and thickly sliced

5–6 tbsp olive oil

100ml water

3 tbsp red wine vinegar

1 rounded tbsp sugar

1 dsp tomato purée

1 heaped tbsp raisins

about 12 green olives, pitted and halved

1 heaped tbsp capers, drained and lightly squeezed dry

2 anchovy fillets, finely chopped

freshly ground white pepper

1 heaped tbsp pine kernels, gently heated in a dry frying pan until golden brown

Spread the aubergines out on a kitchen surface and sprinkle with enough salt to season generously. Gather them up in your hands, mingle together in a colander, place upon a plate and leave to exude their juices for at least 40 minutes. Meanwhile, using a frying pan, and in four separate stages, quietly stew the onion, celery, yellow and red peppers in separate tablespoons of the oil until softened and only *just* coloured. The fifth and final stage will be the washed and dried aubergines. Place all five vegetables in a bowl and mingle together.

To the frying pan now add the water, vinegar, sugar, tomato purée and raisins. Bring to the boil and simmer for several minutes until lightly thickened and the raisins have plumped somewhat. Stir in the olives, capers and anchovies and tip the entire contents of the pan into the bowl of vegetables. Mix in pepper and pine kernels and check for salt. Lubricate with a little more olive oil if you think it warrants it and serve at room temperature with good bread.

Oignons à la Grecque

SERVES 4

As you can imagine, it was a huge joy to see all the late spring-into-summer vegetables and fruits proudly displayed in all the shops and markets of Paris whilst I was there. Amongst the first pink-flecked pods enclosing speckled Italian borlotti beans (I am unsure of the French name for these), tiny, thin *haricots verts*, naturally sweet and fragrant southern French strawberries (we should be deeply ashamed of those now generally on offer over here), myriad salads and pots and pots of herbs, there were also bunches of these pearly white and pale yellow, new season small onions, and also shallots.

Using the onions I made a delicious variation on the classic *champignons à la Grecque*. It is not as if this variation hasn't been done before but, once again, the ingredients inspired its making.

about 35–40 new season (if possible)
   bulbous spring onions, trimmed
   and peeled
1 glass of white wine
150ml tomato passatta
1 tsp coriander seeds

2 cloves garlic, peeled and chopped
1–2 sprigs rosemary
juice of 1 small lemon
salt and pepper
4 tbsp olive oil

Place all the ingredients – except for the olive oil – in a stainless steel pan and
bring up to a simmer. Skim off any scum that forms over the first few minutes of
cooking, then stir in the olive oil and leave to simmer for 30 minutes. Leave to cool
completely and then serve lightly chilled as a first course or as part of a cold buffet.

THE ONE AND ONLY

When I first visited Milan in the late summer of 1985, I had scant knowledge of the city. Of course, I knew there was a famous opera house but remained ignorant of its extraordinary Gothic cathedral. I had also been told of the famous fashion street, the Via Montenapoleone, yet unaware that this street was also home to Cova, the much loved bar and pasticceria and which has since became one of my favourite bars anywhere (Italians have always made the best cocktails anyway — and that's real cocktails not filthy ones made by a trendy, hair-gelled cretin). Whilst G. Lorenzi, the extraordinary scissor and kitchen knife shop diagonally opposite to Cova, should also be noted for its exquisite marrow-bone spoons made from horn and those of mother of pearl, expressly for serving caviar.

As far as cookery is concerned, I had been attempting to perfect the celebrated, saffron-tinged, marrow-enriched *risotto alla Milanese* for some time. My initial attempts had used the wrong rice, ignorantly pre-cooked it and would occasionally incorporate the heinous slug of double cream to unnecessarily enrich that which naturally thickens with indigenous starch and the final *mantecare* — a vigorous incorporation of copious amounts of butter and cheese. Well, one lives and learns… and I hope that I'm a bit better at it, now.

The very same risotto served at Ristorante Gran San Bernado (now, sadly, closed) on the outskirts of the city I remember as particularly fine, with the rice served as the usual, gorgeous golden yellow slop but also served *al salto* (literally, 'to jump'), whereby cold, left-over risotto is crisped in a frying pan until a crusted, flat 'cake'. It is a delight. Also, if you like tripe, eat it at Ristorante alla Collina Pistoiese (Via degli Amadei, 1. 0039 02 86 45 10 85) and which opened for business in 1938. As perfect a traditional Milanese dining room as one could wish for: busy, noisy, chic and packed full of good-looking locals.

2007 — I recently fashioned a risotto using the very fine carnaroli '*gran riserva*' rice, milled by the long established Riso Gallo company. This carefully aged rice — the packet I used is from the 2004 vintage — is grown in the paddy fields of the Po valley, about an hour's drive out of Milan. It was a revelation. Gran Riserva rice is available from Harrods and other epicurean food shops.

However, there is just one place in Milan where it would upset me deeply if I were unable to call by and that is the one and only Peck. Simply, this is the very finest food store I know anywhere. I deeply respect how the Stoppani family chooses not to flim-flam around with attempting to offer foods from all over the world, simply concentrating almost entirely on indigenous produce from Italy — and, naturally, particularly from the north.

There is the most wonderful Parmesan you will ever taste (the three-year-old, especially), so sweet and almost crunchy; the fragrantly lactic, seasonal *burrata* (cream-filled, cow's milk mozzarella); some of the most carefully made prepared food you will ever see, displayed in huge dishes and looking better than many of the same served in restaurants (the *vitello tonnato* is benchmark); various cured hams, it goes without saying, are sublime as are the superb *lardo* (cured belly fat) and fatty pork cheeks; pile upon pile of *cottechino* and *zampone* sausages, essential components of the northern Italian *bollito misto* or to be simply served with lentils on New Year's Eve and also the unique *salame d'orca* — a lightly preserved goose sausage, wrapped in its skin, which is then poached for about an hour and served hot, in thick slices, accompanied by *mostarda di frutta* (fruits preserved in a hot mustard oil syrup, of which Peck's own brand is one of the most pungent I know). And that's not all…

For it is the veal section that truly astonishes: superb thick slices of *osso buco*, each *buco* full of pale pink marrow. There are braising cuts and beautifully butchered roasting joints, all wrapped up in thin slices of fat, tied up into perfect, plump logs and with rosemary sprigs tucked in here and there — just marvellous! Then there are scallopine, fillets and last, but not least, Milan's most favourite of all, the famous veal chop. One has rarely seen such fine examples of such a thing, so neatly trimmed and proudly presented that they quite took my breath away.

Here is the chop, simply cooked with butter and sage — and possibly as much a part of everyday life in Milan as that of an Armani purchase.

SERVES 2

2 well-trimmed veal chops
salt and pepper
a little flour
a thick slice of butter – plus a little extra
a slug of olive oil
10–12 fresh sage leaves
2–4 lemon wedges

Season the chops and dust lightly with flour. Take a large, heavy frying pan and in it melt the butter with the olive oil until it starts to foam. Put in the chops and turn the heat down a little. Allow to sizzle quietly for about 7–10 minutes on each side, until golden and just firm to the touch (a uniform interior pink is ideal). Place on a serving dish and keep warm in a very low oven. Add a little more butter to the pan and turn up the heat once more. When the fats are frothing fling in the sage and stir around until the leaves begin to crisp and curl, whilst also taking care that the butter does not burn. Spoon over the chops and serve at once, with the lemons alongside to (essentially, for me) squeeze over.

PERFECT PIQUANT PORK

I always find it interesting as to how my food-obsessed mind leaps into an altogether higher gastronomic gear when so encouraged by a better diet and healthier living. Recipes and possible dishes just pop into my head at the most alarming rate; I almost look upon this as worryingly masochistic, yet it always seems to happen in these circumstances. Even the simplest inspiration brings on flights of fancy, such as the very one that sparked off today's recipe.

For it was whilst enjoying some perfectly grilled lamb cutlets when one of these gastro-moments occurred. Adorned as the lamb was with very little, I felt the need for some sort of piquancy with which to perk up the singular protein but didn't have any fresh mint, mint sauce *or* jelly, would you believe! So, I compromised with mustard and redcurrant jelly with which to delicately smear the crisp and tender, pink chops. After separately toying with a smear of mustard here, followed by a nugget of jelly there, I eventually both smeared and nuggeted together. I found this a truly delicious combination: sweet, sour and hot, all at once. The brain began to bubble and simmer.

The instant analogy that came to mind was, of course, jolly old Cumberland sauce, into which, I vaguely recalled, a little English mustard powder had occasionally been incorporated by a few of the more daring cooks I have known. When I first came across the suggestion of adding this condiment to my (up until then) clear and ruby-red lotion I was initially loathe to it. But, it very soon became abundantly clear that here was a very good notion indeed, however much it clouded the issue. I then began to think that this particular amalgam would also be better served with pork rather than lamb — although its inspirational vehicle. And, crucially, I just knew that this pork should also be eaten cold.

Both mustard and sweet things have always been good with pork; and, when you come to think about it, it must have been a similar whim which inspired that unique Italian stuff known as *Mostarda di Cremona*, where chunks of very sweet crystallised fruit have been further enhanced by a fiery mustard oil infused into the syrup, the like of which both surrounds the fruits and keeps them moist and sticky for months on end.

And, incidentally, to those who are already aficionados of this most choice of continental tracklements, do you not think that the all-important nose-tingling mustard pungency has been reduced a little of late, in most commercial brands? The one exception to this worrying trend is those made and sold by the wonderful Peck, in Milan. All I can say is purchase plenty when you next visit this most fabulous emporium.

It should also be good and fatty, this cold pork, the sort of pork that I remember as a child being truly excellent in sandwiches. I mean, anybody who cares about really good sandwiches knows full well that a Sunday-supper sandwich constructed from pantry-temperature slices from the left-over roast, wolfed down with a glass of ice-cold milk and all wrapped up inside a woolly dressing gown, whilst also watching *Sunday Night at the London Palladium* remains, without any shadow of a doubt, as the very best sandwich ever.

Cold poached pork belly
with its jelly and
piquant cream

———

SERVES 6

**Please be in the mood and make the
time to cook this recipe. It is absolutely
delicious and needs love and care
lavished upon it.**

for cooking the pork:
1kg piece of fatty belly pork, boned
   (this piece should have a good width to it,
   as it is to be rolled up)
the fatter half of a pork fillet, trimmed and
   skinned
salt and pepper
600g piece of lean belly pork, bones and
   rind intact
1 pig's trotter, split
2 carrots, peeled and chopped
3 sticks celery, washed and chopped
2 onions, peeled (one of them stuck with
   2 cloves)
2 bay leaves
3–4 sprigs fresh thyme
a few peppercorns
1 large glass of white wine
1 chicken stock cube

for the clarification:
200g minced, lean pork
3 egg whites, loosely beaten to a froth
½ tsp salt

for the piquant cream:
2–3 tbsp Dijon mustard
2 tbsp redcurrant jelly
3–4 tbsp pork jelly (see method)
3–4 tbsp crème fraîche
squeeze of lemon juice

Season the inside of the fatty belly pork and the pork fillet. Place the fillet in the middle of the belly, roll it up and tie tightly with several lengths of string. Trim the ends neatly if necessary. Place this, together with the flat piece of lean belly and the trotter into a large enough pan that will take them snugly but with room to spare later, for the vegetables.

Cover with cold water and slowly bring to the boil. Just as the surface of the water is trembling, lift out all the meats with tongs or a carving fork and place in the sink. Rinse all traces of scum from the meats under warm running water and put on to a tray. Chuck out the dirty water, rinse the pan clean and return the meats to it. Re-cover with cold water and add all the other ingredients for cooking the pork.

Slowly bring up to the boil. As before, more scum will appear on the surface, but this time quickly whip it off with a ladle or large serving spoon (it is important that this constantly generated despumation is rigorously removed throughout the entire cooking period of the pork, so as to guarantee a clear stock). Quietly poach the meats for about 1½ hours, making sure that the liquid merely blips and shudders.

Lift out the meats once more and place into a smaller pan in which, this time, they really do fit snugly; I suggest arranging the rolled part upright and curling the flat belly around its edge, almost as an embrace. Drain the stock through a colander suspended over a clean pan and leave there for at least 5 minutes to drip. Discard all solids (they have done their work). Now pour the liquid through a very fine sieve into a (sorry, yet another) clean pan. Leave to settle for 10–15 minutes. Lift off every scrap of fat possible by passing several sheets of kitchen paper over the surface. Ladle just enough of the stock over the pork to cover it, leave to cool and put in the fridge to set. Leave the remaining stock in the pan and allow to cool to room temperature. This is for the jelly. *Note:* You will need *not less* than 500ml of stock for the jelly, so if the pork is not quite covered by the rest of the stock, this is not the end of the world.

Mix together the ingredients for the clarification and tip into the stock. Place over a medium heat and slowly begin to whisk the mince into the stock. Do this for about 5 minutes, or so and then leave to come up to a simmer, occasionally checking that some of the solids have not attached themselves to the base of the pan, where they will scorch and ruin the flavour (I failed to do this once with a shellfish consommé and, as you can imagine, the stench of scorched lobster and crayfish shells was very nasty; it was to be an entire week before my flat no longer reeked).

So, what is occurring now is the clarification process: the egg whites and natural albumen in the minced pork is busy collecting all the impurities in the stock into itself, whilst also adding further flavour anew. As the stock gently blips through this surface crust it should be clear and golden.

After about 30–40 minutes, make a hole in the crust with a spoon and lift some of it away. Using a ladle, transfer the clear liquid that lies beneath through a damp muslin-lined sieve (or use an old thin tea-towel) into a clean pan. Collect all you can. Discard the crust and pour the resultant clear liquid into a bowl. Leave to cool, cover and place in the fridge.

To make the piquant cream, liquidise the mustard, redcurrant jelly and meat jelly (taken from the jelly surrounding the pork, *not* the clear jelly) until really smooth. Add the crème fraîche, briefly whiz once more (excess processing will turn the cream) and sharpen with lemon juice to taste. Pour into a bowl and put in the fridge to set.

To serve, slice each of the pork joints thinly and lay onto a platter or as individual portions (as shown in the photograph). Scoop out spoonfuls of jelly and cream as delicate tracklements. I like to eat scrupulously scraped, hot new potatoes with – if I might be so bold as to say – these exquisite cold cuts.

MRS. DAVID'S HAM

When I was working in a seaside hotel in Pembrokeshire, at the beginning of the 1970s, there was a dish on the menu with a very odd name. I certainly had never heard of *Le Saupiquet des Amognes* before, and when a rather jovial, regular guest asked after a description of this said delicacy, he was told – in all seriousness – that it was 'sliced ham in a cream sauce'. Well, he simply fell about. Kathy, the restaurant manager at the time, couldn't see the humour and went off in a big huff – I seem to remember she had quite a few of these huffs, did dear Kathy.

Humour and huffs aside, it is a supremely good dish this *Saupiquet* thing. Big Sal, the extremely gifted cook at this hotel had unearthed the recipe from the pages of Elizabeth David's *French Provincial Cooking* as, in fact, a great deal of other good things that appeared on the menu were also gleaned from. I suppose this was actually the period when I really discovered E.D. too, come to think of it.

Mrs. David writes: '*Saupiquet* consists of a *sauce piquante à la crème* served with slices of ham fried in butter. It is a modernised version of a famous and very old speciality of the Nivernais and the Morvan districts of Burgundy.' She further goes on to say that the sauce '... is one well worth knowing.' Well, it has certainly been one of those charming and idiosyncratic sauces that has remained dear to my heart ever since: simple to prepare, lovely and creamy yet both light and sharp on the palate. It partners ham superbly, but it is also excellent with salt tongue too. I have always thought that it is sauces such as this, which highlight a particular thoughtfulness in the French cook.

Le Saupiquet des Amognes

SERVES 6

When I have made this before, I have found that cooking one joint of ham is preferable to frying slices of ham, as Mrs. David suggests. I have also taken the liberty of adding some chicken wings and a trotter to the cooking pot, so that the resultant broth has more body to it. You may then use some of this liquor for making the sauce and keep the remainder for a delicious pea soup, perhaps.

for cooking the ham:

1.5–2kg boned and rolled gammon or shoulder joint
900g chicken wings
1 split pig's trotter (optional)
2 carrots, peeled and quartered
2 onions, peeled, one stuck with 6 cloves
4 sticks celery, cut into lengths
2 leeks, trimmed and washed, cut into lengths
8 bruised juniper berries
2 bay leaves
3 sprigs fresh tarragon
a few peppercorns

for the sauce:

4 shallots, peeled and finely chopped
150ml tarragon vinegar
5–6 juniper berries, bruised
200ml white wine
30g butter
1 level tbsp flour
275ml ham broth (see method)
275ml double cream
freshly ground white pepper
a little salt, taking into consideration that the ham broth will already be saline
a little freshly chopped parsley, for decoration (optional)

Put the gammon or shoulder joint into a large pan and cover with cold water. Slowly bring to the boil. Just before the water starts to bubble, and when you will also see that there is a great deal of scum covering the surface, lift out the joint with a carving fork or similar, and rinse under cold running water. Discard the water and wash out the pan. Return the joint to the pot and add the rest of the ingredients for cooking the ham. Cover everything with fresh water and simmer very gently for around 1½–2 hours, skimming off any scum, from time to time, as it settles on the surface. Double check for tenderness after 1½ hours, using a skewer to probe the meat; there should not be any noticeable resistance.

To make the sauce, put the shallots, vinegar and juniper berries in a small stainless steel or enamelled saucepan. Simmer together until the vinegar has all but boiled away to nothing. Add the white wine and reduce by half. Put on one side. In another saucepan, melt the butter and add the flour. Mix together with a wooden spoon and cook very gently, stirring slowly, over a low heat for a few minutes, until this roux has become pale golden in colour.

Measure off the given amount of hot ham broth into a jug and gradually add this to the roux, whisking after each addition, until the sauce is perfectly smooth. Strain though a fine sieve into the shallot/vinegar/wine reduction and bring all this to a gentle simmer. Cook for a further 15 minutes over a very low heat; this will harmonise all the flavours and 'mellow' the sauce. Finally add the cream, whisk together and simmer for 5 minutes, or so until the sauce is velvety and a beautiful ivory colour. Check for seasoning.

Carve the ham as you like to (I like some of the skin left intact), spoon over the sauce and serve with buttery new potatoes and spinach.

PICK YOUR OWN

There are, without question, certain fruits and vegetables of this present season that exactly pinpoint everything that is special about an English summer: strawberries and raspberries, new potatoes and peas; gooseberries and redcurrants, broad beans and runner beans; courgettes and cucumbers and cherries and greengages.

In the garden of a friend in Sussex the other weekend there were scents of apple mint, various thymes and fennel fronds in the air (as well as heady roses and honeysuckle). Small kitchen garden beds were overflowing with cut-and-come-again salad leaves, sorrel and young spinach; one boxed-in bed was a riot of fabulously green flat-leaf parsley which, the minute I clapped eyes on it, immediately superseded my initial thoughts of making some mayonnaise to go with a splendid sea trout. And so parsley sauce it was instead. So fragrant and fresh was the herb, that it quite astonished the dinner guests with its strength of flavour and absurdly verdant green colour, once made into that most English of all savoury lotions.

Earlier in the day, Michael had driven us to a nearby pick-your-own farm (from where, in the spring, I had previously cut basket upon basket of superb asparagus spears – and, excitingly, for the very first time in my life, too) initially to pick big, fat loganberries for his fruit tart. Now, Michael is very good indeed at assembling a fruit tart but, sadly for him on this occasion, those loganberries were not quite ready to be picked. But there were raspberries galore. So that is what went into Michael's tart. And, a little reluctantly, he now had to build two layers. Well, bless his heart!

All right then, how many septuagenarians do *you* know who can a) blind-bake a perfect sweet pastry shell in an oven he quietly loathes (Michael doesn't much care for his Rayburn), b) would actually want to do so in the first place and c) still triumph hugely when caught out with rogue fruit at the eleventh hour? I feel sure there are many young chefs out there who have never even heard of *crème pâtissière*, let alone made some.

There were broad beans for the picking of too, up at the farm – or, rather, had been. Foiled again – either not ready or all gone! Apparently, we were sadly informed that there had been a large crowd of folk meddling amongst them that very morning, stripping the plants almost bare of their furry green pods. We managed but a handful of stunted numbers, which I then proceeded to munch raw on the way back to the house. And, my word, how clearly one can taste the difference between the broad beans one buys even at the most discerning of greengrocers, in comparison with those which I popped into my mouth, whilst motoring through the sunny Sussex countryside. As with freshly picked peas, it is that racing conversion from sugar to starch that takes place in the pod which inevitably disappoints all who are lucky enough to appreciate the difference. I will go back for some more before the season is over.

Broad beans
with cream and mint

SERVES 2

If the broad beans that you are using are super-fresh there seems little point in taking the trouble to remove their individual skins – and by that, I don't mean their furry-lined pods. Generally speaking, the larger and older the bean, the more chance there is that their skins will be tough. To remove the skins, simply blanch them briefly in boiling water, drain, cool and pinch them off using fingers. Only then proceed with the following method.

2kg very fresh broad beans, podded
25g butter
1 small clove garlic, peeled and
    finely chopped

200ml whipping cream
1 tbsp chopped mint
squeeze of lemon juice
salt and freshly ground white pepper

Boil the beans in plenty of salted, boiling water for 2–3 minutes. Drain. Melt the butter in a small pan and add the garlic. Sizzle for a moment and then tip in the beans. Turn them around in the butter for a few seconds and then pour in the cream. Bring up to the boil and simmer until thickened. Stir in the mint and lemon juice, season, and serve up at once. Particularly good with boiled ham and roast pork.

Fried courgettes
with skordalia

—

SERVES 2

While staying in Greece a few weeks ago I became increasingly disappointed by not finding enough evidence of skordalia on the menus of some of the local tavernas we frequented. I am extremely fond of this popular Greek emollient (bread or, sometimes, potato or ground almonds blended together with olive oil, vinegar and much garlic – the Greek version of aïoli, I guess) and soon became a man obsessed as, time after time, the request for a spoonful or two of it was unforthcoming.

Only once were we successful in finding some and, even then, it was not exactly as I like it: too thick with potato – more like cold garlic mash, to be frank. The fried aubergines that accompanied it, on the other hand, were exemplary. We made sandwiches with them, so thick and malleable was the skordalia, and so, in the end, quite delicious for that. Here is the same idea using courgettes, for a change, but with a much nicer skordalia this time, I do believe.

2 large courgettes, sliced on the
    diagonal – about the thickness of
    two £1 coins
salt and pepper
self-raising flour
olive oil, for frying
squeeze of lemon juice

for the skordalia:
50–75g slightly stale, white country
    bread, crusts removed and torn
    into bits
150ml warm milk
2 cloves garlic, peeled, cut in half
    (green germ removed if
    prominently green) and crushed to
    a paste with salt
pepper
1–2 scant tbsp red wine vinegar
about 75–100ml olive oil

First make the skordalia. Soak the bread in the milk for a few minutes until spongy. Squeeze the excess milk out with your hands and put the bread into a food processor with the garlic, pepper and vinegar. Pulse this poultice, adding the olive oil in a thin stream, until thick and paste-like; try not to overwork the mixture, however, as you want to retain a little texture of the bread.

Sprinkle a little salt over the courgettes and allow to drain in a colander for 15 minutes or so. Pat dry with a kitchen paper and grind pepper over them. Heat a good quantity of olive oil in a frying pan (about an inch or so in depth) and fry the courgettes until golden and crisp on each side; I find that using self-raising flour gives a slight puff to the coating. Drain onto several folds of kitchen paper, arrange on hot plates, squeeze a little lemon juice over them and spoon some of the skordalia alongside.

Cherry and lemon pudding

SERVES 4

As perfect a warm summery pudding that I can think of, just now and which celebrates the British cherry season in all its glory. Essentially, this is based upon a cherry and almond tart that I first came across around about the beginning of the 1970s and which hails from the early days of the famous Box Tree restaurant in Ilkley, Yorkshire when it was owned by Malcolm Reid and Colin Long – restaurateurs of rare quality and with enormous style.

Note: The pudding's texture is much improved if you take the trouble to grind your own almonds. Buy whole, blanched and skinned almonds if you choose to take this route.

100g softened butter

400g fresh English cherries, stoned

125g caster sugar

2 tbsp Kirsch

3 eggs

125g ground almonds

juice and grated zest of 1 lemon

a little extra caster sugar

Preheat the oven to 180°C/350°F/gas mark 4.

Grease a wide and shallow baking dish with 10g of the softened butter, tip in the cherries, sprinkle with 25g of the caster sugar and add the Kirsch. Beat together the remaining 90g of butter and 100g of sugar until very light and fluffy and then add the eggs, one at a time, beating them in thoroughly before folding in the ground almonds, lemon juice and zest.

Spoon this mixture over the fruit, level it off and then sprinkle with the extra caster sugar. Bake in the oven for 40–45 minutes, or until puffed up and gently firm to the touch. Leave to cool for 10–15 minutes before eating with very cold double cream, whipped if you like.

Gooseberry fool

——

MAKES 600–700ML

As with such simple tasks as preparing green beans and leaving their spiky bit intact, or failing to remove the skin from new potatoes, the suggestion that 'there is no need to top and tail' a gooseberry is yet another indication that we, as a nation, have become the most slovenly of cooks.

It takes but a few minutes to top and tail goosegogs: you sit down – preferably in a sunny garden in a deck chair – and just get on with it. And if you don't have the time or, perhaps more to the point, the inclination, have raspberries instead. Such an accommodating fruit. Eat them directly from the punnet; then you won't even have to wash-up, either.

Some such rustic-minded cook will soon, no doubt, also be haranguing me over the supposedly pleasurable elements of all those 'bits' – tough, leathery skins and seeds – so seemingly essential to the unrefined (another word for 'easier') gooseberry fool, adding both texture and substance. Oh pish! As far as this one is concerned, a fine fool should be as smooth as silk. And with that in mind, I have seen fit to fashion this particular fool as a kind of de-construction job.

Ergo: put as much carefully whipped cream as you wish into small chilled bowls and then enjoy a super-fine purée of lightly sweetened gooseberries spooned over each. Each ingredient must be as chilled as you dare to achieve the best results. I cannot begin to tell you how delicious is this elegant and refined combination.

1kg gooseberries, topped and tailed and washed
125g golden caster sugar
2 tbsp elderflower cordial
lightly sweetened, vanilla-scented, loosely whipped cream

To make the gooseberry purée, put the fruit in a stainless steel saucepan with the sugar and cordial (if you cannot find elderflower cordial simply use water), cover and place over a very low light. Allow the gooseberries to burst and then simmer for 15–20 minutes, or so, or until the fruit is soft and has released almost all of its juice. Pass through the finest blade of a vegetable mill (*mouli-légumes*) or sieve until only pips and seeds remain behind. Now purée thoroughly in the goblet of a liquidiser until as smooth as silk. Personally, I like to pass this once more through an even finer sieve for good measure.

Note: It is most important that you do not liquidise the fruit before the removal of skin and seeds, as these will add unwanted tannin tastes (bitterness) to the eventual purée. Another notion would be to sweeten the cream with elderflower cordial and then poach the goosegogs with a vanilla pod.

HOT AND COLD

There's no getting away from it, original recipes are a thing of the dim and distant past. Nobody, even in their wildest imagination, is ever again going to be able to create something as remarkable as a hollandaise, a *beurre blanc*, puff pastry, cheesecake, risotto, rhubarb crumble or potted shrimps. What we get up to now is nothing more than a crafty re-jigging.

One of my favourite of all puddings – and it is most definitely an English pud, as the way it cooks is mildly eccentric and smacks strongly of being accidentally discovered – is the one called lemon surprise pudding. I am not about to give you the recipe, as I did so some months ago, forgetting, in the process, to include the sugar… forgive, forgive? However, I myself am less forgiving if, when a recipe is quite clearly filched and mutated, its provenance is not accredited; a note of thanks, a nod to, a debt paid is the least that is necessary.

What I wanted to do with Margaret Costa's lemon surprise pudding (from her 1970 seminal work *The Four Season's Cookery Book*, republished two years ago by Grub Street, £17.99) was to purposefully remove the quite delicious, custard-like pond that collects under a light sponge, so simply turning it into just a lemon sponge, warm and soft, but still with the essence of citrus and the airiness of the original. This one is served with a superb lemon ice cream, the recipe of which was generously given to me by my friend and excellent cook, Hilary Rogers.

Light lemon sponge
with lemon ice cream

SERVES 4

for the sponge:

75g softened butter

1 dsp caster sugar

150g Silver Shred marmalade
  (the lemon one)

rind and juice of 2 small lemons

2 large egg yolks

100g caster sugar, plus a little extra
  for sprinkling

1 tbsp self-raising flour

4 large egg whites

pinch of salt

a little icing sugar

for the ice cream:

8 large egg yolks

225g caster sugar

juice of 2 large lemons

275ml double cream

Note: The ice cream contains raw egg yolks.

First make the ice cream. Beat together the egg yolks and sugar until very light, white and fluffy. Gradually add the lemon juice, continuing to beat (all this is best done using electrical methods), until the mass starts to rise up once more. Lightly whip the cream and carefully fold into the mixture until well amalgamated. Pour into a suitable container, put a lid on and place in the freezer for at least 6 hours, or overnight. The mixture, due to the high proportion of egg, remains delightfully soft and creamy.

Now to the sponge. First grease a – preferably oval (see picture) – porcelain dish with enough of the given quantity of butter to generously cover the inside. Sprinkle with the dessertspoon of caster sugar, moving it around so that it all sticks to the butter, tapping out any excess.

Preheat the oven to 170°C/325°F/gas mark 3.

To make the sponge, first melt the marmalade with 1 tbsp of the lemon juice over a very gentle heat – this will take longer than you think, but it does not have to be completely smooth. Beat together the egg yolks, melted marmalade, lemon rind, remaining juice and butter and 50g of the sugar, until light and mousse-like. Sift in the flour and fold in. In another bowl, beat the egg whites, the remaining 50g of sugar and salt until glossy, and then fold into the first mixture. Pour into the prepared dish, sprinkle with a little extra caster sugar and place it into a deep roasting tin. Pour hot water around the dish so that it comes up to at least two-thirds of the way up. Carefully put into the oven and bake for 40–45 minutes, or until nicely puffed up, spongy to the touch and sporting a perfectly golden surface. Remove from the water and dust with icing sugar. Spoon out at once, into cold bowls, with a scoop of the lemon ice cream alongside.

STRAWBERRY FIELDS

The finest strawberries I last recall popping into my easy mouth were those that I bought from Balducci's, the celebrated Manhattan Italian delicatessen (I guess I should actually refer to it as a 'gourmet food store' in situ, as 'deli' means something quite else, in New York city). Sadly, this fondly remembered treat occurred about 10 years ago now, and although there may well have been a strawberry as fragrant and fine as this eaten another decade before that, I cannot recall the taste of it today. Of that which I am most certain, however, is that it would also have been about a quarter the size.

The Balducci strawberry that I munched whilst strolling along a sunny Sixth Avenue was, as well as being so astonishingly delicious, also the most enormous strawberry I had ever seen; maybe about the size of a large fig? They were, furthermore, quite the most expensive strawberries I had ever purchased, too. A dollar each, to be precise, and though I may have paid five dollars for five of them, that day, the equivalent weight of UK fruit would have over-flown its punnet. But how on earth did they manage to make them taste so fabulous, goddamit?

They hailed from California, naturally. I definitely remember that. They are called 'long-stem strawberries' there. So they called them long-stem strawberries in Balducci's, too, and written as such on stiff, white cards in neat and swirly American script; you know, where even if there happens to be an 's' finishing a word, its little continuation tail usually used for linking up to a following letter still remains intact – almost coquettishly. Anyway, prominently displayed were these scarlet monsters, cosseted within tissue-bedecked trays head to tail fashion, just begging to be bought. And buy, we did.

That which deeply impressed me, however, was quite how the deep, rich red colour of each and every one became even deeper and richer tasting as one munched towards the core. And, of course, the famously spindly long stem also detached itself neatly and properly from its core as all the best behaved, properly ripe strawberries must. Their juice quite literally flowed at each bite – of which there were three! Their sweetness shocked the tooth, so intense was the surprise of it. Breakfast on the hoof has never been bettered.

In Paris, this June, I also bought strawberries. This time to eat on a bench in the Tuilerie gardens, sitting in the morning sunshine. These were delicious too; not *quite* as memorable as those American numbers nor, naturally, anywhere near as gargantuan, but equally, riotously red throughout the fruit with a sweetness and fragrance that further gladdened my already happy heart. They hailed – as almost all the first soft fruits do in that country – from in and around Provence, that particularly sunny kitchen garden of southern France. This variety is small and slightly elongated – the shape of a pear drop comes to mind.

But I do recall thinking that morning, intoxicated as I was by the rare beauty that surrounded my immaculate placement, that a beautiful strawberry has become equally rare, here. Just why is this so? I am sure it has been said before – in fact, I know it has – that the variety known as Elsanta is more than partially to blame for this. I have a sneaking suspicion that it was initially developed within the giant glasshouses of the Netherlands.

It seems to be that it is now almost impossible to find any other strawberry for sale (certainly in supermarkets) that is not Elsanta. Yes, they might s*mell* of strawberries when sniffed through several air holes which puncture the lid of their neat, plastic boxes, but this is merely a con in terms of content and eventual contentment, once the strawberry itself is consumed. The let down, then, is of such enormity, I really am quite staggered as to how the grower, the importer and the final supplier can all truly feel at peace with themselves over this hoodwinking behaviour. The shelf-life of the Elsanta strawberry, of course, remains second to none. How very nice indeed, for the shelf.

2007 – It seems that the Elsanta strawberry is now not quite so ubiquitous as it used to be. And, joy of joys, the enterprising Waitrose supermarket has recently been known to import that delicious French number I mentioned, the Gariguette, in early Spring. Will wonders never cease? Well done Waitrose!

Hot strawberry and almond pie

———

SERVES 4—6

My mum is the only person I have ever known who considered making a hot pie from strawberries. I have never forgotten it, either, as the fragrance of it, wafting from the Aga as it baked, has since remained indelibly fixed in my memory. As most fruit pies go, however, it was a messy old affair; juice ran everywhere (well it does, from strawberries, when heat is applied to them, which is possibly why many cooks see the idea as a non-starter in the first place) from within the pastry shell, dripping onto the oven floor of the Aga – which of course improved the smell no end – and the rest causing the pastry base to become quite sodden by it in the process. This mattered not one jot, to us, the family. And, I should say here and now, a soggy bottom has never tasted quite so good as that of mummy's strawberry one.

So, all of that having been said, the addition of ground almonds as a blotter of sorts, together with my recent understanding of how very sensible is the American style of introducing cornflour to a fruit pie, has now transformed mum's original into a very well behaved pie indeed.

You will need a loose-bottomed, deep tart tin measuring 20cm wide by 4cm deep for this, together with a flat baking sheet, which should be placed in the oven at the start of the proceedings to heat through; this helps the base of the pie to cook through more evenly.

for the pastry:
250g chilled butter, cut into small pieces
425g self-raising flour
pinch of salt
1 egg yolk
approximately 50ml iced water

750g fresh strawberries, hulled
75g caster sugar (reserve a scant tbsp for sprinkling over the crust)
1 flat tbsp cornflour
90g ground almonds
a little milk

Preheat the oven to 180°C/350°F/gas mark 4.

In a food processor, electric mixer or manually, blend together the butter, flour and salt until it resembles fine breadcrumbs. Tip into a large, roomy bowl and gently mix in the egg yolk and water with cool hands or a knife, until amalgamated. *Note:* I do think that, finally, this is the best way to bind pastry together: it doesn't get beaten to oblivion by machine and consequently results in light and crisp pastry. Put into a plastic bag and chill in the fridge for at least 1 hour before rolling.

Lightly grease the tart tin. Roll out two-thirds of the pastry into a circle, making sure to not make it too thin. Carefully line the tin with this, allowing a slight excess to flop over the rim. Chill this once more, for about 20 minutes. Now mix together the strawberries, sugar, cornflour and almonds in a roomy bowl using your hands, until all are well coated. Carefully tip into the pastry-lined tin and lightly tap down until settled.

Brush a little of the milk around the edge of the pastry that lies just above the rim of the tart tin. Roll out the remaining one-third of pastry, but to a slightly thinner degree than the base. Carefully lift onto the pie and, with your fingers, lightly press the two pastry edges together. Using a sharp knife, now cut through the joined edges almost flush up to the rim. Knock up the edges together, again with your fingers, to form a crinkled edge all the way around; you may also depress this edge with the tines of a fork should you feel moved so to do.

Brush the surface with a little more milk and then evenly sprinkle with caster sugar. Make a couple of incisions in the centre of the pastry lid to allow steam to escape, slide onto the baking sheet and bake for about 45–50 minutes, or until the pastry is pale golden, has an agreeably crisp surface and smells simply marvellous. If you feel that the pastry is browning too rapidly, loosely cover with a sheet of foil. Leave within the tin until luke-warm, before removing. Cut into wedges and serve with double cream.

Homemade, loose strawberry jam

MAKES AROUND ABOUT 1.5KG

The friend in whose Greek home I recently stayed is a whiz at making quick jams. These are not as sweet as most, mainly because she prefers her jams less sweet in the first place. It is that they may also then be utilised as something verging on almost a fruit compote to anoint, say, junket, rice pudding or *fromage blanc*. Or, of course, spooned over wonderful Greek yoghurt.

I had my own personal supply of a quietly superb apricot number, of which a jar had previously been placed inside the fridge of my very own kitchen previous to arrival. Neatly adjacent to my bedroom as this was, I happily spooned it over my cool yoghurt each and every morning I was there – and ate it all up within the week. Strawberries can work very well here too, given similar treatment. Have a couple of small saucers stored in the deep freeze, ready for testing the jam for the loosest set.

1kg fresh strawberries, the smaller
   the better, hulled and washed
750g granulated sugar
juice of ½ lemon

Using your hands, carefully toss together the strawberries, sugar and lemon juice in a large stainless steel pan. Leave to macerate for at least 2 hours, by which time the sugar should have dissolved somewhat. Place on a low heat and quietly allow the mixture to liquefy fully, the sugar and strawberry juices having now turned into a good, red syrup. Bring to a fast boil and cook hard for 5 minutes. Remove a teaspoonful of the syrup and place it on the chilled saucer. Push the liquid away from you with your finger; if the surface of it wrinkles very slightly, the jam is ready. If it does not, boil hard again for a few more minutes. Trial and error is the key, here. Allow to cool slightly, lift off any scum that has been generated with a sheet or two of kitchen paper and then decant into well-washed, glass jars. Seal, and store *this* particular jam in the fridge at all times.

Strawberry jam ice cream

SERVES 4

Childishly sweet, yet tasting intensely of strawberries. Think mushed-up Strawberry Mivvi – though you may well have trouble convincing today's children that such a thing ever existed.
Note: **Put a metal bowl in the freezer before you begin the recipe.**

300ml milk
½ vanilla pod, split lengthways
4 egg yolks

250ml double cream
150–175g strawberry jam (see page 179)

Gently heat together the milk and vanilla pod in a solid-bottomed pan. As it comes to the boil, give it a whisk so as to disperse the vanilla seeds into the milk. Cover, and leave to infuse for 20 minutes. Beat the egg yolks with a fork in a small bowl and then mix in a little of the milk to loosen them. Add this to the vanilla-milk mix, whisk together and then cook over a very gentle heat, constantly stirring with a wooden spoon, until the mixture has lightly thickened – do not allow it to boil. Take the chilled metal bowl from the freezer, pour the mixture into it and whisk thoroughly to cool quickly. Now whisk in the cream, too. Stir in the jam, pour into an ice-cream machine, then churn and freeze according to the manufacturer's instructions.

Strawberries
with vanilla ice cream
and crème Chantilly

—

Simply an assembly to finish up with. But, to my mind, an ice cream assembly that has rarely been bettered (yes, okay, chocolate sauce).

A singular scoop of the very finest vanilla ice cream in an individual, well-chilled glass bowl.

A veritable cloud of crème Chantilly spooned on top: very cold double cream hand-whisked in a very cold bowl with icing sugar and vanilla to taste until approaching a cumulous state.

Several perfectly ripe small, sweet strawberries precisely arranged on top, a scant dusting of sieved icing sugar and a silver spoon with which to eat it. Lovely.

RASPBERRY RIPPLE

Without the slightest hesitation, I know that my desert island dessert would be raspberries with vanilla ice cream. No question at all. It is as perfect a marriage of flavour and texture as one could ever wish for. There is just the right amount of interest to each mouthful, with the composure of the messed fruit and gently melting ice cream simply becoming better and better flavoured as one spoons it all about. In essence, a deconstructed raspberry ripple.

Along with many other school chums, the treat of a raspberry ripple ice cream was just about the best thing in the whole world. Those rivulets of very, very sweet raspberry coloured gloop (it really was not much more than that) snaking their way through a block of cardboard-wrapped Walls, was just marvellous. I was partial to the occasional Strawberry Mivvi from time to time, too. And a Jubbly. And that amazing, mad Heart thing. Never cared much for a Zoom, though.

I used to make my own ice-cream wafers, you know. Oh yes. Not actually bake the things you understand, just happily sandwich a thick slice of raspberry ripple from the block of Walls between two wafers. I'd seen it done dozens of times at Granelli's, the Italian ice-cream van on Bury market. Well, I think they were Italian. *All* ice-cream vans that don't say Mr. Whippy are vaguely Italian aren't they?

Anyway, it was in front of *la famiglia Granelli, gelateria di marchetta di Bury*, that I used to drag my scuffed Clarks quite a lot. 'It's no wonder they call you Hoggy at school!', my mother would say as she strode off towards the black pudding stall, with a straining Bodger (our dog) in tow who was very much looking forward to his veritable feast of discarded black pudding skins, licked from the ground around and underneath Jackson's trestle tables.

'A wafer, please. With red stuff?' I whispered hurriedly, standing on tip-toe. Well, that's what I used to call it, this bright red syrup from a squeezy bottle, but the nice woman high up there in the van, called it something else. It was a gabble, really. I couldn't understand a word she was saying. I didn't hear the words 'melba sauce', though, I'm quite sure of that.

These ice-cream wafers were constructed in a metal mould, exactly the size to contain the wafers. Held in the hand, one wafer would be put in the bottom, then filled with this delicious ice cream until it became all pointy, like a small hillock. Finally, the second wafer would be perched on this, the whole gorgeous thing tipped out with great deftness into a square of crinkly greaseproof paper and dribbled with red stuff. It was a bugger to eat; mess everywhere. I have always wanted one of those wafer makers in my kitchen. Still do.

I had an ice cream flavoured with lemon verbena once, at Michel Guérard's restaurant at Eugénie-les-Bains, in south-west France: *La pêche blanche, glâce à la verveine*. Don't you just get a huge thrill when you taste something so new and clever, for the very first time? Well, I do. But have you ever seen fresh lemon verbena? Perhaps some of you grow it in the garden. Most only know it as an herbal infusion, as dried leaves or sometimes in a dusty teabag.

I was in Nice recently, strolling around another market, this time in the Cours Saleya in the old town. I am now grown up enough to want to buy garlic and dried cèpes – and of the finest quality I have ever seen – rather than a dripping ice-cream wafer. Apart from anything else, we were on our way to the restaurant La Merenda, for lunch. But then I saw this lovely bunch of fresh lemon verbena. Well, several branches of it actually, sporting the freshest green leaves and a heavenly, almost oily lemon fragrance; it is also used in the manufacture of soap and bath oils, I am told. Anyway, I bought the lot.

Even though it had been wrapped in damp paper, by the time I returned with it to west London, the leaves had started to curl and desiccate a little. So I let the whole lot dry out on my windowsill in the sunshine. This only took a few days and I am now enjoying my very own, hand-dried, delicious lemon verbena infusions. But just before some of the very last leaves had shrivelled, I used them to make this unusually fragrant ice cream. It is quite superb with raspberries.

Lemon verbena ice cream

I first tried making this without using vanilla, as I thought it would detract from the verbena. Not the case. The verbena clearly seemed to blossom in flavour, once enhanced by the scent of the little black bean. I have since made more ice cream using the dried leaves and with some success, but, finally, the fresher the leaf, the fresher tasting will be this ace ice. *Note:* In the photograph, you may notice a few leaves in the ice cream. In retrospect, I have abandoned this idea as they simply get in the way of a luxurious mouthful. Flavour, not garnish, is all that matters.

350ml milk
a generous handful of lemon verbena
   leaves, massaged and torn with
   the fingers (if they are dried,
   crumble them)
½ vanilla pod, split lengthways
3 egg yolks
125g caster sugar
250ml double cream

Gently heat the milk, together with the verbena and vanilla pod. As it comes to the boil, give it a whisk so as to disperse the vanilla seeds into the milk. Cover, and leave to infuse for at least 1 hour. Beat the egg yolks with the sugar until light and fluffy. Strain the milk onto the egg yolks and whisk together. Pour the mixture into a heavy-bottomed saucepan and cook over a very gentle heat, constantly stirring with a wooden spoon, as if making custard. When the mixture has slightly thickened – do not let it boil – pour it into a metal bowl, or another pan (hot liquids cool quickest in metal), and stir in the cream. Leave to cool completely. Pour into an ice-cream machine and churn according to the manufacturer's instructions. Eat with lovely raspberries.

EX-CEP-TIONAL MUSHROOMS

The first time that I became aware of a mushroom called anything other than just that, was when I had decided to spend most of my very last two school holidays in the kitchens of a local French restaurant, La Normandie (at the time, one of the most highly regarded French restaurants in the land), in the hinterland of my home town of Bury, Lancashire. Having already decided, from the age of about 13 or 14, that cooking in a kitchen appealed to me more than anything else – whatever the school's career advisor might have kindly suggested – my erstwhile holiday homework was soon to be replaced by a far better, far more interesting mode of toil.

At La Normandie I poached some trout and I killed my first lobster. I learnt to bottle, cork-up and label imported French wine (direct from huge barrels) in a proper cellar. I was also allowed to mix several gin and tonics from behind a *real* bar counter and put money into a till that pinged. Furthermore, chef patiently taught me how to perfectly butcher a side of Scotch beef and separate it into its choicest (French) parts: the neatest rump steaks, immaculately trimmed *entrecôtes*, tender little fillets and fatty-edged, fatty-marbled ribs that were to feed two, once grilled until blackened and served with the most gorgeous Béarnaise sauce and *pommes frites*.

And then there were those funny little plastic bags full of what, quite honestly, resembled nothing more than bits of tree bark yet smelt strongly of pig styes; well, just think of this analogy the next time you open a bag of dried *cèpes*… These, in the early 1970s, had to be sent up from London by train (along with dried morels, *jambon de Bayonne*, good olive oil and vinegar) and, for me, were as exciting to open as any Christmas present – albeit vicariously.

And it was whilst using these *cèpes* that I also truly understood how to make a superbly rich cream sauce – unlike anything I had attempted to fashion at home, that's for sure. Would I be staying on at school to take my A-levels? Not a chance, ducky.

It was to be many years later, however, that I would see, marvel at and then finally eat my very first fresh *cèpe*. But as the occasion took place in Italy I should, strictly speaking, admit that it was to be *porcini* that were placed before my friend and I for lunch on that hot sunny day, high up on a mountain overlooking the Mediterranean. And, what's more, they were quite raw – but, my word, how staggeringly good they were to eat!

Salad of raw cèpes
with Parmesan
and olive oil

—

SERVES 2, GENEROUSLY

It is essential to search out the very best and freshest cèpes for the making of this dish, and with particularly firm stems. This is the only dish with which I am very happy to eat Parmesan in its shaved form; simply because this is essential to the success of the dish (sliced cèpes, sliced cheese), rather than as some cretinous, new-wave alternative to simply grating the stuff.

2007 – I am constantly perplexed – well, absolutely livid, to be frank – as to the absurdly popular fashion for making a perfectly decent risotto, finishing it with the traditional, final emollients of butter and grated cheese, vigorously beaten in and then – and then! – girlishly garnish a serving with these wholly inappropriate flaky bits. Grated cheese melts into the risotto as you eat, honey. Flakey bits just stick around. Hopeless. I really loathe rubbish like this.

juice of 1 small lemon
3–4 tbsp extra virgin olive oil
6–8 very firm and fresh, medium-sized
   cèpes, cleaned and very thinly sliced
Maldon sea salt and freshly ground
   white pepper

a few snipped chives
several shavings from a handsome
   wedge of fine Parmesan

In a roomy bowl, mingle together the lemon juice and olive oil until loosely amalgamated. Add the *cèpes* and loosely toss together with the seasoning, chives and shavings of Parmesan cheese. Spoon onto two plates.

Cèpes fried
with potatoes, garlic and parsley

—

SERVES 3—4

About 15 years ago, whilst cooking for Terence and Caroline Conran for a mid-autumn week in their beautiful house in Provence (just prior to the opening of Bibendum, so as to keep my knives good and sharp and torch on damp, as it were), they decided that it would be a nice idea to invite their friend Jean-André Charial, chef-proprietor of the nearby Oustau de Baumanière, in Les Baux, to dinner.

All at once, I was both thrilled and nervous at the very idea. 'I'm off to the market in Arles', I said. 'And *alone*!' (Terence has always been the most frustrating person to shop with in French markets, as all he does is drift off to other vegetable stalls, buying exactly the same lovely vegetables that *you* have bought, and then promptly arranging them all in lovely bowls on a long kitchen shelf when he gets home – where, of course, they look very nice indeed, until they go off, that is.)

So, having once found the most beautiful fresh cèpes in Arles market, along with some waxy La Ratte potatoes, I pondered how very good indeed they might be were they to be fried together – along with much garlic and parsley, *naturellement*. What turned out to be even more satisfying, though, was that Jean-André thought they were very good indeed and, furthermore, appeared to be something quite new to his vastly extensive repertoire. So, that was jolly nice.

200g fresh cèpes, cleaned and thickly sliced
200g cooked, peeled and sliced small, waxy potatoes
2 tbsp olive oil
salt and pepper
50g butter
4 cloves garlic, peeled, crushed and roughly chopped
2 tbsp freshly chopped parsley
a squeeze of lemon juice

Heat the olive oil in a large frying pan until moderately hot (a non-stick pan is good here, to prevent occasional sticking). Throw in the cèpes and potatoes, season and immediately start to toss them around in the oil, whilst also stirring briskly with the aid of a wooden spoon to both separate and nicely gild each component; this will take several minutes. Keeping them on a moderately brisk heat, now add the butter and garlic. Continue to fry and agitate the cèpes and potatoes whilst the butter melts and froths, so allowing the garlic to slightly cook and colour a little. Finally, stir in the parsley and squeeze in a little lemon juice. Serve up at once, tipped out onto a hot serving dish.

Omelette aux cèpes

SERVES 1

One of the finest of all omelettes. And, should you so wish to proudly garnish such a special omelette, save two perfect slices of fried cèpe to lay upon the finished dish. Well, *I* did...

3–4 cèpes, cleaned and sliced
a good knob of butter
salt and pepper

a scrap of garlic
a sprinkle of freshly chopped parsley
2 fine fresh eggs, beaten

Gently fry the cèpes in the butter (using, naturally, your favourite omelette pan) season them well and only stir in the garlic and parsley when they have begun to take on a light, golden colour from the heat of the pan. Now add the eggs in one go, whilst quickly and deftly lifting the solids up from the base of the pan into them (a palette knife is best, here). And then it's a 'lift and tip, lift and tip' action, so that the runny egg may find those parts of the pan where it may begin to set, until a perfect, semi-molten mass has been achieved, and with the *cèpes* only just tethered within.

To expertly complete the fashioning of the perfect omelette, tentatively tip the pan away from you whilst also lifting up the omelette's nearest edge with the palette knife; the omelette should now gently come together — helped along a little by the palette knife — and folding up as a plump, yellow bolster.

Potato soup
with porcini

SERVES 4—6

A few months prior to the publication of Ann and Franco Taruschio's cookery book *Leaves from The Walnut Tree – Recipes of a Lifetime* (Pavilion Books, 1993 – and what a working lifetime that surely was) – I happened to find myself in their kitchen. It was early one evening, just as Ann was spooning out small bowlfuls of this very soup for those who might fancy a taste.

The Walnut Tree was a unique restaurant in Wales, near Abergavenny, that they had opened 'in the bitter winter of 1963', but finally, sadly, they decided to retire from in February of this year. It was unusual to eat something there cooked by Ann, rather than Franco. But (forgive me, Franco) that potato soup with porcini remains as one of my most vivid memories of eating at the Walnut Tree. The recipe that follows is taken directly from their book.

2007 – It was February 2001 when Franco and Ann left their/our beloved Walnut Tree after 38 years. It still exists, but I'm afraid I have since found it difficult to return. So, I never have.

5 medium potatoes
2 cloves garlic
60g butter
salt and freshly ground black pepper
200g porcini, finely diced
1 cup single cream
1—2 tbsp finely chopped parsley
freshly grated Parmesan cheese
1 white truffle, shaved (optional)

Peel and roughly chop the potatoes, boil them in salted water with the garlic. Leave the potatoes to cook until they disintegrate. Pass the potatoes, cooking water and garlic through a food mill, return to the heat. Add half the butter, salt and freshly ground pepper. Beat the mixture with a balloon whisk; if the mixture is too thick add some more water.

A few minutes before serving, add the porcini mushrooms, which have been sautéed in the remaining butter, the cream and parsley. Check the seasoning. Serve with Parmesan cheese and shavings of white truffle, if available.

A GOOD EGG

I find it absolutely bonkers that the finest eggs I can buy locally, originate in Italy. I mean, for heaven's sake! What is the egg world coming to? These Italian jobs really do take the *biscotti*, but what a sad state of affairs it is, that when you want to eat a decent chucky egg, it is an *uovo Italiano*, and six of them will cost you £1.50. Why should it be that three of the simplest pleasures in life — silence, a filter-tipped cigarette and a decent egg — are now so very rare and expensive?

It has been noted by some, that the marigold colour of the yolks of these excellent eggs is, perhaps, a little too astonishing. But then were not the egg yolks one remembers as a *kinder* of a similar Kia-Ora hue? This was not, of course, an issue 30-odd years ago. It would have seemed unusual, to say the least, for my mother to approach Vincent (the farmer up the road), tap him on the shoulder and say, 'Hmmm, Vincent, the yolks of your eggs this week are all pale primrose instead of your usual deep orange colour. And, furthermore, the whites go all wishy-washy in the pan when you fry them. It just won't do! We don't mind bits of crap all over them, but I do expect a decent egg for Simon's brekky.'

Well, of course, she wouldn't have spoken to him like that at all. Apart from the fact that she was far too well brought up and rarely moved to make haughty outbursts (excepting the time when someone slyly slid into her bagged parking space outside Kendal Milne, Manchester, during the January sales). But as far as eggs were concerned, whether they were from Vincent, from Mr. and Mrs. Pearson at the Post Office or even from the village Co-op, an egg was just an egg. Just *always* a good egg. I even remember when eggs were sometimes gingerly placed into a brown paper bag instead of a pocketed carton. Rather that memory of the odd damaged shell, than a polystyrene six-pack of the stale and watery 'free-range' eggs today.

I am told these 25p eggs are organic by my local greengrocer (Michanicou Bros, 2 Clarendon Road, London W11; 020 7727 5191), who receives a twice-weekly delivery — although the supply can be spasmodic from time to time. Mind you, supply spasms, I think, are often a sign of creative produce. Irritating, but caring. So when I absolutely know they are the latest delivery, I snap up a dozen. Apart from anything else, even one week later, eggs as good as these are always going to remain fresher than most you will find elsewhere.

Onward… Now is the winter of our truffle; albeit waning, the final crops are often the pick of the Périgord black. The Alba white spore is hibernating for now, but, God willing and weather permitting, it might deliver a more generous harvest later this year. The 1998 offering was sadly below par, resulting in stratospheric prices of around £1,800 per kilo!

2007 – As you might imagine, or be fully aware, in more recent years the prices for both the white and black truffle has almost doubled.

There are worrying murmurs that the black truffle, too, may suffer a disappointing yield. At around £900 per kilo in Paris recently – admittedly at one of the more illustrious provenders, La Maison de la Truffe in the Madeleine – one of these set me back 50 notes. However, it generously 'truffled' a dozen organic Italian eggs, and there were more than enough shavings to cover six servings of very yellow, very tasty scrambled eggs. So that is £9 per plate, including the eggs, with a quid left over for French butter and brioche toast. Epicurially speaking, I don't see this as an extortionate amount, considering the magnificent treat it is to eat these rarities once or twice a year. I wonder, for instance, how much six ham-and-pineapple pizzas will set you back, plus service, at your local Pizza Hut? Mind you, I'd rather eat one of those less than once – in a lifetime.

You see, when you deposit one small black truffle amongst a clutch of eggs, seal the container and leave them to get to know each other for a few days, the alchemy of this pungent marriage is surely one practised in heaven. Even a truffle the size of a mint imperial will do the job, though you may only manage a dusting, rather than a shaving, of the thing itself. But be assured, the eggs will have captured its soul, imparted directly through their fragile shells by fragrant osmosis.

When I used to cook *œufs en cocottes* (eggs baked in small pots) in Pembrokeshire, in the early 1970s, they were, perhaps, thought of as 'interesting' by the often wary, local clientele; not quite foreign, but certainly continental. Eggs fried, boiled, scrambled or poached were seen as about it really. And their favoured method for the latter, I might guess, was using a special contraption especially made for the job in hand: the egg poacher. Now, this is held by some to be the most ridiculous of inventions. Well, I am not so sure. Why, pray, is it so terribly inadequate to be seen to steam a few eggs – for that is surely the process that takes place here? I don't have one, as it happens, as I like the taste of the vinegar I put in the water when I poach in the conventional manner. Cooking an egg in a buttered, small porcelain dish, resting in a bain-marie, surely amounts to the same thing. As long as it tastes good, and you are happy with your chucky egg, who honestly cares?

Without seeming to be infuriatingly contrary, these days I prefer to cook my little *œufs* in those shallow, eared, porcelain dishes. The reason being, that it is far easier to see how the eggs are coming along as they cook, in a wider vessel, than those that are buried in a deep little dish, submerged by a covering of warm cream – the essential lubricant for all egg dishes cooked in this manner.

Cooking
œufs en cocottes

The simplest form of all is to break one or two eggs into a well-buttered eared dish, season them and spoon over a couple of tablespoons of double cream. Bake for between 7 and 10 minutes in the oven, at 180°C/350°F/gas mark 4. Poke the thing with a tentative finger the first time you go about it, just to be sure that the white has set sufficiently beneath. You should be able to see when the yolk is perfect, sporting its strangely lilac-blue, opaque skin – an immediate indication to those of you who are familiar with the frying and basting of a very fresh, orange-yolked egg. So, that is the elementary baked egg, but here are some further embellishments:

Baked eggs with taragon

SERVES 2

It is best to do this one for a minimum of two people.

So, for two, first lightly butter the dishes and then put 1 tbsp tarragon vinegar in a small (preferably stainless steel) pan and boil until all but evaporated. Add a small knob of butter, several fresh tarragon leaves, 6 tbsps double cream and a little seasoning. Bring to a simmer, stirring, and then remove from the heat when slightly thickened. Spoon a little of this mixture into the dishes, break in 1 or 2 eggs and then cover them with the rest of the hot cream and bake.

Baked egg with spinach

Take a handful of small, young spinach leaves (the larger ones tend to be a bit butch here), season with salt, pepper and nutmeg and briefly fry in a small amount of butter until wilted. Arrange into the dish leaving a well in the centre. Break one egg into the well, lightly season it and spoon over 1 tbsp double cream. Set a sliver of butter on the surface and bake as before.

Œuf en cocotte
aux truffles

Perfume some eggs with a fresh black truffle in a sealed container and keep in a cool place for a minimum of two days. Rub the dish with a cut clove of garlic and smear with butter. Break one or two eggs into the dish, season and spoon over 1 tbsp double cream. Slip three or four slices of truffle into the cream and set a sliver of butter on the surface of the egg. Bake.

Œufs en cocotte pascal

SERVES 2

I have slightly adapted this truly delicious little egg dish, which originates from Elizabeth David's *French Provincial Cooking*. **It is one of the only recipes I like where grain mustard is the preferred condiment, as usually I'm a bit of a smoothie when it comes to the Dijon. Once again, for two people or more.**

Butter the dishes. Chop enough parsley, tarragon and chives (*fines herbes*) to give you about 1 tbsp. Melt a small knob of butter in a small pan and add a scrap of garlic. Over a thread of heat, allow it to flavour the butter for a minute or two and then remove it. Add 5 tbsp double cream now, together with the herbs and 1 scant tbsp mustard. Whisk until smooth, bring to a simmer and remove from the heat. Spoon a little of the mixture into the dishes, break in one or two eggs and spoon the remainder over the top. At this point, you may like to dust the surface with a fine shower of freshly grated Parmesan (not in the original recipe, but especially savoury if you fancy it). Bake, as before.

CREAMY CRUMBLY

✤

Once upon a time, I guess that one of the most important tasks relevant to the simple recipe instructions of 'sprinkling over' or 'stirring in' grated cheese to something baked, or the enrichment of a nice white sauce, was to first locate the grater. The cheese itself – its very name, its taste, its provenance – seemed of little importance.

In the fridge, in the kitchen of our house in Lancashire, it was always Lancashire cheese that we had. We all enjoyed eating this cheese and, therefore, were perfectly happy to grate it for cooking when the need arose. This was simply because it happened to be the particular cheese most widely available to us because of where we lived. Well, yes, Dad did, occasionally, veer *well* off course, indulging us from time to time to the odd tubular smoked cheese from the counter of the hugely suspect, recently arrived Polish delicatessen located at the edge of Bury market's perimeter. And Mum, wishing to also display a similarly independent spirit, would sometimes return from an outing to the food halls of Manchester's swish Kendal Milne department store with an under-ripe (but, of course) wedge of 'French' Brie or maybe – treat of all treats – a foil-wrapped cake of this gorgeous new stuff called Boursin.

So, it was forever to be lumps of Lancashire, in varying stages of higgledy-piggledy vintage and stored within a yellow Tupperware that remained the every day cheese of the Hopkinson family fridge. And, depending upon what Bury market had to offer at the time, that could have been anything from the wet and weeping curds of a crumbly/tasty or crumbly/mild Lancashire, to the slightly firmer wedges of the alternative choice of creamy/tasty or creamy/mild. Oh, the joy of such limited choice! And I really mean that.

Délices au Gruyère

SERVES 4

A delectable little Bob Carrier number here from *The Robert Carrier Cookbook* **(Nelson, 1965). Admittedly, a bit of a fiddle, but once popped in the mouth you will surely admit how worthwhile has been the small chore. A nibble it is not. This is a celebrated canapé.**

Note: **I would recommend making the basis of this dish the day before you wish to finish and serve it.**

75g butter
75g flour
400ml milk
150g grated Gruyère
salt, white pepper, grated nutmeg and
  a little cayenne

2 egg yolks
flour, beaten egg and breadcrumbs,
  for coating
oil, for deep-frying

Melt the butter in a solid-bottomed saucepan and, using a whisk, incorporate the flour until thoroughly blended with the fat. Continue to gently whisk whilst also allowing the fat and flour to amalgamate over the merest flame without colouring. Now, gradually whisk in the cold milk in a steady stream, still over a gentle heat, until the mixture begins to thicken. Once this begins to happen, replace the whisk with a wooden spoon or spatula and keep stirring for at least 5–10 minutes, or until smooth and very thick indeed. Add the cheese and continue stirring until it has fully melted into the sauce and all is glossy and very smooth indeed. Stir in the seasoning and remove from the heat. Leave to cool in the pan for at least 10 minutes and then ferociously beat in the egg yolks one at a time, once more using the whisk. Immediately pour into a clingfilm-lined shallow square or rectangular non-stick baking tin, smooth off the surface with a wet palette knife and then place another sheet of clingfilm directly across its surface. Leave to cool and then place in the fridge overnight.

For the final preparation, first have the oil in the deep fryer heated to a temperature of 180°C. Also, have some flour, beaten egg and breadcrumbs ready in three separate bowls. Now invert the (now) solid cheese sauce onto a work surface, remove one layer of clingfilm and cut little squares – 'délices', in other words – from it with a small, previously wetted knife. Fondle these with flour, then dip them into the beaten egg and, finally, through the breadcrumbs.

To cook, drop them into the deep fryer (say, 6–8 délices or so at a time) and fry for about 1–1½ minutes, or until golden and crusted and with just the merest indication of a minuscule pustule or two of their molten interior showing through their fragile, breadcrumbed coating. Lift from the fat and briefly allow to drain, then gingerly tip out onto kitchen paper. Eat at once.

DON'T MESS WITH ME, HONEY

The last time I talked of cooking scallops in this newspaper, I recall being torn off a strip by e-mail from an irate reader, as sent on to me from the offices of *The Independent*. To such an extent was their ire emptied upon me — along with quite astonishing ignorance, condescension and, most clearly, a strange, underlying pleasure – that it prompted a rare retaliation: I chose to publish the offending letter in full, on these very pages. And never have I received such a full postbag before or since. A magnanimous thank you, to every one who wrote in support.

The crux of the matter, in this case, had arisen simply because standards concerning quality produce that exist between one person and another so often differ, these days. And how! If I happen to come across scallop meat languishing in a plastic dish in its own liquid — as so often presented in this way at the supermarket fish counter — I will not buy them, however reasonably priced they might seem.

And it was surely a case of complacency ('I have decided to cook scallops whatever they look like' – which is not a quote) combined with – I mean, let us honestly face up to this once and for all – this increasing, lack of any integrity or knowledge by the majority of British food consumers, today. Maybe it was simply the reasonable cost of those sad scallops that had, finally, clinched the deal (though I doubt it, to be frank). Nevertheless, it was absolute failure. Angry reader. E-mail sent. All blame directed this way.

So, take note: Soggy, wet scallops sitting in a dish are not suitable for any of the following recipes.

Many recipes given over by folk such as myself and some of my peers, or those from the pages of books assembled by celebrity chefs, or even presented by a few television cooks (truly, as I write, I am listening to Jamie Oliver on *Woman's Hour*, glibly referring to 'five spice' as being an Indian condiment) simply will not work if you don't purchase with integrity. But, although I know full well that I will never be able to do all that naturally brilliant, visual cooking lark, if you so choose to, at least rustle up on your homework…

And, incidentally – and whilst in semi-rant mode – many communicators now supposedly associated with endless cookery advice seem seriously moved to suggest that almost *anything* one might need for assuring success with their given recipes may easily be obtained from the supermarket. Oh yeah? Oh, you mean in Haverfordwest? In Inverness? In Kidderminster? Even in Sainsbury's, Cromwell Road, London for example – its 'flagship store' – not only has leaf gelatine never been available there whenever I have tried to find it, but not one person on the shop floor has ever heard of such a thing. Too many items, perhaps? Too many shelves to even contemplate? Perhaps not nearly enough staff employed who haven't even the slightest, the very foggiest idea, as to what is on them. Those who (brilliantly!) assist in my local Costcutter (minimarket) will both follow me down the aisles and point helpfully or, if it is not in stock, will usually have it in by the following week.

As of this moment, they stock such things as vanilla pods, anchovy essence, both red *and* green Tabasco sauce, pickled walnuts, Roka Cheese Crispies (the finest cheese biscuit in the world), always a ripe Camembert or two and countless other essentials. I am, just now, working on the introduction of packets of leaf gelatine to these exemplary shelves…

This didn't used to be the case when I regularly ventured up to the streets of Soho of a Saturday morning (in the late 1970s and early 1980s) and frequent at least seven, family run, continental delicatessens who would stock such a thing. So I am immensely pleased to say that – for Londoners, at least – if you have recently had trouble finding leaf gelatine, look no further than the still-just-about-hanging-in-there Lina stores in Brewer street, where I was relived to find many packets of it – and purchased several on the spot, just to be sure. This Italian family concern that – against all the odds – continues to stay put (along with I Camisa, in Old Compton Street) can also provide you with several wafer-thin slices of the rare prosciutto crudo known as *culatello*. Try it.

Scallops grilled
in the shell
with
soy, ginger, spring onion, garlic and sesame oil

———

SERVES 2, AS A SUBSTANTIAL FIRST COURSE

Small and sweet-tasting, diver-caught scallops, are often sold within shells that measure no more than about 10–11cm at their very widest. Once prized open, and with the top, flat shell having been neatly freed from its insistently lively muscle (frisky, vibrantly live scallops can be the most determined of shellfish) by means of a sharp, flexible knife administered by a skilled fishmonger, and who should then thoroughly clean the same of all extraneous membrane that surrounds the primary muscle, yet still leave them attached to its curved, bottom shell, are essential to the success of this dish. As per usual, it all depends upon whether you are keen enough to search out such stalwart folk who will perform such a task for you. Mind you, it is the searching out of that taskmaster that is the most difficult, today.

Note: **You will also need 6–8 tbsp cheap, coarse, sea or rock salt to settle the scallops upon as you cook them.**

1 small piece of fresh ginger, peeled, thinly sliced and then cut into the thinnest strips
1 tbsp white wine or cider vinegar
1–2 tbsp sesame oil
10 small scallops, cleaned, and remaining attached to their shells
2 spring onions, trimmed and very finely sliced
1 small clove of garlic, peeled and very finely chopped
1–2 tbsp soy sauce (Kikkoman, for preference)

Preheat an overhead, radiant grill to its hottest temperature.

Soak the ginger in the vinegar in a small bowl and leave to macerate for at least 10 minutes. Spoon the smallest amount of sesame oil upon each scallop simply to coat them. Strew the salt over an oven tray to an even thickness and arrange the scallop shells upon it, scrunching them around so that they fit neatly and horizontally. Grill for no more than about 3–5 minutes, or until the scallops seem clearly stiffened and hot to the tentative prod of an index finger. Remove from the heat, strew with the spring onions and garlic and return to the hot glow for no more than a minute. Dress judiciously with a squirt or two of soy and serve at once.

Mousseline of scallops
with lobster sauce

—

I have noticed, recently, that several occasional food writers, restaurant reviewers and cookery correspondents now choose to refer to La Nouvelle Cuisine as having been nothing more than 'Minimalist French cookery' which '...sort of happened sometime during the 1980s... and should never have been taken seriously in the first place'. Little more than a passing *fol-de-rol*, in other words, cooked up in the campest of restaurant kitchens by bewildered amateurs who fancied (the word is key, in this context) running their very own restaurant.

Just the single, over-cooked scallop splashed with walnut oil vinaigrette and some tomato concasse, exactly centred in the middle of a huge, trellis-patterned Villeroy and Boch plate would – how shall we say – soon be seen as nothing more than *les vêtements nouvelles de l'Emporeur*. For this young man, however, it was to be La Nouvelle Cuisine that was, possibly, the most exciting way onward that a young, keen chef such as me wished to embrace at the time. But then I did, already, know how to cook the old stuff a bit, too.

As far as I can see, almost 20 years on, the very worst interpretations of La Nouvelle Cuisine then, continue to plague us today.

Note: It is important that everything necessary to fashion a fine, hot fish mousse (or from other fine textured meats; chicken breast, for example) should, previously, have been well chilled: this includes all components pertinent to electrical aids – processor bowl, blade, etc – as well as fish, eggs and cream. The simple reason for this is that the slightest increase of natural heat produced by excessive agitation alters the protein structure (and can also curdle the cream), so causing them to slightly 'cook' prior to their intended, gentle coagulation within their moulds. A granular texture to a cooked fish mousse is always a sure sign of this.

Note: I know that this is a laborious recipe, but it is well worth making simply because it is so very delicious to eat. Naturally, if you love to cook it will be a doddle.

for the sauce:

50g butter

1 tbsp olive oil

1 small onion, peeled and
finely chopped

1 clove garlic, crushed

1 small carrot, peeled and
finely chopped

¼ small fennel bulb, finely chopped

the shell debris collected from a
cooked lobster, roughly chopped

salt and pepper

1 scant dsp tomato purée

a generous splash of Cognac

a generous splash of port

1 small glass of dry, white wine

2 sprigs fresh tarragon, chopped

250ml whipping cream

a small squeeze of lemon juice,
to taste

for the mousseline:

200g cleaned, roe-less, very fresh,
very cold scallop meat

1 large cold egg, lightly beaten

250ml whipping cream, very
well chilled

1 rounded tsp fine salt

¼ tsp ready-ground (very finely
ground, in other words) white
pepper, taken from a newly
purchased jar

a little softened butter

To make the sauce, heat together the butter and olive oil and, in it, stew the vegetables until softened. Add the lobster debris, seasoning and tomato purée and stir in. Cook gently, and stirring frequently, for a few minutes more, or until the tomato purée has turned rust coloured and all is glistening nicely. Add the Cognac, port, white wine and tarragon and bring to a simmer. Remove any froth that has been generated from this infusion by occasional dabs from kitchen paper towels and then introduce the cream. Simmer ever so gently for at least 30–40 minutes and then strain through a coarse sieve –suspended over a clean pan – agitating the collected debris as much as you can with a wooden spoon, so forcing as much of its goodness through the sieve to collect below. Return this liquid (the sauce) to a moderate heat and return to a simmer. As soon as the inevitable scum appears on the surface, once more, deftly remove it with a spoon. Allow to reduce slightly, and to thicken, before correcting the seasoning and adding a touch of lemon juice to taste. Finally, pass it through a very fine sieve and put to one side; its ultimate consistency should be that of cold, pouring cream.

Making the mousseline, however, is immeasurably more simplistic. Put the scallop meat and egg into a food processor and purée until very smooth. Remove the bowl as one, and place in the freezer for 10 minutes. Attach to the machine base once more and then add the cream. Mingle together the fish and cream with a spatula to somewhat distribute the two, and then briefly process once more, until homogenised. Tip into a chilled bowl and thoroughly beat in the seasoning using a stiff whisk; you will notice, at this stage, that the mixture will noticeably thicken. Lightly butter 6 small, metal dariole moulds and fill with the mixture. Cover each one tightly with a circle of tin-foil and steam very gently (or placed in a *bain-marie* and baked in a moderate oven) for 20–25 minutes, or until firm to the touch and will leave no evidence of smears when a clean, sharp knife has been fully inserted into the cooked mousse.

To serve, carefully invert the mousse onto warmed, individual plates and then generously spoon the (re-heated) sauce over them.

Fried scallops
with
verjuice and chives

———

SERVES 2

If you happened to read my piece on 'verjuice' the other week, you will know all about this one…

2007 – Verjuice is lightly fermented grape juice and has a delicious sweet/sharp taste to it. If you can find some, one of the very best is that made by Australian, Maggie Beer. Good delis and some farm shops stock it. Or try the net.

125ml verjuice
a little oil
14 small, whole scallops, or 7 large
   ones cut in half horizontally

40–50g chilled, unsalted butter, cut
   into small chunks
salt and white pepper
1 dsp freshly snipped chives

Pour the verjuice into a small, stainless steel pan and simmer over a gentle heat until reduced by two thirds. Set aside. Heat the merest amount of oil in a frying pan and sear the scallops on each side until golden. Remove from the pan and arrange them onto hot plates. Add the reduced verjuice to the (used) frying pan, bring to the boil and begin to whisk in the bits of butter – and while also scraping up any residue exuded from the cooking of the scallops – until liquid and fat have fully emulsified. Finally, check seasoning, whisk in the chives and then carefully spoon over the scallops. Nothing more than some steamed, waxy potatoes as accompaniment here, I reckon.

Scallops poached in butter, milk and onions
with
parsley

———

SERVES 2, FOR A SUNDAY NIGHT SUPPER

A deeply English way of preparing scallops: a soft, lactic, sweet and sloppy sort of thing.

250ml full cream milk (Channel
   Islands is best, here)
50g best butter
1 small onion, peeled and finely sliced
2 cloves
2 blades of mace

1 bay leaf
a scraping of nutmeg
salt and freshly ground white pepper
10 small, cleaned scallops, shelled
1 heaped tbsp freshly chopped parsley

Gently simmer together the first eight ingredients for about 25 minutes, stirring occasionally. Turn off the heat, tip in the scallops and parsley and stir them around for a bit. Now allow the scallops and their liquid to both cook and cool, slightly. Tip into heated, shallow bowls and accompany this delicious fishy slop with thick slices of crusty baguette.

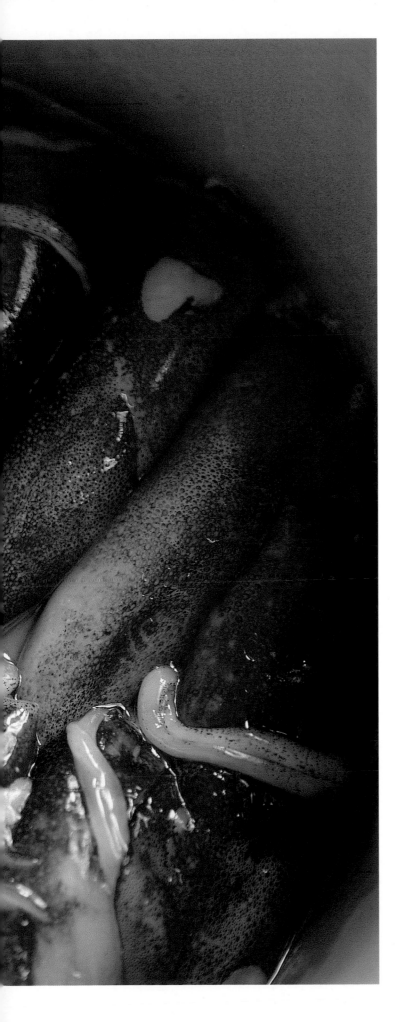

SQUIDS IN

At long last, it seems that spooky old squid is, albeit tentatively, entangling itself around the palate of the timid Britisher. Quite why it has taken us so long to fully embrace the versatility of this internationally popular cephalopod is bewildering to say the least. According to Alan Davidson, from information gleaned from his masterwork, *The Oxford Companion to Food* (Oxford University Press, 1999), squid is 'one of the major food resources of the sea and probably the most important of those which are not yet fully exploited.' Davidson then goes on to mention seven different species of squid, three of which are of the 'family *Loliginidae*' and are 'inshore creatures', whilst the remaining four, 'the family *Ommastrephidae*' prefer the depths of the ocean. And these are only two families out of a known dozen, but 'which (also) accommodate all the edible species'.

Astonishingly, this prolific family duo represents 'three-quarters of the world catch', with at least two of those seven species (*Loligo vulgaris* and *Loligo forbesi*) being common to the fishing fleets of the British Isles. To me, this presents a curious quandary: why is it that, when enjoying coastal holidays in Spain or Italy, the average true Brit seems deliriously happy to consume vast quantities of crisp, batter-clad rings of, respectively, *calamares* or *calamari* yet, once home, immediately reverts to the norm: 'Give us a nice piece of cod, mate and double chips while yer at it' – and as delicious a meal as I can ever think of, no doubt about that. Just why do we never do squid? There must be just squillions of them out there, just waiting to be hauled in. But, no, it's still cod or haddock.

2007 – Well, not now, it isn't, as everyone knows.

Apparently, and with regard to Davidson, once more, '…of the huge world catch' it is 'the Japanese market (that) absorbs about half of it'. At its very freshest – and the Japanese would not contemplate it any other way – squid sliced into ribbons and dotted with orange fish roe contributes as one of the most appealing features to a display of mixed *sashimi*. However, I have never eaten it cooked, as part of the Japanese repertoire. An altogether different kettle of cephalopod, however, are my experiences of Chinese cooking: I cannot recall the last time I ate Chinese food when squid did not appear in some form. The following three recipes are entirely influenced by happy experiences with squid, in the Chinese style.

Squid stuffed with minced chorizo
and baked with rice

—

SERVES 4

A wayward influence maybe, but this preparation actually stems from squid eaten as part of an excellent dinner at the restaurant Fung Shing, in London's Chinatown district. It may have helped that I was eating with Ken Hom at the time, but having returned on subsequent occasions it has rarely been less than absolutely bloody marvellous.

The dish in question involved squid tubes stuffed with pieces of wind-dried sausage, breadcrumbed and then deep-fried to a crisp. I have Europeanised the idea – well, Spanish-ed it, I guess – by using minced chorizo sausage meat as the stuffing and then braising the squid in olive oil, dry sherry and garlic. The addition of rice to the dish is entirely optional, as you might prefer to leave them as they are, serving the little darlings as a feisty first course.

16 small squid
3 tbsp olive oil
4 cloves garlic, peeled and chopped
4–5 mild red chillies
150ml dry sherry
rice (preferably Spanish *Calasparra*)
lemons

for the stuffing:
300g chorizo sausages, skinned
grated rind and juice of 1 small lemon
2 hard-boiled eggs, shelled and chopped
50 fresh white breadcrumbs
salt and a healthy pinch of cayenne pepper
2 tbsp freshly chopped parsley
4 tbsp double cream

Clean the squid by first chopping off the tentacles just beyond the eyes, making sure that they are attached to each other in one piece. Once removed, you will notice the tiny beak protruding; remove this if it is still attached to the cluster of tentacles. Under a slow running tap, remove the insides of the tubes, which are squishy and frankly messy, but are easily lifted out with a finger. Allow the water to run inside the tubes, so removing any trace of innards, including the weird and almost Cellophane-like cartilage. You will also notice two small outside fins towards the thinner end of the tube: do not remove these as they are perfectly edible and, furthermore, there is also no need to remove the thin, plum-coloured membrane. Dry the squid tubes and tentacles in kitchen paper whilst you make the stuffing.

Chop the chorizo sausage meat a little finer than it already is and then mix in all the other ingredients, mulching them together thoroughly using your hands. Using a teaspoon or piping bag, fill the squid tubes with the mixture and secure the ends with a toothpick, weaving it across the opening.

Heat the olive oil in a roomy pan and fry the garlic gently until just beginning to lightly gild. Add the chillies and cook for a couple of minutes more. Remove from the heat, lay in the stuffed squid tubes and tuck in the tentacles here and there. Increase the heat a little and pour in the sherry. Allow it to bubble up and around the squid, cover the pot with a lid and simmer, ever so quietly, for 30 minutes.

Note: If you do not wish to take the rice option, cook the squid for a further 15 minutes, or so and serve as is, with the delicious juices and pieces of lemon on the side.

Preheat the oven to 180°C/350°F/gas mark 4.

Carefully lift the squid out of the oily juices and put on a plate. Tip the juices into a measuring jug. The amount of rice you will need will be exactly half the volume, in weight, of this oily liquid (300ml liquid = 150g rice). So, tip the liquid back into the pan, stir in the rice and reintroduce the squid amongst it. Bring to a gentle simmer, slide into the oven, uncovered, and cook for around about 25–30 minutes; or until all the rice has been absorbed and the surface of the dish has become a mottled crust. Remove, put the lid on for 5 minutes and then spoon directly from the pot onto hot plates. A squeeze of lemon, once more, would not go amiss.

Fried squid

with chargrilled garlic

SERVES 2, AS A MAIN COURSE

It was at Poons restaurant (just around the corner, in fact, from Fung Shing), just off Leicester Square, where I first ate the dish that is now known to many of us addicts simply as 'squid-garlic'. I have been eating this astonishingly delicious speciality, all curly-crusted, hot and salty, ever since they opened (in 1982, I think, although the original Poon's, a bit further around that same corner, had probably been doing it long before that) and have never tired of it in all that time. Recently, the kindly Mr. Poon showed me how it was done, in his small basement kitchen. I was very much excited.

2007 – I was recently informed that this Poons has changed its name to China City. Mr Poon's grandson is now in charge, apparently – and they still do the squid-garlic if you ask for it!

400g cleaned squid (in this case, the larger the fish the better)

oil, for deep-frying (a thermostatically controlled deep fryer will give significantly finer results than oil simply heated in a pan, its temperature only guessed at)

a little salt and freshly ground white pepper

1 small egg white

3–4 tbsp potato flour (or cornflour, but the result is not quite as crisp)

to finish:

50g butter

1 large green chilli, chopped

2 cloves garlic, peeled and chopped

a tiny splash of rice wine (or dry sherry)

3–4 sprigs fresh coriander, leaves only, coarsely chopped

Slice the squid tubes lengthways, so revealing a flat pieces of flesh. Using the point of a small knife, make shallow criss-cross incisions across the inside surface (that was) of the squid, at approximately 1cm divisions. Now cut the flesh into small rectangles, roughly measuring 3cm x 4cm, but one need not feel too restricted here. Place the pieces in a bowl and lightly season.

Heat the frying oil to 350°F/180°C.

Put the egg white into a cup and stir with a fork to loosen its naturally jelly-like consistency, no more. Add the egg white to the squid and, mixing each element together with your hands, massage this slimy albumen over the pieces of equally slimy squid. Sift the potato flour into a roomy bowl and, allowing only a few pieces to drop at a time, constantly turn the squid through it as more are added. Once satisfied that all the squid pieces are well coated, tip them into a sieve and shake off any excess. Have the butter ready melted in a large frying pan, preferably one with curved sides, or a wok.

Fry the pieces of squid in the oil for no longer than 2–3 minutes, occasionally agitating the proceedings so that the morsels do not stick together, Once crisp, the slightest bit puffed up and exhibiting the merest trace of golden coloration around their edges, lift them out, vigorously shake and allow to drain for a minute or so. Up the heat under the melted butter until it begins to froth. Add the chilli and garlic, stir-fry it around until just beginning to colour and then introduce the squid. Briskly toss everything together over a fierce flame now so that all the ingredients become as one sizzling fry-up. Splash in the rice wine (or sherry), stir in the coriander and up-end the whole lot onto a heated serving platter. Eat at once, with a small bowl of chilli sauce on the side, for dipping.

Steamed squid dumplings
with sesame and coriander

SERVES 5–6, AS A FIRST COURSE

At a Poon's off-shoot, the rather soulless restaurant within the old Whiteleys department store, in Bayswater (now a re-vamped multi-floored shopping mall and cinema complex), my unearthing of how this particular kitchen makes their extraordinary cuttlefish cakes (one of many superb dim-sum served here; their cold collation of de-boned, spiced chicken feet is a revelation) was not quite as forthcoming as that of the previous recipe. A hint of, 'Yes, there is some cornflour', and, 'Egg white? Hmm... yeh. Egg white'. But, 'You have to beat the mixture a lot,' eventually seemed to be one of the most important steps. I am even more excited by the following result of my fiddling about and reading a few books. However, that which was originally fried, I have now steamed. And I made it with squid. I must take some in for them, the next time I need my chicken-feet fix.

2007 – I am reliably informed that this branch is no more.

100g pork back fat, diced

75g ginger, peeled and chopped

6 spring onions, trimmed of most of their green parts, chopped

2 cloves garlic, peeled and chopped

2 egg whites

500g cleaned squid, roughly chopped

1 tbsp sesame oil

3 tbsp chopped coriander

1 rounded tbsp cornflour

1 tsp salt

1–2 tbsp sesame seeds

for the dressing:

2 tbsp chilli oil

1 tbsp sesame oil

2 tbsp Chinese rice wine (or, at a pinch, dry sherry)

4–5 tbsp light soy sauce

2 tsp syrup from a jar of stem ginger

Put the back fat into a small pan and, over a very low light, allow to melt until the diced fat is transparent and surrounded by much of its molten excretion. Draw aside and hold at room temperature, but do not allow it to solidify. Place the ginger, spring onions, garlic and egg whites in the bowl of a food processor and purée to a fine paste. Suspend a sieve over a bowl and tip this mulch into it. Now, using a small ladle, force as much liquid as possible out of the fibrous matter to collect beneath. Rinse out the processor bowl, pour in this strained liquor and then tip in the semi-molten pork fat and squid flesh. Pulse for a few seconds to mix and then proceed full steam ahead until all is puréed as fine as possible. Finally, add the sesame oil, coriander, cornflour and salt and blend in with a final, brief whiz.

Note: The inherent texture of both squid and bits of pork fat does not allow itself to be fully broken down by whirling metal blades, however sharp they might be. In other words, just make sure that you do not overwork the mixture hoping for a silky-smooth paste; it just won't happen. And, furthermore, excessive pulverisation can only result in an overheated mixture, which is not a good idea at all.

Have the sesame seeds ready in a shallow dish. Decant the fish mixture into a bowl. Lightly dust your hands with cornflour, scoop out a little of the mixture, mould it into a ball the size of a large walnut and then roll one-third of its surface through the sesame seeds. Place on a plate, seed-side uppermost. Keep making dumplings until the paste is exhausted. Steam in batches, a dozen or so at a time arranged upon small plates, for 6–8 minutes – or until firm and bouncy to a tweak of the fingers.

To make the dressing, whisk all the ingredients together in a bowl. Divide the dumplings between pre-heated shallow bowls and spoon some of the dressing over each serving.

ENGLAND V FRANCE

I am never without a source of fine mustard. Furthermore, if ever I inadvertently find myself without, it will always be someone else's fault, never mine. Mustard is one of my most favourite things. In fact, if she were ever to ask that final, luxury question… 'Well, Sue, it's mustard, actually. (2007 – of course, it's Kirsty, now…) And could it please be the one from Dijon that comes in a pale putty-coloured clay pot, freshly decanted from a brass spigot from the gorgeous Paris branch of Maille, its boutique in the south-east corner of the Place de la Madeleine?

Also, when certain meals on the go are a little difficult to eat – you know, an airline lunch, a *recent* railway breakfast (the standard British Rail 'cooked' used to be excellent), a packed lunch arranged by a difficult Morecambe landlady – the application of a generous smear from a tube of Colman's mustard, can truly make your day: the pie in the sky becomes mildly palatable, those greasy sausages via Crewe are suitably enlivened and Mrs. Staticnylonsheet's meanly made ham sandwiches are helped (in this case only just) by an embrocation of Norwich's finest.

The following two recipes use mustard to the full, both as a driving force in flavour and also to form a quality of emulsion within the finished dish. Mustard has always enjoyed a lasting affinity with cream, luxuriating in its enriching balm. In fact, one of the simplest sauces of all is made by gently reducing some cream in a small pan until slightly thickened, then whisking in a spoonful of fine and smooth Dijon mustard at the very last moment, together with a squeeze of lemon and appropriate seasoning. This is an especially suitable lotion for spooning over slices of freshly boiled ham and boiled potatoes.

Veal kidneys
with
mustard and cream

SERVES 2

A classic French bistro dish if ever there was one; *Rognons de veau à la moutarde* **may possibly be eaten more regularly as a daily lunch dish by everyday Parisians than is some delicious, traditional liver and onions by Londoners. Why is this so?**

1 fresh veal kidney, excess suet and core removed and cut into chunks – or lobes, in fact, having taken care to respect the natural cleavages displayed over the surface of the kidney
salt and pepper
flour
40g butter

1 shallot, peeled and finely chopped
1 tbsp dry vermouth
2 tbsp port
1 tbsp Cognac (optional, but it does add character)
150ml whipping cream
1 level tbsp smooth Dijon mustard
a squeeze of lemon juice
freshly chopped parsley

Season the lobes of kidney and lightly dust with flour. Melt about half of the butter in a frying pan until frothing and briefly fry the kidneys until pale golden in places, for about 2–3 minutes; they should remain very rare. Suspend a sieve over a bowl and tip the whole pan-ful into the sieve. Put aside.

Add the remaining butter to the (un-cleaned) frying pan and gently stew the shallot in it until transparent and softened. Pour in the alcohols and reduce down until they have almost disappeared. Pour in the cream and bring to a simmer, whisking away the while and scraping up any debris and the shallots. Allow to thicken slightly and then whisk in the mustard. Return the drained kidneys to the pan, stir in and thoroughly coat with the sauce. Cook very quietly for a few more minutes until the kidney morsels have tightened up and stiffened a little when prodded with a finger. Do *not* overcook; they should remain pink within. Stir in lemon juice to taste and scatter with much parsley. Serve directly from the pan onto hot plates and eat with boiled potatoes.

Note: You will notice that some buttery/bloody juices will have collected in the bowl underneath that sieve. You *can* add them back to the finished dish, but this may result in a wishy-washy finish. If it's all the same to you, I usually just drink this delicious residue with a soup spoon.

Grilled fillet steak
with
mustard and tarragon butter

SERVES 2

Any grilled food cries out for savoury compound butters. When seen slowly melting over charred surfaces of fowl, fish and meat it quickly has the saliva dribbling. Mustard is a must with steak at any time and in the following recipe the one to use is the coarsely ground seed mustard, once more from Maille and called *Moutarde Fins Gourmets*; **not being a huge fan of very seedy mustards, this one is smoother than most and potent with it.**

2 fillet steaks
oil
salt and pepper

for the butter:
125g best unsalted butter, softened to
    room temperature
1 small clove garlic, peeled and
    chopped
1 tsp tarragon vinegar

4–5 sprigs fresh tarragon, leaves
    removed, chopped
1 rounded tbsp seed mustard
    (preferably *Maille Moutarde
    Fins Gourmets*)
½ tsp Colman's English
    mustard powder
scant ½ tsp salt
freshly ground black pepper

First make the butter. Put all the ingredients into the bowl of an electric mixer (or a food processor using the plastic blade) and beat together until smooth and homogenised. Dampen a sheet of greaseproof paper and spoon the butter onto it in the shape of a rough log shape. Roll up into a tighter log, twisting the ends to form a sort of Christmas cracker shape. Then roll this up tight using a sheet of strong kitchen foil, once again twisting the ends. Put to chill in the fridge.

Heat a ribbed stove-top grill until very hot indeed. Brush the steaks with oil and season them. Grill on both sides until the steaks are cooked to your liking. Put onto a warmed platter, cover with foil and leave to rest for 3–4 minutes. Place each steak onto hot plates, garnish with 2 or 3 discs of butter sliced from the log (any butter remaining will freeze well). Neatly place along the surface of each hot steak and serve. Chips and a green salad? Why ever not.

HAVING A GOOD GROUSE

I was told in mid August, and on good authority, that it will be a bumper season for grouse this year. 2000 seemed to be such a complete wash out that, if my memory serves me well, I only recall eating two grouse over the entire period. This year, I ate four between the 17th and 24th of August and each one was a beauty: plump, deeply flavoured, tender and, naturally, cooked to perfection. Oh, all right then, yes, by me.

Now, please understand, you must not look upon this self-congratulation as flagrant *braggadocio*. And particularly not so in this context. I mean, what could possibly be better than to suddenly receive advice from a very confident grouse roaster when you, yourself, are presented with such birds to roast and simply require a little direction. I used to do this sort of thing in a restaurant kitchen on a daily basis, but now prefer to do it here, at home. And, let's be honest, some further honing of domestic culinary skills can only be a good thing for all of us.

Nevertheless, it has been an immense pleasure to spend much time over the past 20 years or so learning how, exactly, a grouse behaves in a hot oven: as to when it is ready to go in, and when it must then come out. And what ought to happen – but is rarely considered essential – soon after that moment, too.

It is very interesting to note how the presentation of a grouse – or any game bird, for that matter – is now supposed to be handed over from game dealer to customer. Of late, this has caused me much anxiety, for I have recently been informed, on good authority, that the practice of supplying such birds in 'long-leg'

fashion (the important surfaces of the grouse – as in the eating of – having been fully plucked, but with the guts remaining intact and feet still sporting claws and with their 'socks on': a thin, furry coating of feather on lower leg) is, apparently, deeply frowned upon by the present day, British health police. Mind you, as to whether such an authority has, in fact, ever cooked, eaten or ever relished the very idea of consuming a perfectly roasted grouse, for their dinner is, of course, another thing altogether…

Here is a true story. Soon after we had opened Bibendum for business in 1987, and were first putting together the oyster van within the forecourt of the Michelin Building (originally, the 'Tyre Bay', into where motor cars would sidle up requesting pneumatic assistance) it so happened that, on one particular morning, an officious representative also happened to sidle up, questioning, quite reasonably, as to how our new operation would operate within the guidelines strictly set down by her received authority. After various exchanges over quite obvious do's and don'ts concerning this and that, she then pointed at something carefully arranged upon the crushed ice-strewn chilled shelf that had, at great expense, been fixed into the rear portion of a defunct, freshly-painted, deep-blue *deux-chevaux* van. 'What are those', she demanded. 'Those are oysters', I responded, levelly. One should not, however astonished by ignorance, ever make light of *any* question regarding food that is asked of one by such powerful folk.

Roast grouse
with bread sauce and
game crumbs

———

SERVES 20

2007 – **This is one of only two recipes in this book that have appeared in others I have written. The simple reason is that, in each case, the photograph taken by Jason was so marvellous, it seemed a shame not to include it. This one appears in** *Roast Chicken and Other Stories* **(Ebury Press, 1994).**

   I would much rather talk you through the method for roasting a grouse rather than present it in the more usual 'recipe' style. Conversely, those essential accompaniments – well, they are, for me – bread sauce and game crumbs appear as stricter instructions. So, without more ado, gamely read on…

Have your game dealer eviscerate two immaculately plucked young grouse on your behalf and further insist that he saves for you their hearts and livers, which should then be added to the final few minutes of roasting, briefly fried in the roasting butter until pink and then mashed together with a fork and spread upon crisp, bread croutes. Also request of him that you do not wish the birds to be trussed, or decorated – which, in my opinion, is all that it is – with a pointless, small sheet of pork fat in the British tradition; in terms of lubrication, it is simply plenty of hot, frothing butter that is needed to roast a grouse to perfection.

A tentative tethering of the bird's legs as they roast may, if you like (see picture), aesthetically enhance their final appearance on the plate. This can be achieved by simply passing a wooden toothpick through the thinnest part of each leg, its point then deeply plunged into one thigh to secure this temporary stricture. This neat trick – and easily applicable to briefly thrutching *all* small game birds (quails, too) during their subjection to high heat and sizzling fat – was passed on to me several years ago by Franco Taruschio, most lamentably, recently retired from his unique Walnut Tree Inn, near Abergavenny. As is usually the case with naturally inspired culinary folk, the thinking behind it is an altogether sound, practical and swiftly administered notion.

Pre-heat the oven to almost its hottest setting. Smear a little butter onto the base of a solid, preferably cast-iron, deep-sided frying pan or similar style stove-top dish that will also survive the heat from a hot oven; a Le Creuset, say. Lay the two

grouse upon the butter, brush the breasts with a little melted butter or oil and season liberally (the initial melted butter simply helps the seasoning to stick). Finally, top each bird with a further spoonful of softened butter. Slide the grouse onto the middle shelf of the oven and leave there for 10 minutes. Remove, baste generously with the – by now – frothing butter, and return to the oven. Roast for 5 minutes more, together with the livers and hearts, and baste again; incidentally, the most practical way of accomplishing this simple task is to tip the pan towards you, so facilitating a maximum capacity to each spoonful of hot, gently browned, butter to, once more, lubricate the roast.

By this time, the skin of the birds should, hopefully, have become agreeably crisp (and it *is* simply 'crisp', you know, rather than this continuous use of the absurd description, 'crispy') – and crisp grouse skin is just fine, as far as I am concerned. At this point, using thumb and forefinger, gently tweak each side of the two plumped-up breasts pertinent to each grouse with this familiar analogy firmly in mind: the bouncy spring of a freshly shelled, hard-boiled egg given exactly the same treatment. If the similarity fits, the roasting process is complete; if continuing to remain a touch soggy to the fingers, return to the oven for a few minutes more.

Once happy with the result, lift the grouse from the pan and place them onto a hot plate; *keep the roasting pan and residual fat*. Remove the livers and hearts and deal with them as previously instructed. Switch off the oven, leave the door ajar for a moment or two and then return the grouse to rest there for at least 10–15 minutes, the door remaining ajar.

In this state, the two grouse are now ready to be eaten. I used to think that some sort of gravy or some such manufactured moistening was *de riguer*, but now deem this to be quite unnecessary; correctly roasted and rested, the bird will exude its owns juices onto the plate as you dissect and eat it. The only other savoury accompaniments necessary – and which are, as I mentioned earlier, essential ones – consist of copious amounts of bread sauce and game crumbs; and that intensely livery croute, should you have chosen to assemble it, can only further enhance the assembly. Some sprightly sprigs of well-washed watercress, as token greenery are the only other garnish one needs.

Bread sauce

Naturally, more breadcrumbs are now needed for the bread sauce. For this, simmer together 400ml full-cream milk, 3 cloves, 2 bay leaves, ½ a chopped onion, salt and pepper and a thick slice of butter for a few minutes. Cover, and leave to infuse until needed (I would recommend a good 30 minutes). Heat through once more and then strain into a bowl containing 100g fresh white breadcrumbs. Stir together and keep warm over a pan of hot water. Depending upon your preference for a thick or sloppy sauce, add either more hot milk or bread. Check the seasoning before serving.

Game crumbs

Re-heat the pan of grouse-roasting butter over a medium flame and add to it 2 teacups of fresh white breadcrumbs. Season with salt and pepper and fry gently until all the butter has been soaked up. Allow to colour for a few minutes and then add a small glass of medium sherry. Once the frothing has subsided, you will notice that the mixture has become claggy. Don't worry. Turn down the heat and stir fairly constantly with a wooden spoon until lumps begin to collect. In time – about 20 minutes, or so – these will break back down into crumbs once more: the sherry has been driven off by evaporation, its flavour left behind with the butter, and which, in turn, has browned with the crumbs. All should be crisp and a deep, golden brown.

Salmi of grouse

SERVES 2

I have always understood the French style of cooking something *en salmi* (or, sometimes, *en salmis*) to refer to any kind of game – and sometimes ducks – that has been roasted, allowed to relax and cool slightly, carved into joints and its carcases then chopped up into bits to help fashion a rich, winey sauce. Diced vegetables, a little chopped bacon or cured ham, herbs, a relevant aromatic spice or two and a sprinkle of flour to thicken are then added until this unison – after about an hour's gentle simmering and then strained – will have transformed itself into a deeply savoury, deeply dark gravy. The jointed birds are then gently reheated in this until softened and tender, having been fully imbued by its unctuous qualities.

I also ought to mention that, whenever I make *coq au vin*, having once removed the joints from the carcase and fried them, I always then chop up the carcase and simmer it for at least an hour in a bottle of red wine, together with vegetables, herbs, etc., then strain off the wine over the chicken joints; I mean, it can only help to improve the end result, after all.

A grouse prepared in this way would hardly be likely to appear as a *recette particulière* in French cookery books, as grouse is distinctly particular to these islands. However, I really should point out that such a preparation will always be more deeply flavoured when made with old grouse (mature birds), rather than the young birds available just now. Choose your moment, is all I can advise. Furthermore, if you know your game dealer well, he really ought to be able to furnish you with the occasional brace of old birds for – relatively speaking – ready money.

2 cleaned old grouse, livers and hearts left intact
salt and pepper
4 thin rashers of streaky bacon
2 large, flat, dark-gilled mushrooms cut in half
a little softened butter
1 liqueur glass of Cognac
1 carrot, peeled and diced
1 stick celery, diced
1 small onion, peeled and diced

1 tsp tomato purée
1 scant dsp flour
½ bottle of full-bodied red wine
3 juniper berries, crushed
2 cloves
1 bay leaf
1 dsp redcurrant jelly

for a traditional garnish:
6 triangles of fried bread
a little freshly chopped parsley

Preheat the oven to 200°C/400°F/gas mark 6.

Season the grouse, place in a small roasting dish, lay two slices of bacon over the breasts of each bird and tuck the mushrooms alongside. Smear with the butter and roast for 20 minutes. Remove from the oven, baste and then return to roast for a further 10–15 minutes, or until the bacon has become crisp and the breasts of the birds are taut to the touch. Pour the Cognac over the grouse whilst the pan is still hot and ignite.

Once the flames have died down, remove the bacon and chop into dice. Lift the grouse from the pan and set aside to cool. Add the carrot, celery, onion, the livers and hearts from the grouse (chopped) and tomato purée to the pan and stew until the vegetables are tender and the purée has taken on a more rusty hue; stir in the flour and cook for a few minutes more. Pour in the wine, stir in, and then add the juniper berries, cloves, bay and redcurrant jelly. Carve the legs and thighs and breasts from the grouse and set aside. Now chop their carcases into small pieces with the aid of a heavy knife and add them to the winey stock. Bring everything up to a simmer, skim off any scum that forms and simmer for about 1 hour.

Strain the result through a fine sieve into a clean pan. Reduce over moderate heat until fully flavoured and lightly thickened, further skimming off any scum that forms in the process. Remove the skin from the jointed grouse and carefully re-heat in the sauce for 20 minutes, or so. Deeply dip an edge of each croute into the sauce and then into the chopped parsley. Garnish each serving of grouse with three of these. A bowl of buttered, boiled potatoes would be appropriate here, I think.

RABBITING ON

The cooking and eating of domestically reared rabbits in domestic kitchens throughout this country is so woefully neglected that I often wonder if anyone could honestly admit to knowing what they actually look or taste like. Not surprisingly, therefore, the only ones one sees for sale – decent, fat, pink-fleshed critters – are those imported from France.

I first came upon such fine examples many years ago in Arles market in Provence, whilst staying with Terence Conran. 'Bring back some rabbits from the market for lunch, Simon – they are *fantastic*!' I distinctly recall him demanding as I set off down his chestnut tree-lined drive. 'I will get a fire going so you can cook them when you get back…' And what rabbits they turned out to be.

The market itself was a revelation: noisy, bustling beyond belief, cheerful, sunny, deliriously smelly and astonishingly colourful too. There were possibly about ten different stalls selling rabbit (amongst many other things), with each and every specimen as good looking as its neighbour. And although this made choice difficult, it also hammered home to me there and then that here was shopping of the very highest order. I mean, *every* single rabbit as good as the other? Furthermore, the same dilemma occurred when choosing beans, leeks, tomatoes, herbs, butter and so on and so on, goddamit…

So, why are we all these years hence – especially considering how (apparently) demanding, knowledgeable and picky we have become – still so absolutely useless at making markets? But then we have such gorgeous supermarkets instead, don't we. Whilst we have a kitchen drawer stuffed to bursting with flimsy plastic bags, the French housewife has a capacious, woven shopping basket hanging on the back of the door, always at the ready.

2007 – Getting a little bit better with some good farmer's markets now, but still miles to go…

Once our lovely rabbits were safely home I set about jointing them up at once. These should be flavoured as simply as can be, I thought, as I chopped, trimmed and jointed: wild thyme, rosemary and fennel from the hillside (I had already spied these and smelt their heady odour the day before), garlic, a squeeze of lemon juice, seasoning, a little local olive oil and the ends of a few bottles of wine that were hanging around. That was it. Onto the fire after an hour or so's marinating and there we had it.

I have never seen Terence quite so excited with lunch since that sunny day in his French garden. It's about time that I cooked it again, I guess. But I often wonder that those Arles rabbits were not some of the very best cooking I've ever managed. Terrific fire, of course, thanks to TC.

Note: Any self-respecting French housewife would not be seen dead asking that her rabbit be jointed by the stall holder or butcher; she just knows how to do it as a matter of course. There is no reason why this should not be the case here too. Here is how to go about it:

How to joint two rabbits – about 2kg each:

I have purposely chosen to give you two whole rabbits to play around with. These will provide you with five full dishes using every single bit of both of them. Once jointed, you can pop the relevant pieces into sealable plastic bags, squeeze out most of the air, zip them up and freeze for later use. Clearly, however, I suggest that you get on with the brawn straight away as freezing is not exactly practical here and, anyway, once made it will keep, well covered or wrapped in the fridge for 10 days or so. Lovely to have around for an instant first course or a snack with buttered toast.

So, with all that said, here goes:

If the head is still attached, remove it with a hefty blow from a heavy knife. Now cut off each of the shoulders, which are only attached by muscle rather than a joint. Chop off the tiny, spindly extreme joint from each one. Cut straight through the ribcage, about halfway along, around about the point where the meaty saddle part nearest to the (now dismembered) head is tapering off; this is quite clear if you look closely and feel around. Feel around inside the ribcage for the heart and lungs and pull them out, whilst also removing the liver and kidneys – together with most of their attendant fat – from the saddle. Put all these into a roomy pot with the ribcage, neck part, the two tiny shoulder joints and put to one side (you

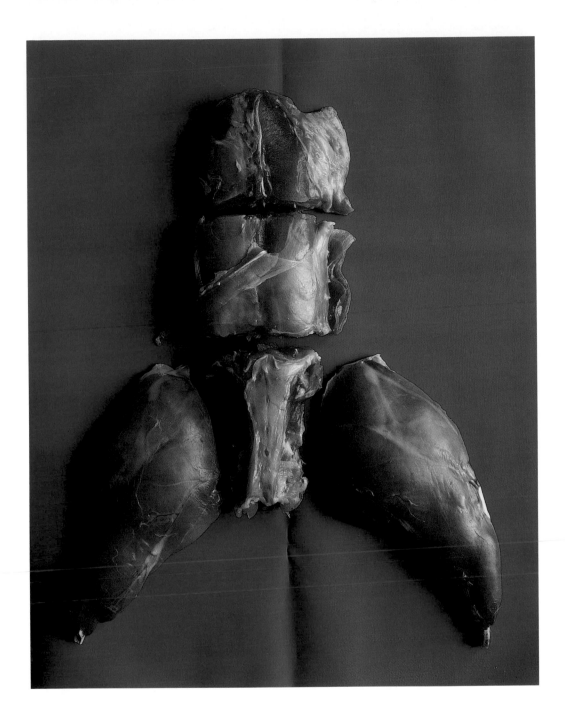

may add the head to this too if you wish, but hew it in two and wash it well first).

Now then, turning to the leg end and with the rabbit's back uppermost, make an incision around the curvaceous part of each leg, revealing as you so do, a sort of pointy and bony central extremity. As you carefully cut down and against this to remove each leg, a neat and obvious ball and socket joint will soon show up on either side. Cut through these to detach each leg. Now, once again, with a heavy blow from the knife, remove the pointy bone (it's pelvic bone, in other words) where this *other* end of the saddle meat stops – and more abruptly this time. If it helps, just think of that area where you place your hands of a morning, immediately above your buttocks, soon after you have got up. You have that stretch, stick out your tummy and moan about the lumbago…

We're getting there. Add the severed pointy bit to the other bits and bobs in the pot. Remove the membrane that adheres to the saddle using a sharp knife, lifting it off in thin strips but without cutting into the meat itself: sort of pierce, lift and separate, if you like; this takes a little practice, but you should get the hang of it quite quickly. Also, remove the majority of the four flaps which extend from the sides of each saddle and add to that roomy pot. So, we should now have four shoulders, four legs, two saddles and a large pot-full of carcase, offal and remnant flesh. Time to proceed.

Rabbit brawn with herbs

———

MAKES ENOUGH FOR ABOUT 12 SERVINGS

To attempt do this jellied rabbit thing reminds me of watching Japanese chef Ikeda (in his eponymous restaurant in London's Brook Street) trim all the flesh from a newspaper-wrapped package of cooked salmon bones. Whatever you might think, the result of all this toil is fantastically worthwhile.

to cook the rabbit:
the pot-full of trimmings and offal
   from both rabbits (approximately
   1.5kg in weight)
1 small pig's trotter, hewn in two
   lengthways by the butcher
150ml white wine
100ml dry sherry
100ml Madeira
1 litre water
400g pork or bacon fat, cut into
   large pieces
2 carrots, peeled
2 onions, peeled, one of them stuck
   with 3 cloves

3 sticks celery
3–4 sprigs fresh sage
3–4 sprigs fresh tarragon
1 whole head of garlic, sliced in half
   horizontally
3 tbsp tarragon vinegar
a little salt

to finish the brawn:
1 tbsp chopped tarragon
4 tbsp chopped parsley
a generous grating of nutmeg
1 heaped tbsp Dijon mustard
plenty of freshly grated white pepper

Preheat the oven to 150°C/300°F/gas mark 2.

Add all the other ingredients listed in the cooking of the rabbit to the pot and gently bring up to a simmer. Religiously skim off all scum that rises to the surface before covering and placing in the oven. Cook for about 1½ hours, or until the meat is falling away from the rabbit bones and from the trotter. Drain into a capacious colander that you have suspended over another pan and leave to drip for 5 minutes. Pass this liquid through a fine sieve into a clean pan and leave to settle for a further 10 minutes.

Now remove all traces of fat from the surface with a ladle and place in a small bowl. Put to one side. Reduce this cleansed stock over a gentle heat until reduced by about two-thirds, continuing to remove any scum that is generated. Leave to cool whilst you deal with the meats and fats. Once these are cool enough to handle, pick out the bits of offal and fat and then strip every single scrap of meat from all bones. Place all of this onto a chopping board, roughly chop using a big knife (*do not use a food processor*) and place into a large bowl.

Now mix all the ingredients for finishing the brawn into the chopped meat and stir in the reduced stock. Taste for salt (you may not need very much at all) and tip into a large terrine dish or large bowl. Smooth the surface using a spatula dipped into hot water and place in the fridge for about 1 hour to begin to set and firm up. Remove, spoon over some of the reserved fat just to cover and return to the fridge to fully set. Do not eat for 24 hours, but when you do, slice it thickly directly from the terrine and serve with hot buttered toast and gherkins.

Braised rabbit legs in red wine
with
smoked bacon, chilli and orange

———

SERVES 2

So inspired was I by chef Stephen Markwick's way with a dish of squid, recently, that I thought a similar preparation might work very well indeed with rabbit and — gadzooks! — it surely does.

2007 — Stephen and Judy Markwick have since sold Markwick's Restaurant, in Bristol. They now have a much smaller place in Clifton called Culinaria, but serving up the same, quite delicious food, naturally.

1 very thick strip of smoked streaky bacon or pancetta, cut into cubes
½ tbsp olive oil
2 rabbit legs
salt and pepper
a little flour
splash of Cognac
2 small oranges, the zest removed from one in pith-less strips (use a potato peeler) and the juice squeezed from both
3–4 small red chillies
½ bottle of full-bodied red wine

to finish:
1 scant tbsp freshly chopped parsley
2 strips pith-less orange zest, finely chopped
1 small clove garlic, peeled and finely chopped

Using a small cast-iron pot, heat the olive oil and fry the bacon in it until golden brown all over. Remove to a plate and reserve. Season the rabbit, dust with flour and quietly fry in the olive oil/bacon fat mixture until nicely gilded all over. Add the Cognac, light with a match and swirl the pan around until the flames have subsided. Strain in the orange juice and add all but 2 pieces of the orange zest. Simmer gently, turning the rabbit legs around from time to time, until almost all of the orange juice has evaporated and the mixture looks a bit sticky.

Now introduce the chillies, return the bacon and add about a third of the red wine. Continue to braise the legs and bacon over the merest heat, whilst also allowing the wine to reduce somewhat before adding more. Once all the wine has been incorporated and the legs are looking deeply dark and reddened, they will be cooked; this entire process should take around about 40 minutes, or so. To complete the dish, mix together the parsley, orange zest and garlic and sprinkle over the rabbit. Very good indeed eaten with some soft polenta.

Lapin à la Dijonnaise

———

SERVES 2

This preparation is possibly the best known and most beloved of all French rabbit dishes. All at once creamy and piquant with the joints of meat succulent and richly bathed in copious amounts of the sauce.

2 rabbit legs
salt and white pepper
25g butter
2 shallots, peeled and chopped
150ml dry white wine
100ml dry cider
200ml whipping cream
2 dsp best Dijon mustard
squeeze of lemon juice, to taste

Preheat the oven to 170°C/325°F/gas mark 3.

Season the rabbit. Put the butter into a pan, set onto a healthy flame and, once hot, add the rabbit pieces. Sizzle gently, letting each side gild before turning over. Once golden all over, remove to a plate and set aside. Tip out all but a spoonful of fat and add the shallots. Cook until pale golden and then pour in the wine and cider. Allow to froth up, then simmer until reduced by half. Reintroduce the rabbit and simmer again. Cover and put into the oven for 40 minutes, turning the rabbit over once.

Remove the rabbit from its cooking liquor and, once more, remove to a plate, shaking off any clinging bits of shallot. Strain this liquor through a fine sieve into a bowl, then return to the (rinsed out) pot. Bring up to the boil and further simmer a little until lightly syrupy. Pour in the cream and simmer until custard-like in consistency. Whisk in the mustard and add the lemon juice to taste. Return the rabbit, simmer for about 10–15 minutes and serve up with some plainly boiled, buttered and parsleyed new potatoes.

Slow-braised rabbit shoulders

with white beans and parsley

———

SERVES 2

A deeply comforting dish, this one. It is to the shoulders of a rabbit that one should look for the most succulent and tasty meat. Here, it falls away from the bone in the most agreeable fashion and it matters not one jot if some of the beans disintegrate somewhat during the cooking, for this also serves to thicken the juices. Jason decided this was the star dish of the five entrants.

120g dried haricot or white kidney beans, soaked overnight in plenty of cold water
4 tbsp olive oil
4 rabbit shoulders
salt and pepper
½ tsp coriander seeds, toasted and lightly crushed
8 cloves garlic, peeled
2 bay leaves
100ml dry sherry
300ml water

Preheat the oven to 150°C/300°F/gas mark 2.

Drain the beans and wash thoroughly. Drain again and reserve. Heat 2 tbsp of the olive oil in a heavy bottomed cast-iron or terracotta pot (*cazuela*), season the rabbit and gently fry on all sides until lightly gilded. Add the coriander seeds and garlic and mingle around with the rabbit until they, too, are moderately coloured. Introduce the bay leaves, sherry, water and the washed beans. Stir all together and add the remaining 2 tbsp of the olive oil. Cover and cook in the oven for about 1–1½ hours, or until the beans are soft and the rabbit is tender and soft. A meal in itself; a green salad if you must.

Quick braised rabbit saddles

with lemon, rosemary and white wine

———

SERVES 2

This last offering is the simplest one of all and is exactly what it says. The flavours are fresh and immediate, what sauce there is comes about from a neat emulsion of oil, wine and exuded rabbit juices with the only other accompaniment then needed being a dish of creamed potatoes with which to eat it.

2 rabbit saddles, trimmed of sinew
salt and pepper
2–3 tbsp olive oil
2 glasses of white wine
3–4 sprigs fresh rosemary
juice of 1 large lemon

Season the rabbit and quietly fry in the olive oil using a roomy, shallow pan, until pale golden all over. Add 1 glass of the white wine and the rosemary. Partially cover and allow to simmer gently until almost all the wine has evaporated; about 10–15 minutes. Turn over the saddles and add the remaining glass of wine together with half the lemon juice. Continue cooking, this time uncovered, for a further 10 minutes and until the juices have mingled nicely and the meat is firm to the touch. Finally, add the remaining lemon juice. Remove the saddles to a chopping board and carve the meat from the saddles (not forgetting the small fillets from underneath too). Serve up onto two hot plates and strain the juices over the rabbit.

LONG LUNCH

The following four-course lunch I have in mind for Monday is based upon the simplest and most accessible of ingredients. Furthermore, the soup, the prawn salad and the apple pie may all be made the day before, then only *just* warming the pie through to enjoy it at its best. All in all, I reckon that here is a Bank Holiday lunch to suit all the family – and a thoroughly enjoyable one to prepare, too.

Simple cream of vegetable soup

SERVES 8 PLUS

This deeply satisfying and tasty soup is based upon one that I first learnt to make as a keen young apprentice at The Normandie, the renowned French restaurant near Bury, Lancashire (as it was then) when I toiled there during a couple of school holidays in 1970. We used to make it in a huge French pressure cooker, which, once its whirring and spluttering valve began to spin and spout steam, cooked the soup in just 25 minutes. About 50 servings, I guess, would result after much mulching through a giant mouli-légumes, careful sieving, seasoning and the all important smoothing of cream finally introduced to bring it all together. This somewhat reduced recipe also makes plenty, albeit of domestic dimensions, as seconds will surely be asked for.

Note: **Please don't be tempted to liquidise this particular soup, as I always find that it turns to gloop.**

½ packet of butter
2 onions, peeled and sliced
4 large cloves garlic, peeled and crushed
3 leeks, white part only, sliced, washed and drained
2 carrots, peeled and diced
4–5 tender and white celery stalks (taken from the heart of the vegetable)
200g white button mushrooms, sliced
2 courgettes, peeled and diced
4 ripe tomatoes, sliced
2 bunches of watercress, roughly chopped, stalks and all
salt and pepper
2 medium-sized floury potatoes, peeled, diced and well washed
2 litres good chicken stock (vegetable stock may be used, but I don't believe it will make as good a soup)
approximately 400ml whipping cream

Melt the butter in a large pan and add the next nine ingredients. Season generously. Allow the vegetables to wilt and begin to stew whilst also stirring occasionally, for about 15 minutes. Once they are all sloppy and juicy-looking, put on a lid and allow to cook ever so gently for about 25 minutes, once again, stirring from time to time. Now add the potatoes and stock and bring up to a slow simmer. Remove any scum that appears on the surface and then continue simmering for a further 20 minutes without the lid.

Pass through the finest blade of a vegetable mill (*mouli-légumes*) into a clean pan, whilst also making sure that every last vestige of juice and liquid has been extracted from the resultant mulch. Now pass through a common or garden round sieve back into the (well rinsed out) original cooking pan, using the back of a ladle; do *not* use a fine sieve, as this will hold back too many necessary solids essential to the soup's final consistency. Quietly re-heat and stir in as much of the given cream until you are happy with both consistency and richness. Adjust seasoning and serve up in heated soup plates. Good bread and butter rather than croûtons here, I think.

Chopped egg
and prawn salad
with
anchovy and English salad
dressing

SERVES 4

Although all the ingredients for this salad are familiar friends with each other and also with you, I remain well chuffed with this particular interpretation. Furthermore, its inclusion here as a light and frisky middle course neatly negates any need for further vegetable accompaniment (apart from the essential potatoes) to the principal dish. And how nice that is.

Note: Waitrose sell 'squat lobster tails' in 200g tubs (100g drained) and I find them absolutely fine for this collation. You may, of course, use prawns as originally stated.

200g drained (and lightly squeezed of excess moisture) prawns or squat lobster tails
4 small hard-boiled eggs, shelled
8 anchovy fillets, chopped
a spoonful or two of mayonnaise
a few shakes of Tabasco
a little salt

for the dressing:
1 hard-boiled egg yolk
1–2 tsp malt vinegar
1–2 tsp English mustard powder
1–2 tsp soft brown sugar
100–150ml whipping cream
salt and freshly ground white pepper

to garnish:
12 tender lettuce leaves, taken from the heart and washed, drained and dried
4 spring onions, trimmed, washed, sliced in half lengthways and immersed in a jug of iced water until ready to use
half a small cucumber, peeled and sliced
1 small carton of mustard cress

Coarsely hand-chop the prawns/lobster tails and eggs together on a chopping board (a food processor will reduce them to a paste in no time) and put in a bowl. Add the anchovies and stir in just enough mayonnaise to merely bind the mixture together. Stir in the Tabasco and check for salt.

To make the dressing, I suggest that you employ the use of your own personal taste buds here, the immovable egg yolk excepted. Mash the yolk in a small bowl using a fork or small whisk until well broken up. Now add just a little each of the vinegar, mustard and sugar and whisk together until smooth. Introduce some of the cream and a little seasoning and then taste it; the end result should be a good balance of sweet and sour. Play around with all of these until you are happy with the result.

Pile the prawn and egg mixture into the lettuce leaves and put on plates. Garnish with the other salad bits and hand the dressing separately at table.

Pot-roast chicken
with potatoes, bacon, garlic and thyme

———

SERVES 4

As fine a one-pot dish that I know. Just watch the family's noses when you remove the lid at table.

50g butter

2 tbsp olive oil

1 fine quality free-range chicken – about 1.5kg dressed weight, with giblets if possible

salt and pepper

130g cubed pancetta or other bacon

12 cloves garlic, peeled and left whole

2–3 generous splashes of vermouth

1 kg potatoes, peeled and cut into large chunks, washed

5–6 sprigs fresh thyme

300ml good chicken stock

Preheat the oven to 150°C/300°F/gas mark 2.

Using a deep, lidded cast-iron pot (an oval Le Creuset is ideal, here) first melt the butter with the olive oil. Season the chicken all over and inside and then slowly brown all its surfaces in the fats, turning the bird over and around, for about 15 minutes. Remove to a plate and add the pancetta and garlic to the pot. Allow both to sizzle and gild slightly and then pour in the vermouth, which will froth and splutter. Introduce the potatoes now and turn them through this fatty residue with a spoon until well coated. Stir in the thyme sprigs and stock and return the chicken to the pot, burying it deep amongst the potatoes. Bring the whole affair up to a bubbling simmer over a low light, put on the lid and transfer to the oven. Cook for 1–1½ hours, certainly until the potatoes are very tender indeed; the chicken itself will also be well cooked, but that is how it is meant to be in this particular instance. Serve directly from the pot at table, carefully lifting the chicken onto a hot serving dish for jointing up. Spoon some of the potatoes – together with copious amounts of juices – around each serving.

A surprisingly fine apple pie

—

SERVES 4

We have never followed the American tradition of adding a modicum of starchy thickener to the filling for a fruit pie. I don't know why this is. Perhaps we worry that it might turn out as something offered up by Mr Kipling. Well, it won't, trust me.

Note: You will also need a loose-bottomed tart tin measuring approx. 20cm wide by 4cm deep.

800–900g Bramley apples, peeled and then, using a sharp knife, the flesh sliced off from them in small pieces and dropped into a bowl
5 cloves
juice of 1 small lemon

175g golden caster sugar (25g of which is used to sprinkle over pastry top after brushing with milk)
1 tbsp cornflour
25g softened butter
375g puff pastry
a little milk

Preheat the oven to 180°C/350°F/gas mark 4, together with a flat baking sheet.

Mix the apples with the cloves, lemon juice, 150g of the sugar and the cornflour. Set aside. Lightly grease the tin with the butter. Roll out two-thirds of the pastry to line the tin (don't make it too thin), allowing for a slight excess to flop over the rim. Tip in the apples – which might look too many but, be assured, they will flop down as they cook – and lightly press them down with your hands. Now brush a little milk around the edge of the pastry, roll out the remaining one-third of pastry, but to a slightly thinner degree than the base. Carefully drape it over the

apples and, with your fingers, lightly press the two pastry edges together. Then, with a sharp knife, cut through the joined edges almost flush up to the rim, knock up the pastry join to form a crinkled edge all the way around and decorate with the tines of a fork. Brush the surface with more milk and evenly sprinkle with the remaining caster sugar. Make 3–4 incisions in the centre of the pastry lid to allow steam to escape.

Place the pie on the baking sheet and cook for 20 minutes. Then reduce the temperature to 150°C/300°F/gas mark 2 and continue to cook for a further 35–40 minutes, or until the piecrust is well stippled with semi-caramelised sugar crystals and that there is also clear evidence of burbling, golden apple juices erupting from within the pie, both through the central vents and around the edges too. Mind you, it is the intoxicating smell, above all, that tells you the thing is ready. Leave to cool to luke-warm before un-moulding. Clotted cream is lovely with this.

SLOPPY VEGETARIANS

If I was forced into being a vegetarian for the rest of my life, I suppose it would not be the end of the world. As long as I had access to those Indian restaurants where some of the very finest vegetable dishes are prepared, I would be quite happy. And, furthermore, some of these are so very good, one forgets they are 'vegetarian' at all. The alternative option – and a worthwhile chore – is, naturally, to cook them for yourself using the correct ingredients, now more readily available than ever before, in supermarkets and the more discerning grocer. Depending on where you live, there are also long established Asian stores, which, once upon a time, were the only outlets where you would be able to find a green chilli, let alone a single leaf of fresh coriander.

I was in Drummond Street the other day, just behind Euston road near the station. I had not been there in years. Here, in small, personally run family grocers (if only there remained native versions of these in every high street in the land), you will find everything you need to make Indian dishes in the comfort of your own home. Smiling proprietors of these are so helpful too, and hugely interested and excited by one's enthusiasm.

But, you see, the real reason I was up in Euston, was that I had this sudden desperate need for samosas. And it was to the Diwana Bhel-Poori House that I was drawn to, for it was here, as far as I remembered, where you could find the finest vegetable samosas in London. Their branch in Westbourne Grove in west London (now, sadly, closed) was where I used to roll up and demand a take-away brown paper bag of nine (they are sold in threes like *dim sum*) together with a couple of polystyrene pots of the essential rusty-red tamarind sauce – a sort of Asian ketchup – for dipping. Potatoes mixed with marrow-fat peas wrapped-up in pastry has never tasted better.

On another occasion, south of the river, this time, at the wonderful Kastoori restaurant (also vegetarian) in Tooting, south London, where an extraordinary tomato curry this place makes is so very, very good, I was inspired to have a go at making one of my own. Anyway, Kastoori's is fantastically good, creamy yet oily and refreshingly sharp and fragrant. Unique and unforgettable. I hasten to add that the following version is a humble effort to reproduce the dish and, I suspect, is possibly nothing at all to do with the way the Thanki family assemble their particular masterpiece. However, I thought that I should have a go, just for the sake of making such an interesting and unusual vegetable curry in the first place. Well, it did turn out nicely, tasted as authentic as I had hoped and Jason's photo certainly seems to capture the right look. Hope you agree.

Tomato curry

SERVES 4

40g butter

2 cloves garlic, sliced

50g fresh ginger, peeled and
coarsely chopped

1 large hot green chilli, chopped
(remove seeds if you like)

6–7 curry leaves (optional – but
they make a huge difference, so
try and search some out)

1 tsp ground cumin

5 cardamoms

10 tomatoes, cored and split in
half horizontally

salt

75g creamed coconut dissolved
in 5–6 tbsp boiling water

squeeze of lime juice, to taste

freshly ground black pepper

Melt the butter in a heavy-bottomed shallow pot or frying pan. Add the garlic,
ginger, chilli, curry leaves, if you have some, cumin and cardamoms. Allow the
spices to gently stew in the butter before laying the tomatoes upon them, skin side
down. Lightly salt their surfaces and spoon over the coconut cream. Loosely cover
and set upon an extremely low light (use one of those heat-diffuser pads if you
can). Much of the juices from the tomatoes will flow out and form a 'sauce', helped
along by the creamed coconut. When this is coming along nicely, baste the
tomatoes with the sauce so that the coconut becomes nicely amalgamated into the
whole. When the dish is ready – about 30 minutes – the tomatoes should have kept
their shape and the sauce will be slightly separated but creamy in parts (if it seems
too dry, simply add a little water). Squeeze over the lime juice and grind on the
pepper. Best served at room temperature as a first course or to accompany some
devilled chicken perhaps.

Spinach, coconut and lentil dhal

SERVES 4

A sloppy soothing dhal is one of my very favourite things to eat. I can eat bowls and bowls of it when the need arises, comforting the soul and filling the tummy with a warm glow. There is also something very, very satisfying over making a pot of food that is so absurdly cheap, too; matters of pence. Once again, the following recipe is a bit of an amalgam of favourite memories from eating good Indian vegetarian specialities. The can of coconut milk is a touch controversial, but it works superbly well here, giving the finished dish a lovely creamy, rich texture.

250g onions, peeled and finely chopped
75g butter
4 cloves garlic, peeled and thinly sliced
1½ tsp whole cumin seed, roasted
1 tsp whole black mustard seeds, roasted
4 cloves
2 tsp ground turmeric
½ tsp chilli powder
200g split red lentils
400ml water
400ml coconut milk
3–4 thick slices of fresh ginger, un-peeled
450g fresh ripe tomatoes, peeled and roughly chopped
250g fresh leaf spinach, washed, trimmed and roughly chopped (the prepared bags from supermarkets are ideal here)
plenty of freshly ground black pepper
juice of 1 large lime
1 tbsp freshly chopped coriander
2 tbsp freshly chopped mint
1 tsp salt

Fry the onions in 50g of the butter until pale golden. Add half of the sliced garlic and the whole spices and continue to cook gently for a further 5 minutes. Stir in the turmeric and chilli powder until well blended, and cook for a couple of minutes. Tip in the lentils and add the water, coconut milk, ginger, tomatoes and spinach. Bring up to a simmer, add the pepper and cook very gently, stirring occasionally, for about 30–40 minutes, or until the lentils are tender and have all but dissolved into the liquid.

Remove the pan from the heat. Melt the remaining butter in a small pan. When it starts to froth, throw in the rest of the sliced garlic and stir around vigorously until it starts to take on a little colour, and the butter starts to smell nutty. Immediately tip into the lentils and stir in (there will be spluttering, so watch out). Add the lime juice, the coriander, mint and salt to taste. Cover with a lid and leave to mellow for 10 minutes before serving, remembering to remove the slices of ginger before you do so. Eat with hot and fresh flat bread, such as naan.

TRICKS OF THE TRADE

One of the wonders of the professional kitchen – and which can never be fully realised in domestic terms – is the endless reliance on 'back-up stuff': intense little essences and powerful reductions, savoury relishes and stuffings, purées and pastes, divers derivative lubricants and juices so usefully generated by the initial cooking of something else entirely – not to mention all varieties of savoury stocks. One only has to afford a cursory glance over some recently published restaurant cookbooks to note how necessary it is to have access to such aids; often, so much so, that one finds it necessary to first master the glossary at the end of the book – the 'see page 293' syndrome and countless other pages of that ilk – before you may even so much as *attempt* the original recipe in question. The instruction 'first read the recipe' in cases such as these is not so much good advice as absolutely imperative.

Two of the following four recipes – 'parsley and garlic purée' and 'duxelles' – fit into this category perfectly. The simplest, homemade chicken broth may be transformed into something quite extraordinary when a spoonful or two of bright green, pungent garlic and parsley purée has been whisked into it at the last minute. This can then also be further enhanced into glorious richness by the addition of a little beaten egg yolk and cream as a liaison, gently re-heated and served up with enormous pride as '…Oh, you know, it's just a little soup Gerald and I like to call our very own.'

This purée may also be spread upon a fillet of fish or the ubiquitous chicken breast before being baked in the oven. Stirred into the resultant winy cooking juices from a big pot of *moules*, it is a revelation. When a few smearings are judiciously spread upon some freshly opened oysters, the same then briefly grilled under a fierce heat, the aromatic result might even tempt the most wary of oyster eaters (large Spanish mussels treated in the same way is yet another option). Simply spread upon a length of split baguette and baked on the top shelf of a hot oven will produce a garlic bread of perfection previously unknown to the remainder of the planet.

Parsley and garlic purée

—

MAKES ABOUT 200ML

Note: **The secret here is the triple blanching of the garlic cloves, which reduces their pungency to a soft and mellow sweetness; almost more onion-like perhaps, but retaining the distinctive whiff of its bolder cousin.**

1 large bunch of flat-leaf parsley, leaves removed

30 large cloves garlic, peeled

250ml light chicken stock

salt and pepper

Bring a pan of water to the boil and tip in the parsley. Cook for no more than a minute or two, quickly drain in a colander and cool thoroughly under cold running water whilst running also your fingers through the leaves to speed up the process. Squeeze out excess water in a clenched fist and then further desiccate within the folds of a screwed up tea-towel. Set aside.

Put the garlic cloves in a pan and cover with cold water. Bring to the boil and drain. Repeat, twice. Return the garlic cloves to the pan, pour over the chicken stock and finish cooking the garlic until very tender and the consistency of the stock has also become nicely syrupy. Tip all into a food processor or liquidiser and add the reserved blanched parsley. Add seasoning and purée until very smooth indeed. Decant into a suitable container that may be sealed (a Kilner jar would be ideal here) and store in the fridge until needed.

Mushroom duxelles

—

MAKES ABOUT 250—300G

One of my earliest tasks as a 16-year-old apprentice chef in the most precise of French restaurant kitchens was to make duxelles for *Coquilles St. Jacques*. Chef Champeau was inordinately proud of the fact that several of his regular customers would always be able to tell as to whether it had been chef, himself, who had made the duxelles, or if the job had been farmed out to someone such as *moi* (this was to be one of his milder put-downs you'll be thrilled to know): the finesse of the chopped shallots, the wafer-thin dimensions of the sliced mushrooms, the bravery of seasoning and the correct amount of reduction of wine and juices resulting in just the right consistency between too sloppy and too dry was, apparently, that which those sycophantic Lancashire businessmen and dreary wives were referring to. Excuse me? In 1970? Near Ramsbottom? But to learn is to have wept over a pan of chopped mushrooms, that's all I'm saying. (*And* they drank copious pints of mild and bitter after dinner *and* their wives 'partook' of the occasional Creme de Menthe a la frappé... I kid you not.)

Anyway, once these 'perfect' duxelles had lined the scallop shell, they were then topped with thinly sliced scallops, fondant béchamel, a little grated Gruyère, a fine sprinkling of dried breadcrumbs – it took me simply ages to get the 'sprinkle' just right – and then baked in the oven until bubbling. And, you know, for me, this remains as one of the most delicious of all scallop dishes, even though many smarty-pant cooks now regard it as a buried dish. Tossers.

Duxelles are also the traditional stuffing spread over and around a fillet of beef before being baked in puff pastry. And, once again, that ubiquitous chicken breast can be quietly transformed by a modicum of duxelles either slipped under the under the skin or stuffed within, before being finished in a simple white wine and cream sauce.

And then there is Michel Bourdin, the legendary chef of London's Connaught Hotel who uses duxelles as part of possibly his most famous creation *Croustade d'œufs de cailles Maintenon*. Here, two impossibly light and buttery pastry boats courageously carry a particularly refined version of this fungal filling, but whose further cargo then involves four *precisely* – and that description has never been more emphatic – soft-boiled, peeled quail's eggs. Finally, all is coated by an immaculate hollandaise sauce. The knife goes in, molten yolk bursts forth (quite ruining a particularly favourite tie of mine on one memorable occasion), duxelles splurge and pastry crumbles. Gastronomic history at its finest.

2007 – Michel Bourdin finally hung up his *torchon* in December 2001, after 25 years of service to one of London's finest and most traditional of hotels. I have only been to eat once since Bourdin left. I miss the old days hugely. The *consomme en gelee* 'Cole Porter' remains as one of the finest examples of haute cuisine that I have ever experienced.

4 large shallots, peeled and chopped

50g butter

350g button mushrooms, chopped,
   stalks and all

salt and pepper

2 tbsp port or Madeira

150ml dry white wine

squeeze of lemon juice

1 tbsp of equal amounts of freshly
   chopped tarragon and parsley

To make the duxelles, fry the shallots in the butter until golden and add the mushrooms. Season and stew together until fairly dry and with any juices from the mushrooms having been driven off. Add the Madeira and wine and simmer until the alcohols have reduced to almost nothing. Squeeze in the lemon juice, add the herbs and then briefly work in a food processor using the pulse button, until the mixture becomes an evenly coarse purée; it should not be too smooth.

Sauce soubise

——

The very word *soubise* – **just say 'sooo-beeze' – seems to instantly suggest smooth and silky, warm and enveloping, soft and soothing; gastronomic balm of the highest order, I guess. It would be quite wrong of me to suggest that this sauce/purée is as useful as a kitchen aid as the previous duo, but it most certainly possesses a remarkable quality in its own right. Sauce soubise is as voluptuous a sauce or purée it is possible to think of. No other vegetable quite so magnificently, so generously, so very helpfully homogenises so very well as that of a mass of buttery, over-cooked onions.**

Sauce soubise also emerges as so wonderfully pale and creamy. But, apart from its use as a splendid sauce (it caresses lamb as if forever a case of first love), soubise can also play a useful role as a stored pot of instant goodness in the fridge of the vegetarian cook: whisked into a vegetarian stock for soup along with an egg yolk for added richness. Treat it as an ingredient.

100g butter
3 large onions, peeled and chopped
salt and freshly ground white pepper
50ml white wine vinegar

100ml dry white wine
400ml whipping cream
2 bay leaves

Melt the butter in a roomy pan and add the onions. Season, and allow them to stew quietly, uncovered, for at least 30 minutes, or until very soft and melting. Stir occasionally and be careful not to allow the onions to catch or colour. Add the vinegar and continue to simmer until there is no trace left of any liquid, be it naturally exuded onion juices or vinegar. Now add the wine and similarly simmer away, but this time arrest the cooking a few minutes before the wine has fully evaporated. Now pour in the cream and add the bay leaves. Finally, bring the mixture to a final simmer and leave to stew for about 20 minutes, stirring from time to time. Once again, don't let the sauce catch; use one of those heat-diffuser pads if you have one.

The penultimate look should be a mass of thickly creamed onions. Pick out the bay leaves and tip the whole lot into the goblet of a liquidiser (a food processor can almost do the job, but you won't get the velvety smoothness that is achieved using a liquidiser) and purée until extremely smooth. Pass through a fine sieve into a small pan, check the seasoning and use as desired.

Skordalia

ENOUGH FOR A SMALL POT - FULL

Originally, I had planned on presenting just the three recipes for this piece, so I guess the following offering is a bonus. I know *skordalia* has made an appearance before, but I thought I would just keep it in reserve in case I hadn't enough to say about the other three… And, what's more, skordalia is able to hold its own alone. It needs nothing more than a crisp slice of cucumber, a cool radish or a stick of celery, to make it sing out loud.

50–75g slightly stale, white country bread, crusts removed and torn into bits
150ml warm milk
1–2 scant tbsp red wine vinegar

2 cloves garlic, peeled, cut in half (green germ removed if prominently green) and crushed to a paste with salt
pepper
about 75–100ml virgin olive oil

Soak the bread in the milk for a few minutes until spongy. Squeeze the excess milk out with your hands and put the bread into a food processor with the vinegar, garlic and pepper. Pulse this poultice, adding the olive oil in a thin stream, until thick and paste-like; try not to overwork the mixture, however, as you want to retain a little texture of the bread.

MIXING MEMORIES

As a fresh-faced teenage cook, I will always remember Mum telling me how she had scrimped and saved over many months to collect the necessary cash (nursery school teaching, I think it was) to furnish herself with one of the very first, very exciting electric food mixers, newly manufactured by the hugely innovative Kenwood company. All I know is that it was an enormous benefit to my earliest, culinary exploits.

Although the arrival of the Kenwood mixer must have been around about the close of the late 1950s I, myself, cannot recall the exact moment when this new-fangled apparatus actually appeared as a permanent feature of our kitchen. I know that it lived on a work surface by a sunny corner with a window and adjacent to the dripping bowl. There were utensil drawers below and its attachments lived in one of these, just above the dog's basket. As to what might have been kept in there before the mixer arrived, I haven't the faintest idea.

There might well have been nothing, of course. Kitchens, after all, were quite the plainest of household rooms in the 1950s. Any paraphernalia then was restricted to a hand-cranked mincer, a rolling pin, one or two wooden spoons, a rusty sieve, a corrugated implement for chopping carrots, less than several stout knives and — which remains one of my most favourite culinary toys to this day — the miniature lawn-mower-like contraption with a dozen tiny sharp wheels which crushed and pulverised parsley rather than chopped it. However misguided might have been the thinking behind its efficiency, I can only say that the flavour of Mum's delicious parsley sauce remains fixed in my memory forever.

When not in use, mum's brand new Kenwood mixer was always well tucked up and protected by a black and white, Gingham cloth affair that she had personally cut out into a pattern and stitched together to fit the machine; yes, people did that sort of thing in those days. I mean, the dust!

Only last Christmas, in fact, I easily forced left-overs through its 40 year old (at least!) mincer attachment to make rissoles for Boxing Day. *And* I remembered to put some stale bread through at the end, to both add bulk and bind to the mix and also clear the machine of all traces of lingering meat, just as Mum had originally taught me to do all those years ago. And this wasn't simply a case of post rationing thrift, it was, and remains, nothing more than common sense.

Of all the most useful operations that the Kenwood managed, however, was the ability to beat up egg whites into a stiffness that, previously, would have been seen as completely inconceivable to the domestic cook. Only hand whisking and a stiff elbow, as demanded by professional hotel chefs, would previously have come anywhere near to the mechanical endurance of the domestic whirring of a Kenwood motor. Sometimes, truly, we do not know how lucky we are.

Le Mont Blanc

———

SERVES 4

My life as a hugely glamorous food writer occasionally requires that I am required to respond to all manner of interesting gourmet questions asked of me by my adoring public. This could take place at a Chelsea wine and cheese party, for example, or while mingling amongst the euphoric recipients of a post 'Fresh Soup' awards party. In fact, it would not surprise me at all if someone even chose to sidle up to me on my occasional bus route between Barnes and Hammersmith Broadway, begging of me that I should gastronomically enlighten them in some exciting fashion.

Constantly prepared that I am for such a confrontation to actually take place, have no doubt that I will be well prepared with diverse intelligent and creative responses to any query that may happen to come my way. As an example, a particularly well rehearsed discussion over how much I dislike chestnuts has long been honed to perfection, all ready and waiting for the inevitable '...And finally, Simon, is there, perhaps, anything in cookery that you absolutely loathe?'

And chestnuts, in every possible way, were always there as the instant answer (just secondary, that is, to the taste of honey, the thought of ever even *thinking* to make a vegetable stock, not bothering to remove the spiky end of a French bean before cooking or serving a new potato with skin remaining attached). Until recently, that is. Until I ate the Mont Blanc as served at the Angelina tea rooms, on the rue de Rivoli, Paris.

After much work, I do believe that I have now finally come quite close to emulating this remarkably delicious confection of sweetened and puréed chestnuts, whipped cream and meringue in the privacy of my own kitchen. And I do hope you will like the results; let's face it, for something to convert me to liking chestnuts, this must be worth eating.

Note: The contraption I used for achieving the essential 'worm-like' look for the classic Mont-Blanc (see photograph on previous page) may be purchased from good kitchen shops. In the professional kitchen this is known as a potato 'ricer'.

for the meringues:
4 egg whites
pinch of salt
225g caster sugar
a little softened butter
plain flour

for the chestnut purée:
275g cooked chestnuts, puréed until perfectly smooth
1 x 250g tin sweetened chestnut paste (*crème de marrons*)
1 tbsp icing sugar
1 dsp natural vanilla extract

for the whipped cream:
300ml double cream (very cold)
1 tbsp caster sugar

Preheat the oven to 140°C/275°F/gas mark 1.

Using a scrupulously clean mixing bowl, whip the egg whites with the salt until soft but able to hold a peak. Beat in half the sugar, a tablespoon at a time, until glossy and stiff. Now fold in the rest of the sugar, using a large spatula with authoritative scoops rather than mimsy movements; the air must be contained, but the sugar does also need to be thoroughly mixed in.

Lightly grease a flat baking tray with the butter and sift over a spoonful of flour. Shake around a bit to disperse the flour in an even coating and then tap off the excess (the kitchen sink is the most contained area and affords the least mess). *Note:* I have *always* found this coating to be the most effective non-stick method, however arcane you might think it to be.

Spoon out the meringue mixture and shape into individual sized 'nests' (a worrying description, I know, but for once apt, here) with a definite, deep indent in each of their middles. Bake in the oven for about 1¼-½ hours; the point at which the meringue reaches a pale coffee hue is how I like it. Leave to cool for a few minutes on the baking tray before placing on a wire rack to cool.

Fully process all the ingredients for the chestnut purée together until super smooth and set aside. Whip the cream and sugar until thick. To assemble, place each meringue nest on a plate, fill it with whipped cream to a generous, dome-like height and squiddle (a fair description, here, I think) just the correct amount of chestnut purée through the metal press over each serving, masking the cream — but not the meringue nest — completely. Chill for at least 30 minutes — and 60 minutes maximum — before serving.

Meringues
with
whipped cream and stem ginger

—

SERVES 4

For me, this will always be more of an elevenses thing rather than a dessert or 'sweet from the trolley' (similar thoughts apply to the Mont-Blanc, too). Perhaps an affair of the fork and a frothy coffee, as opposed to the finale to a full-blown, three-course dinner.

I also prefer that the meringues for this turn out a pale coffee colour with a slightly crackled surface and chewy-soft and sticky within. Shape the meringue mixture as squiffy as you please, using a tablespoon to form their shape. Then again, if it so pleases, do feel free to use a nozzle and piping bag for that distinctly decorative look.

for the meringues:
4 egg whites
pinch of salt
225g caster sugar
a little softened butter
plain flour

to fill:
400ml double cream
3 tbsp ginger syrup
3–4 globes of preserved ginger, thinly sliced

Prepare the meringue mixture and method of baking them in exactly the same way as in the previous recipe. This time, however, spoon out the meringue mixture in whichever form suits your mood. Bake and cool as before.

Loosely whip the cream with the ginger syrup (decanted from the jar of stem ginger), stir in a few slices of stem ginger and then use the cream to sandwich the meringues together. Finally – and simply to pretty the offering – decorate each serving with a slice of stem ginger.

EGGPLANT EXIT

This week's article is to be my last for this highly respected, *Independent* organ. I truthfully feel that although I *do* often have a great deal to say, of late I have found it increasingly more difficult to find the right way to say it. It also occurs to me that my initial brief had begun to drift further into discontent too – and, yes, this has been noted – rather than in celebration of good things, passionately (I hope that, above all things, there was always a little passion) discussed. And, finally, the mild guilt of repetition – though that is something that may have affected me, more, rather than you.

It will have been nearly 8½ years since Emily Green (at the time, its equally highly respected restaurant critic) suggested to this retiring cook that he might just entertain the idea of composing a column or two for the Saturday page, as the most reasonable alternative to composing salads in the Bibendum kitchen. 'Mr. Hopkinson Cooks his Goose' ran that very first by-line, together with a serviceable photograph and my early attempts at describing, in a journalistic medium, all that I knew about a roast goose stuffed with mashed potato – although anyone with the mildest leanings, gastronomy-wise, knows full well that it was the unique, mad, lovely and late Peter Langan who first alerted us to such a feast, but I think – I sincerely hope – that I said so at the time.

Over the years I have been assisted along the way by the essential, initial encouragement of Hilly Janes, soon to be followed by the hugely inspirational, guiding and forthright Allan Jenkins. Then it was to be Lisa Markwell's sensitive and reassuring voice, together with Andrew Tuck's spirited enthusiasm for the relationship between cook and snapper on the page. The snapper, of course, being the remarkable Jason Lowe, without whom my scribble would have been as a bird without wings. I am forever indebted, to thee. And, of course, to Emily Green, she who set me up good and proper in the first place. Thank you, from the bottom of my heart. And last but not least to you, dear readers, for bothering to read in the first place and, from time to time, writing back so thoughtfully (scallop wittering excepted, naturally). Bless you.

Here, finally, are some aubergine recipes. Possibly my favourite vegetable in every sense: good shape, lovely colour, countless varieties, great versatility, year round availability, keeps very well, nice and shiny to look at and it also feels rather gorgeous too… Go on, fondle an aubergine. Cheerio, for now.

Salad of grilled aubergines
with
garlic cream dressing and basil

—

SERVES 2

A lovely dish for a weekend lunch eaten out of doors.

1 large aubergine, peeled and cut into
   thick-ish slices
salt and pepper
12 garlic cloves, peeled

juice of ½ small lemon
fruity olive oil
10–12 basil leaves
a little extra olive oil

Lightly salt both sides of the aubergine slices and put into a colander to drain for 30 minutes. Rinse briefly and pat dry with kitchen paper. Put the garlic cloves in a small pan and cover with cold water. Bring to the boil and drain. Refresh with cold water, again, to cover, add a little salt and simmer until very tender. Drain once more and then purée in a food processor with the lemon juice, seasoning to taste and 4–5 tbsp of olive oil, added whilst the motor is running as if making mayonnaise by this method. Once you are happy with the consistency – sort of sloppy but just pourable – check for seasoning and reserve.

Brush the aubergines with olive oil and – using a ribbed, cast-iron, stove-top affair – gently grill them on both sides until cooked through but only lightly burnished by the bars beneath. Lay them onto two plates. Spoon the garlic sauce over them and place a basil leaf onto each slice. Anoint with a little extra olive oil and serve warm.

Nasu dengaku
(or Japanese grilled
aubergine with miso paste
and sesame)

———

SERVES 4

A brief few words about ingredients.
The white miso paste can be found in
health food shops, as can the *mirin* too,
sometimes. The *dashi* soup stock
usually comes in sachets and simply
needs boiling water added to it (it is
actually a nice drink in itself). This also
can be obtained in health food shops,
but a lightly flavoured chicken or fish
stock would do at a pinch. Sake will,
naturally, give the best results here,
but dry sherry may be used as a
substitute. Whilst bearing all this in
mind, if you are lucky enough to have a
Japanese store nearby you will, of
course, be quids in.

2007 – **Many Japanese ingredients are
now available at the larger
supermarkets.**

2 large aubergines
peanut oil
1 dsp sesame seeds
lemon

for the miso topping:
200g white miso paste
2 tbsp sake (or dry sherry)
2 tbsp mirin
2 tbsp caster sugar
1 large egg yolk
6–7 tbsp dashi
1 large knob of fresh ginger, peeled

To make the miso topping, put the first five ingredients into a double boiler and
whisk together. Gently cook, stirring all the time with a wooden spoon, until
visibly thickened. Now stir in the dashi little by little, until the consistency is one
of double cream. Remove from the heat and plunge into a bowl of iced water, so as
to stop the cooking. Grate the ginger and put into a small tea-towel or J cloth.
Squeeze the juice into the miso mixture and stir in. Leave to cool completely.

Pour some peanut oil into a large frying pan to a depth about 1cm. Heat until very hot
and put in the aubergines cut side down. Cook until the surfaces are an even gold
colour and then turn over. Cook for a further 2 or 3 minutes and then tip out any
excess oil. Turn the heat down to very low, cover and stew for a further 5–7 minutes,
or until the aubergines are tender when pierced with a sharp knife. Pre-heat an
over-head grill. *Note:* You may also deep fry the aubergines, if you wish – and which,
in fact, is exactly how the Japanese go about it. However, I would only attempt this if
you have a proper, thermostatically controlled machine designed for the purpose.

Spread about a tablespoon of the miso mixture over each cooked aubergine half,
covering the surface evenly. (*Note:* It is difficult to make small quantities of this
mixture, but it will happily keep in the fridge in a screw-top jar for a few weeks –
or freeze it.) Sprinkle the aubergines with the sesame seeds and place under the
grill for a few moments to burnish the miso and to also toast the sesame seeds.
Serve at once with pieces of lemon for squeezing over.

Iman Bayeldi

SERVES 4

There are various ways in which to approach the preparation of this sumptuous dish, but the one which asks that you make slits along the length of the vegetable and into which you are supposed to force the onion and tomato mixture has always defeated me in practical terms. I like to use masses of onions and an excess of chopped parsley in my particular interpretation – both integral ingredients – but choose to omit the often asked for pine kernels, simply because I do not which for unwanted textural intrusion to inhibit the silky-smooth mass that is the finished dish.

500–600g aubergines

salt and pepper

150–200ml olive oil

350–400g onions, peeled and very thinly sliced

4 large cloves garlic, peeled and chopped

250g ripe tomatoes, cored, peeled and roughly chopped plus a few extra slices of tomato

4–5 heaped tbsp freshly chopped parsley

200ml fine quality tomato juice

5 tbsp plain yoghurt mixed with 2 tbsp chopped mint, to serve

Cut the aubergines in half lengthways, make a criss-cross of deep cuts into their flesh (taking care not to pierce through the skin underneath), lay them out and sprinkle their cut surfaces with only enough salt to generously season them. Leave them like this for 10 minutes and then turn them over onto a wire rack (with a tray positioned underneath) and allow their dark brown juices to drip out for a further 30–40 minutes, or so. Squeeze out any excess with your hands and dry the aubergines thoroughly with kitchen paper. Now heat about 3–4 tbsp of olive oil in a roomy, shallow pan (that may also be transferred to the oven) and fry the aubergines cut side down until golden. Flip them over and put the pan in the oven. Bake for 30 minutes, or so until soft all the way through when pierced with a sharp knife. Remove and allow to cool.

Whilst the aubergines are cooking, gently fry the onions and garlic in 4–5 tbsp of olive oil until the palest golden but very soft indeed; this will take anything up to 30 minutes. Tip in the tomatoes, season and continue cooking until all has become a soft and slightly sticky mass. Stir in the parsley. Scoop out most of the flesh from the aubergines so leaving a finger-width wall of skin and flesh. Chop this coarsely and thoroughly mix with the tomato and onion mess. Check for seasoning and pile back in to the aubergine shells, smoothing over the surface. Cover each stuffed aubergine with a couple of slices of tomato, sprinkle with a little salt and pepper and pour over any remaining olive oil. Pour the tomato juice around and slide the pan back into the oven and bake for a further 30 minutes, or until the tomato slices have burnished a little. Leave to cool to room temperature before eating; as they so do, it is a good idea to occasionally baste them with the tomato and olive oil sauce from beneath. Hand the yoghurt and mint at table.

INDEX

Acknowledgements

—

I would like to thank the following – both past and present – for their invaluable help.

At *The Independent*, to Emily Green, who offered me the column (December 1994) in the first place and also to Hilly Janes, who broke me in, so to speak. Much later, it was to be Lisa Markwell who looked after me until the final hurdle, when I stopped writing my column in the Spring of 2002. In between, however, it was to be Allan Jenkins who truly held my hand. For it was he, most particularly, who gently cajoled and inspired me to write the right stuff. Thank you so much.

At Quadrille, thanks to Clare Lattin in public relations and to Lisa Pendreigh, senior project editor, who left no stone unturned over my imperfect manuscript. My grateful appreciation also goes to Lawrence Morton, whose design of the book delights and thrills throughout. And, of course, to Jane O'Shea, my publisher, who I have felt able to turn to at any time, with ease, and always been greeted with nothing but the greatest enthusiasm. Thank you.

Also a long standing and very fond thank you to Anthony Goff, my agent for nearly 25 years, now, for being so patient and helpful at all times.

Finally, bless you, dear Michael Birkett, for keeping all the cuttings in the first place. The book would not have happened without them. And, of course, to Jason Lowe, for taking the wonderful pictures that Michael kept.

PS. And if it were not for the incredible feat performed by one Laura Hynd, who searched through each and every one of Jason's negatives, we might have been in a right old pickle.

First published in 2007 by
Quadrille Publishing Ltd,
Alhambra House,
27–31 Charing Cross Road,
London WC2H 0LS
www.quadrille.co.uk

The material in this volume was previously published in *The Independent* Saturday magazine between December 1994 and April 2002.

Text © 2007 Simon Hopkinson

Photography © 2007 Jason Lowe

Design & layout © 2007 Quadrille Publishing Ltd

Editorial Director: Jane O'Shea

Creative Director: Helen Lewis

Project Editor: Lisa Pendreigh

Designer: Lawrence Morton

Photographer: Jason Lowe

Production Director: Vincent Smith

Production Controller: Ruth Deary

Cataloguing-in-Publication Data: a catalogue record for this book is available from the British Library

ISBN 978 1844 00 502 4

Printed in China.

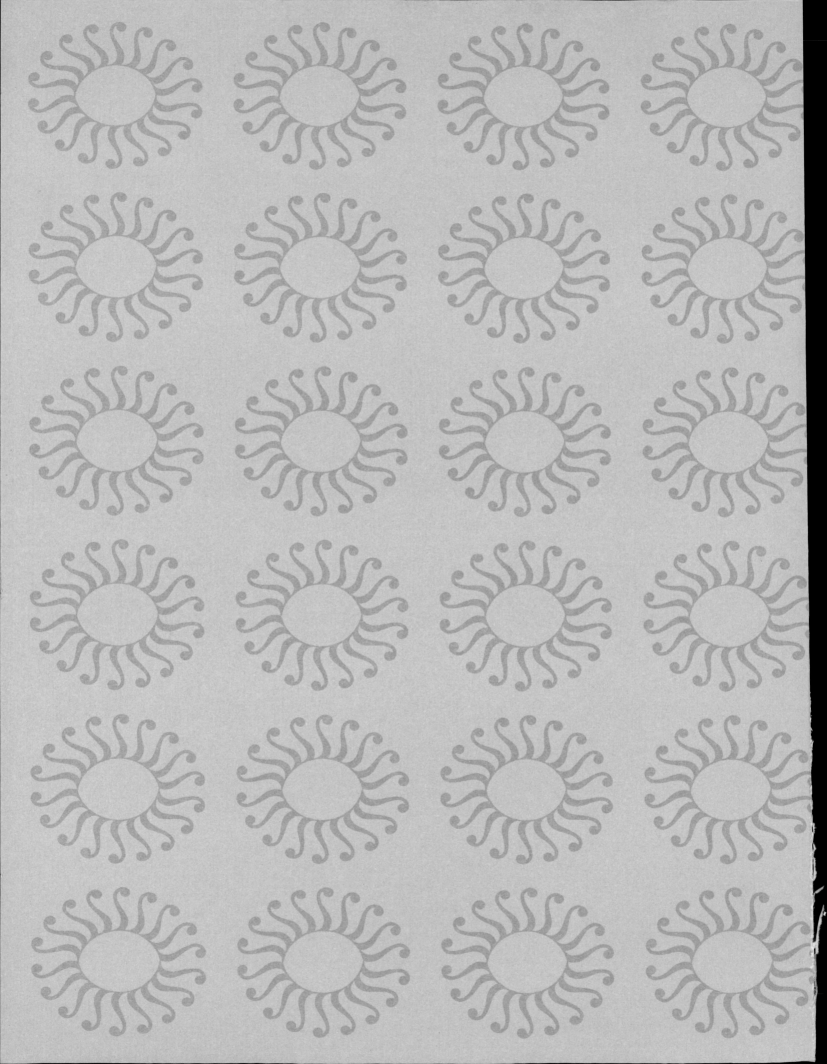